The State

Its Nature, Development and Prospects

Gianfranco Poggi

Polity Press

Copyright © Gianfranco Poggi 1990

First published 1990 by Polity Press
in association with Basil Blackwell

Editorial office:
Polity Press, 65 Bridge Street,
Cambridge CB2 1UR, UK

Marketing and production:
Basil Blackwell Ltd
108 Cowley Road, Oxford OX4 1JF, UK

ISBN 0 7456 0571 0
ISBN 0 7456 0879 5(pbk)

British Library Cataloguing in Publication Data
A CIP catalogue record for this book is available from the British
Library.

Typeset in 10 on 12pt Times
by Colset Private Limited
Printed in Great Britain by T.J. Press Ltd, Padstow, Cornwall

Contents

Preface

Over ten years ago I published *The development of the modern state* (Stanford, 1978). That book is still in print, and I hope it will remain so, for the one the reader is now holding is a new and different book.

As its subtitle indicates, it reconsiders the question of how the state came to be and attained its contemporary form(s); but whereas my treatment of that question accounted for most of the previous book, it is now treated only in chapters 3 and 4; and, while the two books share a typological approach to that theme, they conduct somewhat different arguments.

As to the rest of this book, it mostly deals with topics not discussed in the previous one. I start from the notion that there exists a plurality of forms of social power, one of which – political power – constitutes the institutional content of the notion of the state itself (chapters 1 and 2). After reviewing the 'story' of the state, I confront the question of how one might evaluate it and explain it (chapters 5 and 6). My treatment of the contemporary liberal-democratic state is more extensive in this than in the previous book, and considers different aspects of this topic (chapters 7 and 8). In chapter 9 I offer a summary discussion of the communist party-state, which *Development* had not even mentioned – a discussion made rather more tentative by the fact that between the time I first drafted it and the time I wrote its final version, the Soviet and East European political scene witnessed unforeseen developments of great significance. I mention these, but do not even seek to suggest what their final import might be. Finally, my last chapter presents a number of arguments to the effect that 'the state of the state' is not a healthy one today, but ends up with a timid two cheers for the old beast.

As has been the case with all my previous books, this one has also arisen out of my teaching practice, for its content has been developed within courses I have taught at the University of Sydney in 1984, at the University of Edinburgh in 1986, and at the University of Virginia in 1989. I thus owe a great deal to the audiences of those courses for the contributions they made to my thinking on my subject.

Desmond King, a colleague at Edinburgh, read drafts of all the first few chapters and offered a number of helpful criticisms on them. Other such criticisms have been offered by John Meyer, of Stanford University, and by my old friend Beppe Di Palma, of the University of California (Berkeley). Victor Zaslavsky's comments on my chapter on the Soviet party-state put me further in his debt. Tony Giddens followed the progress of my writing patiently – for the manuscript took much longer to write than either he or I expected – and commented thoughtfully on successive drafts. Both my daughter and my wife read the penultimate version of the book and sought to improve the final one.

I am very grateful to the Center for Advanced Study in the Behavioral Sciences, of which I am currently a Fellow, for allowing me to complete this book in a most supportive and friendly setting; and to the Center for Advanced Study of the University of Virginia for the financial support provided by the National Science Foundation under grant BNS87-00864.

Center for Advanced Study in the Behavioral Sciences,
Stanford, California
1 December 1989

Part I

Part I

1

Social Power and its Political Form

I

What is social power?

Our effort to understand 'the modern state' may begin with a brief discussion of a much wider, more basic concept – that of social power. Unfortunately, this not a matter of starting out from a notion that is simple and unproblematic; on the contrary, 'social power', and indeed 'power' itself, are also complex and controversial notions.[1] We may, however, disregard the attendant complexities and controversies, and seek to convey straightforwardly the universally significant, raw phenomenon, to which the notion of social power points.

That is: in all societies, some people clearly and consistently appear more capable than others of pursuing their own objectives; and if these are incompatible with those envisaged by others, the former manage somehow to ignore or override the latter's preferences. Indeed, they are often able to mobilise, in the pursuit of their own ends, the others' energies, even against their will. This, when all is said and done, is what social power is all about.

Yet we may feel that we are going overboard in our willingness to accept a rough-and-ready understanding of the phenomenon in question; that, in particular, the word 'somehow', used above, is too generic to be of much use. We might then seek to differentiate somewhat the notion of social power, by asking ourselves how, on what grounds, the favoured people manage the feat in question.

Three forms of social power

We might give first, again, a generic answer, to the effect that social power rests on the possession by those people of some resources which they can use to have their own way with others. Our question then becomes – what are these resources?

Most answers to this question[2] (in this formulation or others) end up by distinguishing three forms of social power. Here, for instance, is the version of this distinction offered by the Italian political philospher Bobbio:

> We may classify the various forms of power by reference to the facilities the active subject employs in order to lay boundaries around the conduct of the passive subject . . . We can then distinguish three main classes of power: economic, ideological and political. Economic power avails itself of the possession of certain goods, rare or held to be rare, in order to lead those not possessing them to adopt a certain conduct, which generally consists in carrying our a certain form of labour . . . Ideological power is based upon the fact that ideas of a certain nature, formulated . . . by persons endowed with a certain authority, put abroad in a certain manner, may also exert an influence upon the conduct of associated individuals . . . Political power, finally, is grounded in the possession of facilities (weapons of all kinds and degrees of potency) by means of which physical violence may be exerted. It is coercive power in the strict sense of the term.[3]

Except for characterising as 'normative' the form of power Bobbio labels 'ideological' – a term which is too laden with potentially misleading connotations – I subscribe to this tripartite distinction.

The role of coercion

The state, our object of concern throughout this book, is a phenomenon principally and emphatically located within the sphere of political power. Thus we may from now on in this chapter, limit ourselves to this form of social power – and notice how Bobbio's definition of it (but not only Bobbio's) connects it, starkly and perhaps shockingly, with weapons, violence, coercion. *Shockingly*, I suggest, because on the strength of this definition the bandit, who makes people hand over their possessions at gunpoint, may appear as the prototypical political figure.

A bandit, however, normally threatens, and thus has his way with, a few individuals, for a strictly limited time, and can compel them to perform only few, narrowly circumscribed activities. If we concern ourselves instead with manifestations of power which affect larger numbers of people, encompass a large range of activities (and inactivities) and do so for longer periods of time, this disqualifies the bandit from consideration. It does not, however, exclude the reference of the phenomena we are concerned with to violence and coercion; at most, we might say, we can redefine the prototypical political figure as not so much a bandit as a warrior, availing himself of the military superiority he and his retinue enjoy over an unarmed, military ineffective population, not just to terrorise the latter but to rule over it.

But again (even ignoring the difficulty often found in distinguishing between the bandit and the warrior . . .) one may continue to find it shocking that the phenomenon of political power should be connected as directly with violence and coercion as the reference to the warrior suggests. After all, the manifestations of political power most of us routinely experience – the tax assessment notice, the fine for traffic violation, the blather of politicians at the hustings or on television – seem to have very little to do with violence and coercion.

Yet there are good grounds for relating conceptually the whole phenomenon of political power to the unpleasant realities evoked by the figure of the warrior. Ultimately, it would be difficult to think of any significant embodiment of that power, no matter how much it may differ from the warrior in its appearance and its concerns, no matter how dignified by law and consensus (think of a judge or of a popular statesman), which does not owe its political identity to the fact of relating however indirectly, to violence and coercion. The American sociologist Peter Berger has phrased this point as follows:

> The ultimate and, no doubt, the oldest means of social control is physical violence . . . Even in the politely operated societies of modern democracies the ultimate argument is violence. No state can exist without a police force or its equivalent in armed might. This ultimate violence may not be used frequently. There may be innumerable steps in its application, in the way of warnings and reprimands. But if all the warnings are disregarded, even in so slight a matter as paying a traffic ticket, the last thing that will happen is that a couple of cops show up at the door with handcuffs and a Black Maria.[4]

In the light of this, what we should consider as unique to political power, as conceptually intrinsic to it, is control over the means of violence, rather than the direct and frequent recourse to their employment. In any case, the non-coercive aspects of political experience, or indeed of political power, are numerous and significant. Various authors quote Saint Augustine's provoking query, 'what are kingdoms but robberies on a larger scale?' as evidence of his bitter awareness that coercion is the defining feature of the political form of social power, and omit a clause that qualifies that dictum: 'what are kingdoms, if justice be removed, but robberies on a larger scale?' The qualification is important: the fact that, as it were, the bottom line of political power is constituted by coercion, can be transcended, in moral terms, by the uses to which that power, and indeed coercion itself, is put. Presumably these uses, in Augustine's mind, can make a kingdom rather different from a large-scale robbery.

Commands

I shall quote another religious text as a pointer to the complexities of political power. This concerns the centurion episode in the life of Jesus, as narrated in the three synoptic gospels; the gospel according to Luke has the centurion – a minor Roman military official – beseech Jesus on behalf of his sick servant in the following terms:

> Lord, I am not worthy that you should come under my roof. But just say one word, and my servant will be healed. For I, too, am a man under authority; and I say to one of my servants, 'go' – and he goes; and to another, 'come' – and he comes; and to another, 'do this' – and he does it.

This text, however indirectly, points to a central feature of political power once it is stabilised, standardised into authority: its exercise takes the form of the issuing of commands.

Now, a command on the one hand is always explicitly or implicitly complemented by an 'or else' clause, a pointer to the command-giver's ability to use coercion in order to overcome recalcitrance or resistance on the part of the person receiving the command. On this account, there is a distinctive (and sinister) factuality to commands, an implicit (and sometimes explicit) reminder that 'we have ways to *make* you obey . . .'

On the other hand, a command is a thoroughly intersubjective operation: by means of it, one subject seeks to initiate and control another subject's activity. It is also thoroughly symbolic in nature, and presupposes the other subject's ability to entertain and interpret the message addressed to him/her. On account of both its intersubjective and its symbolic nature, every command implicitly acknowledges that compliance with it is, when all is said and done, a contingent matter, requiring both that it be properly understood and that the person to whom it is addressed be willing to obey it. (As Roman jurists used to say, *Etsi coactus tamen volui*: I may have been compelled, but in the final analysis I committed my will.)

Legitimacy

The significance of these non-factual aspects of command – that is, of the routine expression of political power – is witnessed in the emphasis which political and social theorists have often placed on the notion of legitimacy. Once more, this is a complex notion, raising difficult conceptual questions. Once more, a few elementary considerations suffice to justify that emphasis. Consider the following line of argument:

– Normally, commands are not given for the sake of giving them; whether or not they evoke obedience is not a matter of indifference to the giver of a command.

– The latter, then, is interested in restricting the element of contingency attached to compliance. He/she can prefer to do so by making explicit the 'or else', 'we have ways . . .' component of the command. A Roman emperor used to express this preference by saying of his subjects, 'let them detest me, as long as they fear me.'

– Normally, however, command-givers consider a compliance exacted through fear (or, for that matter, evoked primarily by a consideration of the direct, immediate advantage compliance may bring to the person receiving a command) as less reliable, more brittle and niggardly than a compliance willingly granted by a person convinced that the command-giver is morally entitled to expect obedience, and correspondingly feeling morally obligated to grant it. Thus:

– A political power relationship, other things being equal, is made more secure, and its exercise more effective and less costly, to the extent that it can credibly appeal to principles establishing such an entitlement and such an obligation. It may be said to be legitimate to the extent that it can do so.

The German sociologist Max Weber (1864–1920) added a particular twist to this line of argument, which had long been agreed upon by political and social theorists.[5] He reasoned that if legitimacy was a significant, consequence-laden property of stabilised political power relationships (if, indeed, it contributed materially to their stabilisation), then the precise nature of the typical principles presented (and accepted) as grounding the entitlement to command and the obligation to command, was also likely to be of some consequence. He thus used variations in those principles (among other things) as ways of characterising various aspects of what we may call, paraphrasing William James, the varieties of political experience.

Certainly, throughout history, the phenomenon of political power, based ultimately on the unequal availability to individuals or groups of facilities for practising coercion, and normally qualified and limited by reference to principles of legitimacy, has become embodied in very different arrangements. Its comparative significance with respect to other forms of social power, or indeed with respect to other pheonomena not involving any power relations, has also varied greatly.

This book does not survey the range of variation which the arrangements concerning political power have covered in the course of history. All the same, its theme – the modern state – is wide enough to afford the reader a glimpse into the diversity and complexity of the political power phenomenon. I shall devote the balance of this chapter, however, to a few further considerations concerning political power and political experience in general.

II

The rivalry between forms of social power

We saw earlier that there are three major forms of social power: economic, normative and political. Their bases differ very significantly, being respectively the control over critical material resources, over the content of social beliefs, values and norms, and over material and organisational facilities for sustained coercion. Yet, at bottom, the operations of all three powers revolve around the same object: the ability to control and direct the use and development of a society's ultimate resource – the activities of the individuals making up its population.

For that very reason, it is probable that the three powers (or rather, the groups which have built up one or the other of them as a facility for the pursuit of their own interests) will contend with one another. Their contest will have two overlapping aspects. On the one hand, each power will seek to restrict the autonomous sway of the others, diminishing their autonomous impact upon that ultimate object. On the other hand, it will seek to enhance itself by establishing a hold upon as great as possible a *quantum* of the others, by converting itself to some extent into them. (If you can't lick them, let them join you, as it were.) In the course of both aspects of the contest, each power will seek to emphasise the significance of its own resources, the saliency of its peculiar uses. What do these amount to in the case of political power?

The distinctiveness of political power: paramountcy

A first answer can be given by referring to, as I have phrased it above, that power's peculiar uses. These uses normally consist in safeguarding a given society's territorial boundaries against aggression and encroachment from outsiders; and in imposing restraints upon those individuals or groups within a given society which use or threaten to use violence or fraud in pursuing their special interests.

It can be claimed for political power that it has a functional priority over others, for only in so far as it discharges those tasks can individuals can go about their business – and that includes the exercise of whatever other form of social power they possess – in a (relatively) peaceable and orderly manner. For this reason it is sometimes claimed that political power is paramount with respect to other forms of social power. This point is made as follows by Bobbio:

> Let us first consider the relations between members of a given collectivity. There may be strong disparities of economic power among them, and those deprived of means of production may be clearly subordinated to those possessing them. Ideological power may also be much in evidence, in that most members of the population routinely subscribe to and abide by the beliefs and values put abroad by the dominant class. In either situation, however, there may be circumstances, no matter how infrequently, in which only the resort to physical coercion can prevent the insubordination or disobedience of the subaltern groups of the collectivity.
>
> Let us consider, further, the relations between different collectivities. Here, ideological constraints and inducements are not likely to be of much significance in maintaining the status quo; whereas one collectivity may well apply economic sanctions in order to induce the other to adopt a certain line of conduct. Yet, in this context the decisive instrument for the realisation of the will of one of the parties will be, in the last resort, the employment of force – waging war.[6]

The distinctiveness of political power: ultimacy

A second answer considers the particularities of the resource in which political power, as we have construed it, grounds itself – violence. We can define this as the application, or threatened application, of physical force, affecting the existence, bodily integrity, and freedom from restraint of individuals by being brought to bear upon them, their property, or other individuals with whose existence and wellbeing they are significantly concerned.

In the light of this definition, political power can be said to have a quality we may call ultimacy. Violence – or the threat of it – appears as the facility of last resort in shaping and managing interpersonal relations, for it operates by causing sensations and activating emotions which all sentient beings experience, and which in their rawer forms do not even presuppose the quality of humanness in those on whom it is brought to bear.

This feature of violence – in German, one might characterise it as *voraussetzungslos*, that is, capable of operating in the absence of any presupposition – probably accounts for what we have called before the'factuality' of commands. This feature is emphasised, for instance, in Rüdiger Lautmann's discussion of the use of force on the part of police officers:

> One forgets too easily, that the police have to do with power in a very immediate sense, as physical coercion employed against men. When the door to a dwelling is smashed through, or a man is captured, overpowered or killed, it makes little difference from a purely external viewpoint, as far as the person affected is concerned, whether this is done at the hands of a criminal or of a guardian of order. [my translation][7]

Another German author, Wolf-Dietrich Narr, has emphasised the peculiar features of physical violence and the uniqueness it confers upon a power grounded in it: 'Physical violence has the particularity of producing consequences directly, immediately, without the recourse to media of communication; normally, speculations about its causes and forms are superfluous . . . it addresses the integrity of the human body in direct, immediately graspable and comprehensible fashion.' Besides, the forms of violence – culminating in killing – which are typically at the disposal of those exercising political power have a distinctive absoluteness about them.

> There is a wide range of gradation in the recourse to physical violence. Spouses hit each other, and so do children. A fist fight erupts in a tavern. But in each of these cases the physical nature of the individual in only partly compromised, even though one's body may be black with bruises. It makes a decisive difference if instead it is not just part of the body that suffers damage, but the human body as a whole that is affected or threatened, as happens with imprisonment and with killing or the threat of killing . . . Whoever is in a position, credibly to threaten others with physical annihilation, has at his disposal a sanction potential which is incomparably superior to all other sanctions. Not just the quality of existence, but existence itself is at stake. Whoever within a society has such power to annihilate, determines what ultimately happens. Having it, on this account, constitutes the very core of the political experience. [my translation][8]

A further feature of violence, recently emphasised by Popitz, is what he calls its boundlessness. He quotes Solzhenitsyn: 'To the disadvantage of the ruled, and to the advantage of the ruler, man is so constituted that, as long as he is alive, there is always something else one can do to him.'[9]

Another contemporary German author characterises as follows the unique features of 'means of physical coercion':

> They are more universally employable than other sources of power, because they operate indifferently with respect to the moment in time, the situation, the subject and the theme of the activity which is to be motivated . . . One can reasonably expect that violence must reach a high threshold, before it makes sense, to those affected by it, to choose instead to challenge it and to engage in a struggle, however hopeless. And its means do not markedly depend on other structures, for they presuppose, to be effective, only a superiority of physical force, not status superiority, group membership, traditions, role complexes, availability of information or institutionalised value conceptions. [my translation][10]

Finally, this grounding in violence imparts to particularly intense moments of political experience – warfare, the 'no holds barred' confrontation between factions unrestrained by constitutional rules in their struggle respectively to hold and to grab power – a specific quality of momentous irrationality.

Lenin liked to use the expression *kto kogo?* – meaning 'who whom?', who defeats, who kills whom? – to emphasise the unavoidable moment of momentous contingency in the outcome of armed confrontation. Weber reminds us of 'the utterly universal experience that force always begets force, that everywhere the most idealistic and (even more so) the most revolutionary movements become mixed with social and economic interests in establishing domination, that the recourse to force against injustice has as its final outcome the triumph not of higher right but of greater force or shrewdness.'[11]

In dealing with political power, then, we are dealing with a particularly loaded human reality. Consider the following. As we have seen, it is possible to see political power as being paramount with respect to other forms of social power, by pointing to its distinctive 'missions' – the defence of the territory from external aggression and the ordering of relations internal to it. Yet, together with these two minimal aims (and indeed, sometimes, instead of them), political power can pursue almost any others one can conceive; and in doing so it may impose very heavy burdens on society (and on the other social powers). Worse, it need not perform those two functions well, if at all; it can, in particular, generate much of the disorder which it claims to be intent on curbing. (There are unfortunate similarities, in this respect, between the warrior, whom we have recognised as the prototypical political figure, and the bandit, to whom we have tried to deny that recognition.)[12]

Such reflections on the nature and effects of political power have for a long time inspired a number of critical questions, which in various formulations have been the object of sustained attention over the millennial course of Western social and political theory. Let us consider a few of the most fundamental and provoking among such questions.

Why political power?

That is, on what grounds does political power constitute a constant, wide-ranging and (as we have seen) momentous aspect of human existence? What basic requirements of human existence, if any, does political power fulfil? What intrinsic human potentialities does it express and assert? The answers to these and similar questions have been very varied. Consider a few:

– According to Aristotle, who probably articulates a view widely held within Greek civilisation, political experience is the key aspect of human nature, the highest dignity of our species. Only humans, as free and rational beings, have the capacity to develop through rational discourse the designs for living characteristic of the collectivities in which they live. The most noble and distinctive of these is the city – that *polis* from which politics and related terms derive. And ideally it is the citi-zens' peaceable, open-ended public argument that produces the valid, enforceable understandings of virtue proper to each city. Because this is an ideal, it is only occasionally and imperfectly fulfilled, and the Greeks were the first to adopt institutions intended to fulfil it. At the same time, it is an ideal inherent in human nature, at least as a potentiality; and other forms of political experience, which negate and restrict the free participation of individuals in determining the models of conduct valid for the collectivity, give only inadequate, corrupt expression to that potentiality.

In the Greek view of political experience, its specific power aspect (the 'vertical' dimension, as it were, of the experience)[13] is seen as subordinate to other aspects embodying its 'horizontal' dimensions, and emphasising the coming together in discourse and in shared endeavour of rationally thinking and freely associating individuals. Essentially, the task of power is to make binding upon each collectivity its specific designs for living, and to uphold their exclusive validity in dealing with other collectivities; their vertical, power component, however, becomes salient to the extent that citizens' involvement and the open-ended and public nature of discourse are restricted or excluded. (It is in Roman political thinking that that component becomes preponderant *vis-à-vis* other aspects of political experience.)[14]

– Starting from a different vision of human nature, which emphasises the savage and greedy passions motivating the individual, one can construe political experience in a radically different manner, and make the power phenomenon utterly central to it. The whole political realm is here conceived as a remedy to the built-in liabilities of human nature, rather than as the fulfilment of its best potentialities. (Hobbes is the sharpest articulator of this view.) Human beings are seen as naturally prone to exercise fraud and violence upon one another in the pursuit of their egoistical interests; this results in a condition of painful, fearsome insecurity for all men and women; and the answer to that is seen in the construction of political institutions, seen essentially as arrangements for generating and storing coercive power and making it more effective, exclusive and formidable.

As Popitz puts it: 'it is never possible completely to eliminate a basic aspect of human experience – the fact that individuals, in confronting one another, experience concern, fear, anguish.'[15] In particular, since all human beings are potentially violent and intrinsically exposed to each other's violence, it is in the interest of individuals to vest in an artificially constituted sovereign all capacity to exercise violence, as that sovereign's exclusive, unchallengeable prerogative.

– But one does not need to connect political experience and political power directly with human nature. An answer under other aspects similar to Aristotle's connects them instead with certain conditions which human collectivities may but need not attain – particularly, with their attaining a certain threshold of size and complexity. Should this happen, arrangements must be made to sustain those qualities of durability and cohesiveness which smaller, homogeneous collectivities derive directly from each member's natural commitment to custom and affiliation with their kith and kin. One such arrangement consists in vesting in some individuals the responsibility and the facilities to enforce rules, and possibly to make them, in order to guarantee that the collectivity will respond in a coherent, reliable manner to new circumstances, opportunities and threats. On the basis of arguments of this kind,[16] the emergence and development of political power (as of other forms of social power) appear to be based on the services that power renders to human collectivities.

– On a very different construction, political power reflects and embodies some people's exclusive ability to rule over others – an ability which is not artificially conferred upon them (as it is on Hobbes's sovereign) but which they naturally possess and spontaneously prove by imposing their own rule. Superior human beings acquire political power as a result and expression of their disposition to lord it over inferior ones; and the primordial political experience is the forceful subjugation of peaceful and defenceless settled peasant populations by armed, mounted nomads, intent upon domination and exploitation.

– Finally, the answer developed by Marx and Engels (to be considered later in its application to the genesis and development of the modern state) grounds political power in the class division which is common to all historical societies and arises from the division of labour and/or the institution of property in the means of production. Political institutions are at bottom an instrumentality (and occasionally a stake) in the class struggle. As such, they are destined to be made dispensable by the ultimate outcome of that struggle – the construction of a socialist, classless, non-divided society.

How far political power?

This question, which has attracted much attention on the part of Western political and social theorists, and which furthermore has greater pragmatic significance than that of the whys and wherefores of political power, concerns its scope. That is, assuming, on whatever grounds, that political experience is a significant, indispensable and/or unavoidable aspect of the human condition, how great should its domain be? On how many other aspects of human experience should political power impinge? How many collective resources should it absorb and deploy?

These queries derive their significance – one might say, their pathos – from two considerations. In the first place, as we have already remarked, political arrangements and political activities can be brought to bear on practically any aspect or facet of human experience. Weber has phrased this point as follows:

> It is not possible to characterise a political organisation – and thus, in particular, 'the state' – by reference to the *ends* to which it orients its activity. On the one hand there is no end, be it the provision of food or the protection of the arts, which has not been pursued, albeit occasionally, by some political organisation. On the other hand, there is no end, be it the assuring of the individual's security or the enforcement of laws, which has been pursued by all political organisations. It is for this reason that the nature of such an organisation can only be defined by referring to a *means* which may not be exclusive to it, but which is specific to it and intrinsic to its essence (and which occasionally becomes an end to itself) – force. [my translation][17]

In the second place, as the same quote indicates, the actual scope of political power has varied enormously according to historical circumstance. Thus, what it should be in any given circumstance is a question of considerable moment, and Western political and social theory has often addressed it by seeking to formulate general, intrinsically valid principles from which to derive an answer appropriate to any given 'here and now'.

The search for such principles has taken two main routes, which, however, are not incompatible and have sometimes both been followed within the same argument. Along one route, one seeks to assign substantive boundaries to political power, by specifying a finite set of ends which it should encompass. (A great German liberal thinker, Wilhelm Humboldt, formulated this line of approach in the title of a book of his, literally, 'Ideas for an attempt to locate the boundaries of the state's activities' – translated into English as *The limits of state action*.)[18]

Theoretical statements of the scope of political power attained along this route have often sought to determine (against Weber's advice) the finalities intrinsic to the nature of political activity, mostly reducing these to the maintenance of law and order within the collectivity and the securing of its boundaries against external encroachments. Alternatively, they have sought to specify the appropriate competences of other spheres of social life and/or the natural, innate entitlements of individuals, and derived the legitimate boundaries of political power from the principle that it should respect those competences and secure those entitlements. (See for instance the so-called 'subsidiarity principle' of Catholic social theory.)

In a more secular frame of mind, some contemporary writers have sought to determine which goods (broadly understood as all things, activities and conditions which people find useful and gratifying) are by nature collective: that is, which goods cannot be effectively produced and secured via the self-interested activities of individuals operating on the market and/or cannot by enjoyed by isolated consumers, but need to be produced and secured through political, coercive arrangements.[19] Their thesis is that political power should involve itself exclusively in providing for such collective goods, leaving the production and distribution of all others to the markets. Thus the maximum welfare of the collectivity would be enhanced: for, arguably, markets by their very nature cause a society's resources to be put to their most efficient uses.[20]

The second route to the determination of the scope of political power emphasises not so much the ends of political activity – in the terms of my last quotation from Weber – as the modalities of the employment of its specific means: that is, once more, coercion. Exactly because coercion can be put to so many uses, and the recourse to it has the peculiar and disturbing features we have indicated above, it is critical that it should be exercised in as restrained and controlled a manner as is compatible with its effectiveness. To this end, its employment should as far as possible be guided by general rules, specifying by whom, in what circumstances and to what extent it should be employed. In this way, it is intended, the sway of force can be reduced, moderating its tendency to be used excessively and/or arbitrarily, that is, according to the interests and preferences particular to those exercising it, instead of those underwritten by the wider community.

Ideally, indeed, coercion should figure within political activity as a background potentiality, and in the foreground should stand instead processes of a different nature, which appeal directly to loyalty, custom, shared advantage, conviction and obligation. Even commands should – says Hegel – appeal as much as possible to *Einsicht und Gründe*, that is (literally) 'insight and grounds', rather than fear. They should, as it were, be issued in the form of articulated speech, rather than by shouting or by gesturing threateningly. (As a Neapolitan is supposed to have replied to his Saracen captors, who had placed before him the stark alternative, either to convert to Islam or to be impaled: 'Impaled – no. Other than that – let's argue.')

Thus, a concern with 'due process' should characterise institutionally permitted, legitimate coercion, and screen the normal conduct of political business from naked force. This yields procedural rather than substantive limits upon political power. But the former often presuppose and strengthen the latter, particularly those substantial limits expressing the notion that individuals have claims to autonomy and socially valuable interests of their own, which politics should respect and protect.

Political action and morality

A further question which has attracted much attention in Western political theory concerns the relations between political action and morality. Both ancient and Christian philosophy (and theology, in the latter case) consider that political action falls straightforwardly within the domain of morality, but each construes their connection differently. In antiquity, as we have seen, the *polis* is an utterly central site of moral experience, for it is through distinctively political processes that virtue itself is defined and the institutions making the practice of it binding upon individuals are established. Socrates was accused of impiety because he threw doubts on that connection; but in the event himself, according to Plato's *Crito*, chose to die by drinking hemlock rather than negate the connection by escaping, as his followers were beseeching him to do. Christianity inverts the relationship: political, public concerns should reflect the priority of moral principles oriented chiefly toward the individual conscience and the soul's salvation; political responsibilities constitute (at best) a subordinate extension of the morality grounded on those principles.

Modern political theory, however, suggests that the reasoning and practice relevant to the political realm may legitimately (not just as an aberration, as Christian thinking conceded) diverge from the reasoning and practice dictated by morals. What is politically mandatory and lawful may differ from what is morally binding and meritorious.

Machiavelli formulated the divergence in terms of the relationship between the ends and the means of political action: 'Most particularly in the action of rulers, the criterion of judgement lies in the ends. Thus, let a ruler so act as to acquire and secure the state: whatever means he adopts to such effect will always be judged honourable and receive every-body's praise', no matter how blameworthy he may appear from the standpoint of morality.

Weber emphasised the contrast between the realm of political action and that of morality by suggesting that each is the appropriate ambit of a distinctive 'ethic'. Under the 'ethic of intention', appropriate to morality, whether an act is good or bad depends exclusively on whether it conforms with a categorical norm binding on the individual conscience: you do what it is your duty for you to do, and let the consequences of your dutiful action take care of themselves. Under the 'ethic of responsibility', appropriate to the political realm, you do what you must do in order to actually produce the wanted consequences; you must strive to determine these, take charge of them, rather than devoting yourself to the fulfilment of principles, however worthy: 'There is an abyss between acting according to the ethic of intention, whose religious expression is: "the Christian shall act as a just and leave the outcome in God's hands", and acting according to the ethic of responsibility, whereby one must respond for the (foreseeable) consequences of one's actions.'[21]

We may once more turn to Bobbio for an account of the contrast formulated by Weber. That contrast is particularly evident in the fact that, at any rate in the modern state, citizens are forbidden to visit violence upon one another; and yet are expected to be willing to engage in violence in dealing with foes in wartime, and also, if they are state agents, in dealing with other citizens. Bobbio suggests:

The difference may reflect the fact that in relations between individuals, violence never (except in the case of self-defence) constitutes an inescapable last resort; while in the relations between collectivities one may normally claim that it constitutes that. But in turn, the reason why individual violence is not justified lies in the fact that normally individuals are, so to speak, placed under the protection of collective violence . . . Hence, individual violence lacks justification exactly to the extent that collective violence is seen as justified. In other words . . . morals can afford severely to condemn interpersonal violence in so far as one can safely assume that the accepted, routine practice of collective violence guarantees the individuals' normal existence.[22]

It is, one may note, on such grounds that one may argue the paramountcy of political power: its operations must be assumed if a civilised existence is to go on at all. In this sense, contrary to the Christian position indicated above, the institutional practice of politics is presupposed if private morality is to be practised, rather than politics being simply an aspect or extension of private morals.

III

The institutionalisation of political power

The multiplicity of the questions we have raised, however cursorily, in the second section of this chapter, and the diversity and complexity of the answers we have sketched, emphasise a point made above: political power is a momentous, pervasive, critical phenomenon. Together with other forms of social power, it constitutes an indispensable medium for constructing and shaping larger social realities, for establishing, shaping and maintaining all broader and more durable collectivities.

So far we have considered political power in its generic aspects. From now on, our attention is focused on the most massive and significant of its modern manifestations, the state. Before that, however, we may reflect that the state itself constitutes only one modality of a somewhat wider phenomenon – the institutionalisation of political power.

That wider phenomenon comprises three aspects, according to the German sociologist Heinrich Popitz:

> First, there is the growing *depersonalisation* of power relations. Power no longer stands or falls with one particular individual who at any given time happens to have a decisive say. It connects progressively with determinate functions and positions which transcend individuals. Then, there is growing *formalisation*. The exercise of power becomes more and more oriented to rules, procedures and rituals. (This does not exclude *arbitrium*. But one may speak of *arbitrium*, or of favour, only in so far as arbitrary decisions and acts of favour stand out over against what is done as a rule.) A third aspect of the institutionalisation of power is the growing *integration* of power relations into a comprehensive order. Power gears itself into the existent conditions. It embeds itself, and becomes absorbed into the social edifice, which it supports and by which it is in turn supported. [my translation][23]

In the next three chapters, first by developing a conceptual portrait of the state, and then by reviewing summarily the main phrases in the development of the European state, we shall see to what extent and in what particular ways that development has institutionalised political power.

2

The Nature of the Modern State

An organization which controls the population occupying a definite territory is a state insofar as (1) it is differentiated from other organizations operating in the same territory; (2) it is autonomous; (3) it is centralized; and (4) its divisions are formally coordinated with one another.[1]

This definition, occurring in the introductory chapter of an important book on *The formation of national states in Western Europe*, offers a useful preliminary characterisation of our object, which I shall comment and enlarge upon in the first part of this chapter. On account of that book's theme, however, the definition comprises only those fundamental (and abiding) features of the modern state already embodied in the early stages of its development. In the second half of the chapter, therefore, I shall consider some additional features, reflecting primarily the experience of the last two centuries.

I

Organisation

To begin with, the state is 'an organisation'. That is, to express this point in the manner suggested in the first chapter: for there to be a state, political power must be vested in and exercised through a set of purposefully contrived arrangements – a body of rules, a series of roles, a body of resources – seen as concerned with and committed to a distinctive, unified and unifying set of interests and purposes.

In a later chapter we shall see how implausible it has become, in view of the enormous expansion and internal diversification of contemporary states, to consider the agencies and groups active in each as constituting *one* organisation. This makes it difficult for us to realise, retrospectively, how keenly, and how successfully, the protagonists of 'state-building' sought to entrust the conduct of political business to a single organisation, and to distinguish that from all other entities harbouring and ordering social existence. To convey the novelty and the daring of that vision, the nineteenth-century historian Burckhardt attributed to the Italian Renaissance the view of 'the state as a work of art'; and numerous seventeenth-century and later writers spoke of the state as a machine.

Previously, in the Christian West, the possession of political power had been embedded in other forms of social power; its practice had been the prerogative of privileged people *qua* privileged people, just another expression of their social superiority. By the same token, the loyalties which it sought to evoke were part and parcel of other people's general condition of social dependency. *Qua* organisation, on the other hand, the state unifies and makes distinctive the political aspects of social life, sets them apart from other aspects, and entrusts them to a visible, specialised entity. Thus individuals can claim the prerogatives involved in the exercise of rule only on grounds of their position within that entity.

The institution of hereditary kingship, which in its original forms vested sovereignty in a given individual purely on account of his/her birth, seems to personalise power utterly. Yet, as Simmel pointed out long ago,[2] this is a misleading impression: the very fact that the accident of birth can assign to any individual at all, no matter what his/her personal qualities, the supreme political position, indicates that the position itself, not the individual holding it, is the pivot of the system. *Yo, el Rey*, the words with which traditionally the Spanish monarch announced his binding commands, is a formula which expresses the dependency of even the most exalted and absolute form of rule on the occupancy of an office.

Differentiation

Turning now to differentiation – a concept to a large extent implicit in that of organisation itself – this is at a maximum when the organisation in question performs *all* and *only* political activities. Historically, the most visible and contested aspect of differentiation has probably been the process whereby the state has become secular. A state is secular (at any rate in one interpretation of this notion) to the extent that it disclaims any responsibility for fostering the spiritual wellbeing of its subjects/citizens or the welfare of religious bodies, and treats as irrelevant for its own purposes the religious beliefs and the ecclesiastical standing of individuals.

The 'separation between state and civil society' is another, broader way of expressing the state's organisational differentiation, connected with its development in Western Europe in the eighteenth and nineteenth centuries. It conveys the state's recognition that the individuals subject to its power also have capacities and interests of a non-political nature, which they may express and pursue autonomously, and its commitment to disciplining and ordaining the resulting private activities only in a general and abstract manner. This pertains in particular to the citizens' economic activities, for the production and distribution of wealth are largely assigned to the institutions of private property, contract and the market, with respect to which the state claims to operate as an outside guarantor rather than as an interested party.

Coercive control

What, then, is implied in the understanding that the state 'controls the population occupying a definite territory'? First, the control a state exercises over a population typically involves coercion, with its characteristic ultimacy, already discussed in the first chapter. In other words, whatever else and whoever else is involved in controlling a population, the state specialises in last-resort control, one potentially affecting the interests individuals have in the integrity, safety, and freedom from pain and restraint of their own bodies and those of their loved ones. Second, the state claims the monopoly of such control, which can only be exercised by individuals mandated or authorised by it; and through such individuals seeks to organise, to make particularly formidable and purposive, the practice (or the threat) of coercion.

Sovereignty

A further feature of Tilly's definition – autonomy – expresses, in somewhat more muted fashion, what is often encoded in the more controversial and loaded notion of sovereignty. The controlling organisation is a state in so far as it is (among other things) sovereign: that is, it claims, and if necessary is willing to prove, that it owes to no other power its control over the population in question; that it responds to no other organisation for the modalities and the outcomes of that control. It exercises that control on its own account, activating its own resources, unconditionally; does not derive it from or share it with any other entity. That control cannot be challenged or limited by appealing to a body of juridical rules, for typically such rules are themselves an aspect of the state's control activites, and an expression of its sovereignty. (Autonomy means in fact the ability to produce one's own rules.) To be effective, a challenge to a state's title to control its own population and territory must *de facto* deprive it of its ability to exercise it; thus, when all is said and done, any challenge must take the form of armed confrontation, of trial by force.

Territory

We can now consider the reference to territory made in our opening quotation, but neglected to far. The basic implication of the sovereignty (or autonomy) of the state, is that the state has exclusive control over a portion of the earth – *its* territory, over which it routinely exercises jurisdiction and law enforcement, and whose integrity it is committed to protecting against encroachment form any other political power.

The state's relationship to the territory is a complex one. It has its 'hard' aspects: in particular, the territory must normally possess geographically distinct, fixed, continuous boundaries, and be militarily defensible. But it also has 'soft' ones; the portion of the earth in question is often idealised as the motherland or fatherland, considered as the very body of the state and as the cradle and home of its population. In the course of the development of the modern state, that relationship ceases to be thought of as one of ownership: as an Italian jurist suggests, the state does not *have* a territory, it *is* a territory.

Typically, a state's territory is continuous, has no enclaves, and is relatively large. The most visible aspect of the development of the modern state in Europe was the drastic simplification of the continent's political map, which around 1500 comprised some 150 independent political entities, and around 1900, about 25.

Centralisation

This feature is largely implicit in others already discussed. To qualify as a state, the organisation in question must be a unitary one; all political activities, as we have seen, must originate from it or refer to it. Individually or collectively, members of the population may hold other forms of social power; but they cannot exercise political power, except in the capacity of agents of the state itself, or by influencing the activities of such agents. Within the territory, a number of public bodies may exercise political faculties, but they derive all such faculties from the state. As to the key political resource, in the modern state the 'use of force is regarded as legitimate only in so far as it is either permitted by the state or prescribed by it'.[3]

Federal states represent a major exception to this rule, because they systematically divide governmental powers not just between different organs of the central state (see the next point) but between the latter and other political entities (sometimes called states). Historically, however, centralisation applies to them too, as a trend in the actual relations between the two levels.

Formal coordination of parts

The final defining feature of the state in our quotation ('its divisions are formally coordinated with one another') connects with previous ones. *Qua* organisation, the state is a complex entity, within which parts are distinguishable. For the sake of its unitary nature, of its 'centralised' character, it is essential that such parts should dovetail, that explicit arrangements should specify the competences of each part and their related faculties and facilities. As a result, the parts appear not as independent power centres, but as 'organs' which assert and enhance the state's own power by bringing it to bear in a more purposeful, competent manner, on behalf of the state as a whole.

The states system

I should like to round off this elaboration of the definition of the state offered by Tilly by making explicit a very important implication of the nature of the state as characterised by it. In particular, two features of the state discussed above, the state's sovereignty and its territoriality, jointly produce a most significant consequence: the political environment in which each state exists is by necessity one which it shares with a plurality of states similar in nature to itself. Each state is one unit lying next to others within a wider entity, the states system. But it is important to see that these units do not consider themselves, and do not conduct themselves in relation to one another, as organs of that wider entity, as they would if the latter had established and empowered them and were in a position authoritatively to regulate their conduct. Sovereignty entails that all states are (to an abstractly equal extent) primary, self-positing, self-sufficient entities; it is not the states system which brings them into being, but on the contrary their independent existences which generate the system.

Thus the relations between states are not structured, monitored and sanctioned by a hight power, for no such power exists: the state is the highest level *locus* of power present in the modern political environment. Those relations result instead from the open-ended, competitive pursuit by all states of the greatest amount of security and of the realisation of their own interests which they can command through their own resources. Thus those relations express, and revolve around, the *quantum* of power each state possesses relative to all others.

A basic way in which states seek to increase that amount is to neutralise or decrease the opposition of others to their own interests by means of alliances. But the plurality of potential allies, the changing concrete content of those interests and the fact that alliances are not authoritatively sanctioned by an overarching power, cause them to be intrinsically provisional and open to revision. Inter-state relations are thus necessarily open-ended, fluid, highly contingent. They reflect and engender continuous tensions and rivalries, and these (once more, in the absence of a superior power moderating them and settling them bindingly) may occasionally engender open enmity. The latter confirms the ultimate grounding of the state's power in organised coercion; for enmity typically expresses itself in attempts to overpower the opponent by main force, and has as its most dramatic manifestation the armed clash of the contendents – warfare.

The peculiar configuration of the states system as a plurality of a juxtaposed units recognising no shared subordination to any other political entity engenders a sharp discontinuity and contrast between the quality of political experience within and political experience between states. Relations internal to a state reflect, in principle, its unchallengable superiority as the sole fount of political power, imparting to political experience (and indeed to social experience at large) a unique quality of orderliness and peacefulness. All other subjects are made to renounce force as a means of asserting their own interests against opposing ones; and differences are settled by the state's enforcement of a binding criterion of judgement, normally supplied by law. (Writers describing the attainments of early state-building often use imagery which has strong overtones of architecture, of comprehensive and stable design – the image of the pyramid of power, of the state as an edifice, as a machine, as a clock.)

In contrast, the external relations of states are marked by tension, instability, disorder; its several units are all forced by the nature of the system they form to maximise their own power advantage over one another. And the only way to settle the resulting conflicts is, ultimately, for the parties to fight it out, to seek to overpower each other. In other words, what each state forbids its citizens to do to one another, all states must stand in readiness to do to each other. In fact, as we have seen in the first chapter, the state may expect citizens to serve its own power interests in the international context, by displaying at its bidding, in dealing with the enemy, exactly those qualities of aggressiveness, bellicosity and ferocity that it expects them to restrain and repress in their dealings with one another.

The 'Modernity' of the state

A final comment on Tilly's definition is that, in my view, it suffices to establish the peculiarly modern nature of its referent. In fact, it suggests that although one often speaks of 'the modern state' (I have myself made use of this expression) strictly speaking the adjective 'modern' is pleonastic. For the set of features listed above is not found in any large-scale political entities other than those which began to develop in the early-modern phase of European history.

In previous large-scale political entities, political power was institutionalised in a different manner, and mostly to a lesser extent. Those entities mainly expressed and extended the particular powers and interests of individual rulers and dynasties; in them, as I have already suggested, political prerogatives were undifferentiated components of privileged social standing. In general, those entities were structured as loose confederations of powerful individuals and their groups of followers and associates, with uncertain or varying spatial boundaries. On that account, the conduct of political activities lacked those characteristics of intensity, continuity and purposefulness which follow from entrusting such activities to an expressly designed, territorially bounded organisation.

Alternatively, there had existed complex, organisationally sophisticated entities exercising political prerogatives over relatively well-defined territories; but these were constituted as 'empires',[4] and as such did not conceive of themselves as existing side by side with other such entities and as making up with these a wider system analogous to the states system. Rather, each empire saw itself as having political charge of the world as it conceived of it. Also, the political activities routinely performed within such entities were exclusively military and fiscal, and, significant as they were, they did not order social life with the purposefulness and intensity that (modern) state do.

II

If, as I have just suggested, the definition of the state elaborated so far begins to apply only with the advent of the modern era, then in later stages of that era states acquired features not comprised within that definition. Some of these deserve to be taken into account in the conceptual portrait I am here drawing, for they are shared, to a lesser or greater degree, by the majority of contemporary states, at any rate in industrial societies. I have in mind the following features, some of which are closely related to one another:

Nationhood

Normally, the population of a given state shares significant commonalities other than the control exercised upon it by the state; it is supposed to constitute a distinctive collective entity on grounds other than political – to be a people or a nation, not just a population.

There is nothing intrinsically modern about the fact that the population which constitutes the referent of a system of rule also possesses other collective identities. But in pre-modern systems such non-political commonalities as existed used to be narrow, locally based ethnic ones; and these had to be replaced, redefined or complemented by others, in order to characterise a broader referent suitable for an emergent state system of rule.

There are several connotations of the notion of nationhood which make it particularly suitable for that task. It has, so to speak, a primordial ring to it (after all, the root of 'nation' is the same as that of *nat*ure and of 'being born' – *nasci*, in Latin), and to that extent it potentially expresses an intense, emotionally charged sense of belonging. On the other hand, in the course of its historical development that notion ceased to denote an exclusively primordial bond among those to whom it applied; it came to encompass, beside an ethnic bond, also a religious one, or a linguistic commonality, or one grounded on the sharing of institutional legacies, or of something as vague as historical experience or a sense of destiny. Nationhood could thus be attributed to the larger and larger populations of larger and larger territories; in fact, the sense of nationhood was soon to be generated by a large population's sharing of the same territory, whose boundaries were determined by the military successes (and failures) of a given centre of rule.

But a territorially bounded commonality is a relatively universalistic one; it groups individuals primarily on the basis of the physical location of their activities, and as such it is relatively indifferent to other aspects of their circumstances, or is focused on solidarities which transcend the differences and conflicts generated among them by those other aspects. A strongly felt, acted-upon sense of nationhood could thus not only, as it were, vault over local, particularistic affinities, but also moderate the trans-local, interest-based contrasts typical of the market relations which economic modernisation made more and more significant.

Generally speaking, a successfully constructed national identity facilitates communication between the people sharing it, creating a backdrop of shared assumptions and understandings to their interactions. More specifically, it can be argued that if strangers meeting on the market share a strongly felt sense of nationhood, this induces among them something of that sense of trust that in local communities is based on extensive, prolonged, mutual acquaintance, and can thus facilitate their entering into contractual relations with one another. Furthermore, the extent to which national affiliations, specially if overlapped with ethnic ones and intensified by inter-national animosities, can curb the class consciousness and the combativeness of subaltern groups has long been the bane of Marxist working-class movements.

These reflections on the political significance of the relatively wide and lasting sense of mutual belonging which nationhood both presupposes and generates, suggest why, at any rate in the industrially developed and modernised parts of the world, the structures primarily involved in political acitivities appear as the historical product of two overlapping but conceptually different processes – state-building and nation-building.[5] Early on, the former process largely preceded the latter; in the later, 'nationalist' phase, it was often claimed that the previous existence of the nation established the necessity and the legitimacy of the burdensome and often bloody enterprise of giving it a state of its own. But mostly the two processes overlapped. Some aspects of state-building, for instance the development of a public education system, expressly sought to generate in the state's population a sense of nationhood which could not be presupposed, but which once brought into being would in turn inspire and favour other aspects of state-building.

In other parts of the world, particularly since the Second World War, state-like political structures have sometimes been erected by political-military movements claiming to act on behalf of previously suppressed national identities and interests. The claim may have been valid in some cases, but in others it merely reflects the aura of legitimacy surrounding the nation as the modal political community associated with modernisation. For here the invocation of nationhood flies in the face of irreducible and stubbornly more significant ethnic and religious affinities. It has been suggested that in such cases it might be more appropriate to speak, if anything, of state-nations rather than of nation-states.[6]

Democratic legitimation

Most contemporary states have a democratic legitimation. By this I mean the following: the state not only claims to complement and uphold politically the other, pre-and non-political commonalities that bind its people together; it also claims to see in the people its own constituency, and thus the ultimate seat of all the powers that it exercises. Furthermore, the state claims to see its own existence as justified by the services it renders its people, and the people's compliance with the political demands placed upon it as constituting both a dutiful acknowledgement of the services rendered it, and a necessary condition of further services being rendered. Finally, the services in question are chiefly of an economic nature; they consist primarily in the contribution the state makes, or claims to make, towards promoting the country's industrial development and the growth of its national product. Or, as Luhmann puts it, in contemporary society 'the primacy of the economy shows itself in politics through the extent to which judgement of political success is made to depend on economic successes.'[7]

Citizenship

The notions of nationhood and of democratic legitimation find institutional expression in a particular bond between the persons making up the population and the state – citizenship. This is a set of general and equal entitlements and obligations vested in individuals with respect to the state. The content of the set varies historically, as does the definition of who counts as a person for this purpose; women, for instance, have been largely excluded from that definition until our own century. But generally those who do count have a right to take an active role in some aspects – however infrequent and insignificant – of the state's activity (typically, by taking part in elections). Furthermore, further opportunities for more significant and more demanding participation are in principle open to the generality of citizens through their voluntary involvement in political parties. Citizenship thus means that individuals at large possess (among others) specifically political capacities, interests and preferences, the exercise of which allows them to affect to a greater or lesser extent the content of state activity.

The state and law

Especially (not exclusively) in Western societies in the eighteenth and nineteenth centuries, the institutional development of the state lay particular emphasis on the state's relationship to law. This is a complex phenomenon, comprising two apparently contrasting aspects. On the one hand, law adds to the two social functions it performs everywhere, the allocation of control over goods and the repression of conduct defined as anti-social, one which is much rarer – the organisation of political power and the programming of (some of) the modes of its exercise.[8] On the other hand, the state, which for a long time had played a critical role in enforcing law, acquires more and more fully and exclusively the prerogative of making it.

Thus, while law becomes involved in shaping significant political processes, at the same time it loses the autonomy from rulers it had previously enjoyed, as a set of principles and norms deriving their content and their validity from religion, tradition and the spontaneously developed practices of corporate groups; it openly becomes the product (and, unavoidably, the instrument) of policy.

The balance between, so to put it, the *juridicisation of politics* and the *politicisation of law*, is an unstable and variable one; but whatever its vicissitudes, clearly the mutual involvement of those two phenomena, politics and law, becomes deep (particularly in the nineteenth century), and impinges significantly on the nature of both phenomena. This is indicated among other things by the ideological charge attached to expressions such as rule of law, *Rechtsstaat*, legal positivism. (This last, in particular, seeks to eliminate an opposing, ancient view of the nature and sources of the law, which invoked 'natural law'. Faced with the centuries-old question, whether law (*jus*) derived its validity from being just (*jus quia justum*) or from being commanded (*jus quia jussum*) it comes down sharply on the second side.)

So far as concerns us here, the main point is that increasingly the state comes to employ juridical instruments (from the constitutional charter to the statute to the administrative ruling to the judicial sentence) in order to perform the most diverse political tasks. It is by means of law that the state articulates its own organisation into organs, agencies, authorities; confers upon each different competences, facilities, faculties; establishes controls over the resultant activities; attributes to individuals the capacities, entitlements and obligations of citizenship; extracts from economic processes the resources with which to finance its own activities, and so on. 'Public law' is the term (of Roman origin) employed in Continental Europe to refer to the growing body of legislation and regulation dealing with such matters, which is sometimes the concern of specialised courts.

The state, thus, 'speaks the law' in almost all aspects of its functioning. An implication of this (though perhaps not an inevitable one)[9] is that the state's activities, in order to be imputable to it, and to produce the intended effects, must in turn constitute the dutiful execution of legal commands, although some of these are abstract and general enough to leave space to discretionary judgement and political initiative. In any case, in this perspective, the formation of valid legal commands, constitutes the highest manifestation of sovereignty. (Even in the popular understanding of power, 'laying down the law' is seen as its most significant expression.)

As a consequence, particularly in the mature state of late nineteenth and early twentieth century Continental Europe, a sophisticated form of legal speech becomes the medium of many decisional processes internal to the state, as well as of much public argument concerning the nature, the scope and the general or specific targets of state action. For this reason, Max Weber saw in the modern state the embodiment *par excellence* of what he called 'legal-rational domination'; and in one of his lengthier definitions of the state he assigned the first place to the following characteristic: 'It [the state] possesses an administrative and legal order subject to change by legislation, to which the organized activities of the administrative staff, which are also controlled by legislation, are oriented.'[10]

Bureaucracy

This last quotation leads us directly to a further feature of the modern state, again one particularly marked in the later phases of its development – the bureaucratic nature of the state's administrative apparatus. This can be seen as an attempt to reduce the potential contrast between on the one hand the fact that the state is a unitary entity, and on the other hand the fact that it is highly composite, comprising a number of diverse parts.

Though all the activities of a state are seen as ultimately powered and directed from a single centre, and as sanctioned by its monopoly of legitimate coercion, those activities differ hugely in their form and content, as well as through having to be carried out under very different circumstances. Correspondingly, the various organs and offices making up the state differ greatly in the concrete activities they conduct, authorise and control, and for that reason tend to become relatively autonomous of one another. Each seeks to maximise the state resources it commands, and to assign priority to its own concerns over all others.

Bureaucracy is a relatively effective means of controlling these tendencies (*relatively*, because it can never utterly suppress them, and indeed beyond a certain point may well intensify them). It entails that the complex of organs and offices making up the state is layered in two ways. First, ultimate decisional powers are vested in a supreme organ which is the very seat of sovereignty, and is itself non-bureaucratic (the Crown, Parliament, the ruling party). In the second place, all other organs and offices, mostly charged with administration, and particularly likely to become more and more numerous and diverse, are purposely structured according to a particular model of organisation – the bureaucratic model.

In this model, all activities of the state (except the making of a few, most momentous decisions of a strictly political nature, directly concerning the state's internal security and the maintenance of public order) consist either in the framing of general directives, or in the articulation of these into less general ones, or in the implementation of the latter. To these levels of generality of directives there corresponds a hierarchy of offices, empowering those issuing the more general (and thus the more abstract) directives to mandate their specification into less general ones by lower offices, to oversee their implementation, and to verify *ex post facto* whether such specification and implementation has been properly and successfully carried out. In other words, organs and offices in charge of more general directives can activate, control and sanction the operation of lower ones. To the extent that this possibility is realised, it confers upon the state what has been called 'infra-structural power'. That is, the political centre can monitor, activate and sanction the most diverse social activities, taking place over the whole territory, and do so according to directives which are of its own making, and are thus intrinsically changeable.

A further aspect of the bureaucratic model bears closely on another, previously discussed feature of the state, its relationship to law. In the model, the critical qualification for the holding of any office is the knowledge of the appropriate directives, as well as the mastery of the intellectual techniques for interpreting them, specifying them into less general ones, ascertaining the contingent situations on which they are to be brought to bear, and finally seeing to their execution. The presumption is that to the hierarchical arrangement of offices corresponds also a hierarchy in the possession of such knowledge and of those techniques. Both are assumed to be learnable, teachable and testable.

In the course of the development of many European states, it has often been assumed that the most relevant knowledge for the performance of the state's administrative activities was legal knowledge. There are various reasons for this assumption: the degree of systemic coherence imparted to legal knowledge by the universities; its intellectual sophistication and cultural prestige; and finally, something I have just indicated – the intrinsic affinity seen to exist between the political enterprise and the phenomenon of law.

The significance of law in orienting administrative conduct, however, should not be overstated. In the first place, in English-speaking countries it has never been as great as in other Western countries. Even here, furthermore, it has had to contend with the growing significance, especially in the twentieth century, of non-juridical forms of knowledge. Even where law was taken most seriously, its application to concrete circumstances called for sound knowledge and reliable information concerning factual conditions, not just legal norms. Thus, from relatively early on in the development of the state, efforts were made by individual states to collect data on demographic and economic conditions (the term 'statistic' bears witness to this) and to keep themselves abreast of developments in the material and organisational technology of production. Of course, states also sought, more or less successfully, to develop and apply know-how relevant to their two overriding (and overlapping) concerns – the collection of taxes and the organising, equipping and deploying of armies and navies.

For this reason and others, all administrators had to make some allowance in their practices for the increasing social significance and political relevance of bodies of non-juridical knowledge. However, they differed considerably in the extent to which this consideration affected the recruitment, training and career structure of officials, as well as the philosophy behind the structure and practice of the administrative units themselves. Over time, there thus emerged considerable differences both *between* states in the extent to which their administrative apparatus routinely concerned itself with the technical effectiveness, as against the juridical correctness, of its own operation, and *within* a given state in the prevalent orientation of individual parts of its apparatus.

Other important differences, again both between and within states, concerned the extent to which administrative action, whatever the grounds to which it officially referred, was in fact determined primarily by considerations of expediency, such as securing the continuing tenure of power of governmental elites, widening the discretion and fostering the status and economic advantages of the administrators themselves, or shaping public policies to suit the requirements of the dominant socio-economic interests.

For all this, it remains the case that, especially on the Continent, the structure and mode of operation of the bureaucratic model, particularly in the intermediate phases of state-building, attached considerable significance to law, and especially to a specialised, increasingly complex body of public law – administrative law.

III

A thoroughly institutionalised system of political power

Having thus given a relatively diffuse conceptual portrait of the state, let us reconsider briefly the statement by Popitz quoted at the end of the first chapter. Clearly the state, as portrayed above, embodies to a high degree all aspects of institutionalisation Popitz mentions.

To begin with, we can see the *depersonalisation* of political power reflected, for instance, in the nature of the state as an organisation, that is as a set of positions that shape and constrain the conduct of inhabitants, to the point of rendering relatively insignificant their individual identities. The same phenomenon, of course, is entailed in the bureaucratic model: here are depersonalised both the officials, mainly chosen through public, purportedly objective, examinations, and guided in their activities by their knowledge of rules and circumstances; and the citizens with whom the functionaries deal, and who so often complain of being treated as cyphers or as anonymous entries in a file.

The primary way of *formalising* the exercise of political power in the state is the conscious effort to standardise it by means of laws – from broad constitutional principles and conventions to the minute regulation of the operating procedures of the remotest provincial office. 'Rituals', mentioned by Popitz as an alternative mode of formalisation, are not inexistent, but much less significant than in other, more archaic, large-scale systems of institutionalised power.

The final aspect, the *integration* of political power into a greater social whole, is reflected for instance in the predominance of states whose populations claim a sense of nationhood; in the near-universal preference for a democratic form of legitimation (as understood above); and in the growing significance of citizenship as a set of mutual claims and reciprocal involvements binding together the state and the individuals.

The thorough extent to which political power has become institutionalised in the state is of course the product of protracted, complex and diverse historical processes. We shall consider these, albeit, schematically, in the next two chapters.

3

The Development of the Modern State (1)

The task of this chapter and the next

The development of the modern state[1] is an integral aspect of a wider, complex and momentous historical phenomenon – the advent of modern society in Western Europe – which an increasing number of students consider not amenable to rigorous explanation. Some of them have taken to calling it 'the European miracle':[2] an expression suggesting, together with a degree of Eurocentric arrogance, a sense of bafflement as to the causes of the phenomenon, rather than the assured feeling that a definite set of causes has been (or can be) convincingly identified.

I mention this as a disclaimer that what follows should be seen as a proper historical explanation of the development of the modern state. What I offer is instead a schematic account of the main phases of that development, emphasising the discontinuities between the phases as well as the cumulative character of the whole development rather more than a properly historical treatment would allow. Also, I take little notice of the differences the development presents in different regions of Western Europe.

What is being offered is in the first place a streamlined reconstruction of the major innovations affecting political institutions – that is, the arrangements for building up and exercising political power. In the second place, some consideration is occasionally given to concepts and theories more or less self-consciously developed by the political actor and/or by their advisers, spokesmen or supporters, in order to criticise existing arrangements, and to propose or oppose alternative ones. What is missing from the present account, however, is any sustained considera-tion of concomitant developments in other spheres of social life, although often enough such developments made the new political arrangements necessary and possible, and in turn were influenced by the changing political environment.

I

Feudalism: origins

The political modernisation of European society began – at different times between the twelfth and the fourteenth centuries, according to which part of Western Europe one considers – against the background of a complex set of arrangements mostly referred to as feudal. Thus, in order to make a start in our argument, we must determine the meaning of that disputed label.[3] What arrangements concerning political power can be reasonably labelled 'feudal'?

The early roots of feudalism lie in the political institutions of Germanic tribal populations in the era preceding the great barbarian invasions.[4] Those institutions were focused on the imperatives of military command: a tribe's warriors (which generally meant all free men) generally acclaimed one of their number king, on account of his qualities as a chief, and mostly for the purpose (and for the duration) of a single major military undertaking. (The mutual implication between war and political arrangements, and thus the significance of the relation between political experience and violence, already stressed in our first two chapters, are continuously echoed in the story summarised in this and the next.)

The concern with war and leadership in battle also inspired a special relationship between the king himself and the best of the tribe's warriors, signalled by the name of *vassi* attached to the latter. This was an intrinsically honourable relationship, for both parties – the king and the *vassus* – owed one another aid and counsel. Collectively the *vassi* constituted an elite group: the king's *trustis*, to use a Germanic term, or his *comitiva*, to use a Latin one.

Some of the great barbarian invasions of the Roman empire were carried out by alliances between several tribes; and again military considerations, and the requirements of conquering and ruling over sizeable parts of the former Roman empire, influenced the constitution of larger Germanic kingdoms. Here the strengthened powers of the king found expression also through new sets of offices (collectively called, in Latin, the king's *palatium*), generally held by that same elite element, the *vassi*. In most cases, however, even the two overlapping institutions of *palatium* and *trustis/comitiva* were not sufficient to the task of establishing and consolidating large-scale, durable political structures;

for tribal affiliations and the rivalries between leading dynasties cut across both arrangements, continually weakening and periodically undoing them.

Feudalism: the key arrangements

The great exception is represented by the Frankish kingdom. Beginning in the late seventh century, a new dynasty of Frankish rulers, the Pippinids, made good use of the vassalic bond to secure the cooperation of members of the warrior elite not just in military tasks, but in other aspects of the governance of the territories under Frankish rule. They did so by grafting onto the vassalic bond an institution of Roman (and ecclesiastical) origin – the *beneficium*. That is, they endowed each vassal with a grant of land which, in due course, came to be called *feudum*, 'fief'.

By exploiting the land he held in fief (chiefly via the unpaid labour of the rural population settled on it), each vassal was made capable of equipping and training himself and his followers for the practice of war, of defending and policing the territory, administering justice and seeing to the local implementation of the ruler's policies. But while he performed these activities on the ruler's behalf, in doing so he also acquired considerable prerogatives of his own, and a growing autonomy *vis-à-vis* the ruler himself. For typically the fief, and sometimes a larger portion of land surrounding it, became 'immune' from the powers originally vested in the grantor, and which now devolved on his 'enfeoffed' vassal.

In turn, major vassals, those holding their fiefs directly from the emperor, the king, or a ruler of comparable significance, often established with other, lesser warriors and chieftains the same relationship in which they stood to those higher potentates. Here, of course, they appeared as the higher party (generally called in Latin *senior*, and in vulgar languages *Herr*, lord, *seigneur*), granting fiefs to lesser members of their own privileged social stratum, and placing upon them, via a vassalic compact, the same obligations they had undertaken *vis-à-vis* their own (over)lord, including those concerning tasks of governance.

This means that, over a larger territory – in principle, even one as large as the Carolingian empire – the performance of those tasks was entrusted largely to a structure connecting the members of a privileged group of warriors and landlords, bound to one another by honourable, contractual obligations of aid and counsel. The structure might have two or more tiers, and on each tier the concrete tasks of governance were assigned to a less exalted member of the group, who exercised it over a smaller parcel of land.

At all levels, the structure could operate consistently and reliably, and thus secure seasonably coherent and dependable practices of rule over the larger territory, only on certain conditions: for instance, that the vassal would actually perform his obligations toward the lord, and vice versa; that the lord would actually be able to deprive a miscreant or inactive vassal of the possession and enjoyment of the fief, and assign it to another vassal; that on a vassal's death the fief would return to the lord, or be transferred to the vassal's heir only on condition that he would comply with the obligations originally undertaken by the vassal himself.

The feudal entropy

One can easily see how improbable were those (and other) conditions on which depended the effective and coherent functioning of a feudal system of rule. For the historical context was one where timely and effective communications between the parties to the vassalic compact, and in particular the transmission of instructions downwards and information upwards, was made impossible by, for instance, widespread illiteracy and the decay and insecurity of the road system. Also, it was of the essence of the compact that each vassal would maintain an autonomous military capability in order to perform his obligations; but, by the same token, he would also be able to offer armed resistance to his own lord's attempt to force upon him his obligations if he neglected them, or to deprive him of his feudal holdings. (In fact, feudal law in some circumstances not only allows but expects the vassal to resist his lord.)[5]

Furthermore, in the overwhelmingly agrarian economy of the European middle ages, agricultural surplus was the dominant source of economic power. Thus, no individual vested with a feudal claim upon that surplus could afford to be deprived of it, lest he forfeit his military capability and his privileged social standing. Nor for that matter could he disregard any opportunity to increase his feudal holdings, even if in order to pursue them he had to disregard or contravene his obligations toward his lord, or assume incompatible obligations toward other lords. Hence, the incentive to hold on to his position of advantage even by violating the terms under which it had been originally acquired, was very strong.

Finally, the vassal's interest in securing for his heirs the possession and exploitation of the fiefs he held ran counter to the original assumption that each vassal would feel a strong personal obligation to fulfill the vassalic compact. For as a fief went from heir to heir, the bond between each successive heir and the original grantor of the land (or *his* heir) became less and less cogent and enforceable.

For all these reasons, feudal arrangements were intrinsically unable to provide a coherent institutional basis for a stable, wide-ranging system of rule. Because of this, imaginative and powerful rulers sought to complement those arrangements with others. But these mostly could not withstand, in the long run, the inherent entropy of feudal arrangements: that is, their tendency to disperse and fragment political power, abandoning its exercise – at the periphery of a larger system – to the narrow interests of petty chiefs and dynasts, who often struggled with one another, or banded together only to resist their lord's commands.

The Carolingian emperors, for instance, tried to build alongside and across the network of feudal arrangements at whose apex they stood, a system of territorial offices (those of 'count' and 'marquis'), and of inspectorates (the *missi dominici*, or envoys of the lord), which would counter the entropy inherent in that framework. But the economic and cultural conditions of the age forced the Carolingians to fall back upon the vassalic bond and the fief in appointing the holders of those offices, and in making their operations economically possible. Thus, the entropy often triumphed. In the long run – by the early eleventh century, for instance, in the central territories of the Carolingian empire (which were to become France) – political power was to a large extent held and exercised by a multitude of petty chieftains, who put their key resource – the possession of a military stronghold (a *castellum*) – primarily at the service of their economic greed.[6]

Combating the entropy

But 'to a large extent' does not mean 'totally'. Almost nowhere in Western Europe did the political ordering of social existence rest exclusively on feudal structures (that is, at bottom, on the private arrangements between powerful individuals), and it was nowhere wholly at the mercy of their entropy. In the first place, over the centuries the Christian Church had established a system of ecclesiastical offices which constituted a supplementary structure of communication and leadership. Church leaders (bishops, abbots) at various times also performed critical tasks of political command and saw to public needs.[7] Furthermore, the Church, because of its international (as we would now call it) character, constituted an invaluable vehicle for a sense of commonality and shared purpose which reached across wide and little-travelled spaces, and across diverse ethnic identities and social ranks.[8]

In the second place, as medieval historian currently emphasise, the memory of the Roman empire, though increasingly remote, continued in various ways and to a sometimes surprising extent, to inspire a sense that there had been, there could be, ways of governing wide territories other than via networks of mutually obligated individuals. The Church appealed to that sense, as shown for instance by the correspondence between the jurisdiction of several dioceses and that of Roman municipal constituencies. Secular rulers, too, appealed to that sense in order to emphasise the distinctiveness of their position – and nowhere as explicitly as in the idea of a renewed, Christianised, and thus 'Holy', Roman empire.

But also at lower levels, within that empire, and after its failure as an effective system of rule, many people never entirely lost a sense that governance could be, and should be, the responsibility and the prerogative of a set of specifically public offices, operating according to explicit, comprehensive, uniformly enforced rules. And that belief repeatedly inspired (or at any rate was called upon to justify) rulers ambitious to consolidate their power, increasing its reach and its scope.

The fulfilment of such ambitions, however, could not depend exclusively, or even largely, on the persuasiveness of appeals to the Roman idea of a *res publica*, guarded by a distinct set of political offices and prerogatives. Unavoidably, that fulfilment depended chiefly on whether such ambitious rulers could defeat both the vested interests which ran contrary to their own ambitions, and the competition of other rulers who shared them. I speak of defeating advisedly, for typically such ambitions could only be fulfilled through decisive, successful military confrontations – a further reminder of the military aspects intrinsic to the political enterprise. Though the confrontation between competing claims to more extensive and penetrating political power takes place at different times and through different vicissitudes in different parts of Europe, in the long run its outcome is approximately the same in all major circumstances: slowly the struggle for power sifts through the multiple power centres established during the feudal era, allowing a few of them to extend their reach over larger and larger territories.

II

Beyond feudalism

But this outcome should not be seen only in quantitative terms. In the process of attaining it – and indeed in order to attain it – the successful centre of political power normally underwent also a qualitative transformation. Furthermore, this became more and more marked even after that centre had ceased bringing new territories under its rule. The transformation did not so much *extend* that rule as *intensify* it. That is, it made the exercise of political power more continuous, regular and purposeful.

Various social changes determined this process of intensification of rule – from the improvements in the road systems in various parts of Europe, to the growth of literacy, to developments in the material and social technology of warfare, to the increasing significance of economic processes mediated by money and centred on the towns.

The intensification of rule, in turn, presented a variety of aspects; among these, I would like to emphasise the emergence of (partially) new, shared understandings and explicit arrangements concerning the acquisition and exercise of political power. For, by and large, rulers who respect those understandings and observe those arrangements are thereby further empowered and legitimated *vis-à-vis* their subjects; whereas rule exercised without such understandings and arrangements becomes by the same token contentious and potentially precarious.

Let me clarify what is new here; for even under feudalism, rule was carried out in the light of shared understandings and under established arrangements. Yet these, in principle, concerned only the relations between powerful private individuals (*particuliers*, to use the French expression) – the lord and his vassals – who represented only themselves, or at best their respective dynasties. Furthermore, those understandings and arrangements were rudimentary and poorly articulated; taken together, they constituted an obscure, vernacular body of custom. Finally, under feudal arrangements the two principals largely went their separate ways in the routine exercise of rule, each attending primarily to building up his own economic and military resources. Except for a vassal's occasional involvement in the expeditions of his lord's army, and in the sessions of his judicial court, the two were not expected routinely to cooperate in rule.

The polity of estates

These arrangements are strongly modified by the advent of the post-feudal, early-modern system of rule which is often designated by the German expression *Ständestaat*, possibly best translated as 'polity of estates'. In a number of larger territories, particularly enterprising and successful rulers constructed new kinds of political relations with various parts of society, establishing different understandings and arrangements under which to rule.

In the first place, in the polity of estates the rulers present themselves primarily not as feudal superiors, but as the holders of higher, public prerogatives of non- and often pre-feudal origins, surrounded by the halo of a higher majesty, often imparted by means of sacred ceremonies (for example, the *sacre du roi*).

In the second place, the counterpart to the ruler is typically represented not by individuals, but by constituted bodies of various kinds: local assemblies of aristocrats, cities, ecclesiastical bodies, corporate associations. Taken singly, each of these bodies – the 'estates' – represents a different collective entity: a region's noblemen of a given rank, the residents of a town, the faithful of a parish or the practitioners of a trade. Taken together, these bodies claim to represent a wider, more abstract, territorial entity – country, *Land, terra, pays* – which, they assert, the ruler is entitled to rule only to the extent that he upholds its distinctive customs and serves its interests.

In turn, however, these interests are largely identified with those of the estates; and even the customs of the country or the region in question have as their major components the different claims of the various estates. Thus, the ruler can rule legitimately only to the extent that periodically he convenes the estates of a given region or of the whole territory into a constituted, public gathering. By addressing such a gathering and becoming involved in its deliberations – according to a body of increasingly explicit and sophisticated rules, and with reference to an established set of competences and faculties – the ruler can, jointly with the estates, determine policy. Naturally, such a gathering tends to come the seat and the occasion of a bargaining process, between a ruler seeking new faculties and resources, and estates keen to reassert their traditional privileges; and the outcome of the bargaining reflects, in the end, the balance of power between the parties. But the process itself is clothed in formalities which to an extent constrain that outcome, and compel the ruler to articulate the grounds of his claims.

Typically, a ruler comes to the gathering to ask for money and other resources (mostly needed, once more, for the purpose of waging war). But he cannot do so without justifying his demands by reference to traditionally recognised public ends to the pursuit of which he intends to commit the money and the resources. Such ends must go beyond the interests of the ruling dynasty, and further those of the land itself and of its people – as represented, of course, by the estates, that is by its *pars melior* (better part). The estates, furthermore, possess autonomous facilities and faculties of rule, differing from estate to estate and from region to region.

> Practically all the functions which the contemporary state claims as its own, were then parcelled out to the most diverse bearers – to the church, the landowning nobility, the knights, the towns, and various other privilege-holders. By way of enfeoffment, mortgage, immunity, the realm had lost, one after another, almost all regalian rights and transferred them to what we would today conceive of as private bearers.[9]

These dispersed political prerogatives are routinely employed in the pursuit of each estate's special interests – the noblemen's exploitation of the rural population by means of seigneurial rights, for instance, or a town's control over the markets and fairs periodically held within it, or the monopolistic practice of a certain trade or craft on the part of its practitioners constituted into a guild. However, once they have consented to a larger, country- or region-wide initiative of the ruler's, the estates place those prerogatives at the service of that initiative. Thus the ruler's policies, in order to mobilise wider resources than those he possesses *qua* landlord, or those he administers *qua* holder of a non-feudal title, must be systematically mediated by and through the estates. In this sense it can be said that polity of estates is marked by a 'power dualism'.[10] 'Both parties – rulers and estates – consider themselves in possession of a higher right. Both have at their disposal a full-fledged apparatus of power of their own: officials, courts, finances, often even their own armies and their own envoys . . . The rulers must deal with the estates as one would with associates having equal entitlements as oneself'.[11]

III

Toward absolutism: intellectual aspects

In the polity of estates, political prerogatives were claimed as rightfully theirs by this or that social group, and mobilised largely in the service of interests peculiar to it. This constituted its backward-looking aspect, bestowed upon it by the more and more remote feudal past. Also the fact that rulers periodically needed to address the holders of autonomous powers and obtain their assent and cooperation in their political undertakings, can be seen as a reminder of the contractual nature of the feudal bond – although, as I have pointed out, the relations between the two parties in the polity of estates were more frequent and regular, and encompassed wider concerns than under the feudal dispensation.

In any case, in those parts of Europe where the state developed earlier and more effectively, that development took primarily the form of a progressive reduction of the political prerogatives of the estates, and of their concentration in the hands of the ruler. The ruler undertook to exercise these prerogatives in a comprehensive and relatively uniform manner over the whole territory, via an apparatus of rule which depended on him alone. The progressive erosion of the characteristic dualism of the polity of estates led to what can be considered the first major institutional embodiment of the modern state, the so-called absolute state.[12]

Needless to say, any reasonably comprehensive causal account of the development of the absolute state would have to call upon a large number of non-political factors, and among these it would probably give priority to military and economic determinants of the process. But, as I indicated at the beginning, this chapter and the next do not seek to give such an account. Rather, I prefer to mention some intellectual aspects of the process, by pointing at a few ideas which, explicitly or implicitly, played a significant role in the story.

As we have seen, the polity of estates operated against a background of established tradition – largely a legacy of the feudal phase – so it is hardly surprising that the dynamic leading to its transcendence in the absolute state had a distinctly intellectual edge to it. For in early-modern Western Europe – that is, in an increasingly literate, secular, sophisticated intellectual environment – the arrangements for rule became the object not just of contentions between actors with different interests and resources, but also of self-conscious debate over the contrasting claims.

Although what ultimately settled those conrasts was the power superiority of one party, which enabled it to have its way over the resistance of the others, each party had an interest in articulating its own claims as convincingly as possible, if only in order to operate in fact as a party, that is as a collective force, an alignment of like-minded individuals. The burden of clearly articulating its claims lay most heavily upon the party, or parties, proposing innovations, and thus having to overcome the resistance of the status quo, of established, traditional arrangements (although paradoxically even the innovating party was often under a compulsion to rest its claims on the appeal to some respected tradition).

Throughout the early phases of the development of the state – those corresponding, in this synthetic review, to the polity of estates and absolutism – two overlapping traditions of discourse were mobilised by the forces chiefly identified with that development: Roman law, and the Graeco-Roman republican tradition.

The later phases of the polity of estates thus saw a protracted and sophisticated intellectual argument over the proper arrangements for rule, from which emerged, among others, the idea of sovereignty.[13] As other writers have pointed out,[14] that idea operated on two fronts. One the one hand, it contrasted the claim of Papacy and of Empire to constitute a universal commonwealth which both empowered and limited the activities of all Christian rulers; on the other, it challenged the dispersion of political prerogatives inherited from feudalism and still characteristic of the polity of estates.

In the context we are considering, the battle for sovereignty had already been won on the first front: the empire and the papacy themselves constituted no more than particular, territorially limited systems of rule, with ever fainter claims to universal jurisdiction. The real target of that battle was the dualism of the polity of estates, which acknowledged a plurality of territorially distinct entities, but within each entity tended, as we have seen, to divide facilities and faculties of rule between the estates themselves and the ruler.

Thus, the latter's claim to sovereignty no longer meant primarily, as it had done previously, that the ruler acknowledged no superiors, but rather that he acknowledged no peers – except, of course, outside his territorially limited sphere of power; for each sovereign entity exists side by side with other such entities. The key intellectual argument for sovereignty is that law and order can only be maintained within each territory if one power alone possesses a distinct prerogative – whether this be conceived as the power 'to make and unmake law' (Bodin), or as the exclusive control over coercive force (Hobbes). The argument gained immeasurably in cogency from the experiences of the wars of religion on the Continent and of the seventeenth-century revolutions in England: both sets of events show the costs of a country's not possessing a centre of unchallengeable, ultimate, paramount power, before which all others must bow.[15]

It is essential, according to the argument, that sovereignty should be enjoyed by a center of power qualitatively different from all other social forces, because exclusively concerned with a distinctive set of interests, of a specifically political nature. In this respect, that argument is complemented by another, focused on the Renaissance notion of *ratio status* (*raison d'état*).

Two aspects of the latter argument are relevant here. The first aspect – to which that notion chiefly owed its notoriety and controversiality – is its negative content, to the effect that the pursuit of specifically political interests (those concerning the acquiring and securing of power within 'principalities', to use Machiavelli's expression, and their territorial expansion) lies outside the constraints of morality and law, and, in particular, can legitimately make use of unrestrained force and of premeditated deceit.

The second aspect is less obvious: it relates the above exemption from morality of rulers *qua* rulers to the expectation that their actions should indeed be rational, that is, controlled by considerations of effectiveness, and should in fact be oriented to a specific, overriding set of interests. Only the emphatically public nature of rule, the fact that its concern with internal order and external might gives it paramount significance with respect to all other social interests, authorises the powers responsible for it to violate moral dictates applicable to everybody else and to all other pursuits.

This emphasis on the distinctiveness of the tasks of rulers constitutes the most significant difference between the Western absolute state and despotism. For the former aims in principle to gather unto itself – and, typically, to vest in the sovereign – only specifically political faculties and facilities, leaving individuals and collectivities in possession of their established resources and claims, as long as they do not entail a parcelling out of sovereign prerogatives.

The notion of the absoluteness (in the sense of not-boundedness) of the monarch's power reflects the claim that he is the fount of the law – as in the principle *quod principi placuit legis habet vigorem* (whatever pleased the ruler shall constitute valid law) – and as such he is 'not bound' by it. But the law in question is only public law, that is, a body of statutory rules specifically concerning the exercise of political powers, which for that very reason may be overridden by their maker whenever by observing them he would jeopardise the paramount interests of order and security. Such law leaves undisturbed, in principle, those claims of individuals and groups which embody their private interests, and give firm shape to the highly diffrentiated structure of Western European society.

Thus, the concentration of *imperium* in the monarch presupposes and complements the dispersion of *dominium*, that is, of property and possession, among his subjects.[16] Indeed, a prime concern of the *imperium* holder is understood to be the preservation of the inequalities of economic power and of social standing resulting from *dominium*. (After all, the monarch himself has a private capacity, typically that of a particularly wealthy and most noble landlord.) However, when the specific rights and privileges constituting those inequalities occasion contention, the task of adjudicating the resulting controversies falls increasingly upon public courts expressing and bringing to bear the ruler's power – although some of those courts (for instance the French *parlements*) had originally been estate bodies, and occasionally confirmed that origin in opposing the king's centralising designs.

These are the essential terms of the new power equilibrium characteristic of the absolute state. The basic relationship between the monarch and the estates is no longer fixed by assigning to each party unequal amounts of political power, and by requiring the concurrence of both in the making and execution of policy. The distinction becomes a more abstract one: in principle, all political power is vested in the monarch, while politically powerless subjects can go on enjoying and exercising powers of a different nature, as long as they do not infringe upon the monarch's prerogative.

Thus the arrangements whereby policy making and administration were shared between the monarch and the estates became progressively weakened and displaced. But in this very period both the military rivalries between rulers, and a multitude of social, economic and cultural developments were increasing rather than diminishing the demand for policy making and administration. Thus new arrangements had to be put in place, which clearly assigned to the political centre the responsibility for meeting the demand and for extracting and allocating the requisite resources.

The monarch and his court

One can perhaps distinguish two aspects of this process. On the one hand, the monarch and his court became established as the sole centre of policy formation; on the other, a new administrative system was constructed which bypassed the estate-based system in connecting the centre with the country at large.

The French kingdom in the seventeenth century – its golden age – constitutes the best locale for observing the first aspect of the process, which enhanced the centrality and superiority of the monarchical institutions and emphasised the exclusive nature of the monarch's powers. This aspect is most forthrightly stated in a document of 1766, in which Louis XV rebutted the claim to autonomous power of the courts called *parlements*:

> In my person alone resides the sovereign power, and it is from me alone that the courts hold their existence and their authority. That . . . authority can only be exercised in my name . . . For it is to me exclusively that the legislative power belongs . . . The whole public order emanates from me since I am its supreme guardian . . . The rights and interests of the nation . . . are necessarily united with my own and can only rest in my hands.[17]

Again, two phases may be distinguished here, which (simplifying the matter considerably) can be made to coincide with the two successive reigns of Louis XIII and Louis XIV.

The task of Louis XIII (assisted and indeed guided first by Richelieu then by Mazarino) was chiefly to neutralise the resistance and whenever necessary forcibly to overcome the open rebellion of the higher nobility and of other estate powers. (Both resistance and rebellion coincided at times with the challenge to monarchical supremacy posed by religious dissidence.) He achieved this by what would be called, in the jargon of twentieth-century political science, a non-decision, – that is, over most of the seventeenth and eighteenth centuries, the French monarch never chose to convene the Estates-General of the realm.

Another, more visible strategy, well known to readers of *The Three Musketeers*, was his repression of duelling. Even persons whose status entitled them to bear arms could no longer wield them in order to secure and enforce their own rightful claims to honour and advantage. Duelling was proscribed as constituting a microscopic form of private warfare, in order to preserve to monopoly of law enforcement held by public institutions. On a larger scale, and in positive term, the military reforms undertaken under Louis XVI by Le Tellier began to establish the French state's rigorous and effective control over its armed forces.

But Louis XIV's task was not just to continue his predecessor's policies, but to further their success by making of himself, his councils and his court, the visible, uncontested fulcrum and pinnacle of the polity. The elaboration of a subtle and sophisticated body of rules for court conduct, with the concomitant construction of Versailles, represented in many ways the masterpiece of Louis' kingship, for they served a number of functions.[18]

To the country at large the court appears as a floodlit stage on which wondrous events are enacted, as a lofty pedestal from atop which the Sun King radiates the light of his majesty. For the nobility, life at court provides a set of status and economic rewards which partly compensate for its loss political prerogatives. At the same time, life at court separates the noblemen taking part in it from their original base in the country (as well as from the capital, given the distance between Paris and Versailles). Finally, it places them in competition with one another; the resulting rivalries among the nobles pose no threat to the Monarch's position, for the main object of contention is his favour, and are thus enacted in such a way as to continuously reassert his superiority; also, they allow the contendents to form at most narrow, shifting cliques and cabals.

The king stands at the summit of the whole setting as the living and acting embodiment no longer just of his dynasty but of a larger and more abstract entity – the French state. This is the most plausible meaning of the possibly apocryphal utterance 'L'état c'est moi', which certainly cannot be interpreted as collapsing the French state into the private identity of the physical individual Louis Bourbon. For, as I have phrased this point elsewhere,[19]

[the] King of France was thoroughly, without residue, a 'public' personage. His mother gave him birth in public, and from that moment his existence, down to its most trivial moments, was acted out before the eyes of attendants who were holders of dignified public offices. He ate in public, went to bed in public, woke up and was clothed and groomed in public, urinated and defecated in public. He did not copulate in public; but near enough, considering the circumstances under which he was expected to deflower his august bride. He did not much bathe in public; but then, neither did he in private. When he died (in public) his body was promptly and messily chopped up in public, and its severed parts ceremoniously handed out to the more exalted among the personages who had been attending him throughout his mortal existence.

Patrimonial administration

Overlapping with the court, there also develops, in the direct service of the king, under the ancient denomination of 'councils', a number of exalted bodies of a new kind – the early prototypes of ministries, in the modern sense of a group of officials appointed, not to render occasional advice to the ruler, but to ensure the continuous, knowledgeable management, on his behalf, of a specific set of political and administrative affairs.

In due course the French king's councils were to become the stem of a ramified set of offices of similar nature operating over the country at large; but France in the seventeenth century does not provide the best locale for what I have called the second aspect of the construction of the absolute state – the development of a novel set of administrative arrangements.

There was much that was too archaic about the administrative system of *ancien régime* France. In particular, in order to provide the ruler with the revenues he needed to make war and to maintain his court, many honourable and lucrative offices could be *bought* by private individuals. This patrimonialisation of what were in principal public positions, and thus of the administrative system, was further accentuated when (as was possible during long phases of the *ancien régime*) those who had bought offices and paid an additional charge – called the *Paulette* – could even transmit those offices to their own heirs.

More widely, administrative *patrimonialism* represented for a long time, under absolutism – and by no means only in France – a legacy of the two systems that had preceded it: feudalism and the polity of estates. Under those systems, administrative tasks in the periphery were largely monopolised by privileged individuals and bodies, who treated them as one aspect (and one instrument) of their general position of social and economic advantage. Noblemen raised and equipped troops, led them into battle, or exercised judicial powers, by virtue of *being* noblemen, and in the pursuit of the same interests they had *qua* landlords. The legal discipline of markets was vested in the same bodies of tradesmen and merchants which authoritatively regulated the production and distribution of the goods to be marketed, and which thus had both the interest and the opportunity of limiting and controlling competition to their own direct advantage.

To bring these arrangements under a simple, general formula, we might say that in the polity of estates (as, even more clearly, under feudalism) the key institutional arrangements for the performance of political and administrative tasks consisted in vesting in individuals and bodies the *right* to perform them. In such performance those individuals and bodies were legitimately guided by their *interests*, and constrained chiefly by the concurrent, traditional rights vested in *other* individuals and bodies. Such a formula was still to a large extent embodied in the administrative arrangements to French absolutism, at any rate outside the military sphere.

An equally simple and general formula indicates the direction toward which a more advanced form of absolutism might seek to steer its own administrative system. Here, individuals performing political, judicial and administrative tasks would do so in the course of discharging *duties* they had undertaken toward the state; they would thus act not as private individuals, but as public functionaries. Their performance, accordingly, would be guided primarily not by their interests as individuals, but by *knowledge*. The object of such knowledge would be not (as in the polity of estates) an assemblage of diverse, locally grown, tradition-grounded rights, but a coherent *system* of abstract, general commands, mandating appropriate action in the light of objectively ascertained circumstances.

If necessary, the operational content of those commands would be specified in a directive imparted to a given functionary by a superior and more knowledgeable one. The former's obedience would normally be motivated by a commitment to the higher, *public* interest supposedly embodied in the commands and the related directives. It might be objected that it would be unrealistic to expect individuals not to consult their own private interest. The rejoinder to this is that in a well-ordered system it would not be in their interest to consult their interest; for higher functionaries would invigilate the conduct of lower ones, and make their personal advancement dependent upon their demonstrated ability to serve the public interest objectively.

Prussian absolutism

The formula I have just described is still part of the official philosophy (whether credible or not) of the administrative systems of contemporary liberal-democratic states – the philosophy of what I have already called the bureaucratic model of administration. Such states have inherited the model from the nineteenth century, when it came closest to actually inspiring the construction and operation of working administrative systems. A century earlier, a somewhat rudimentary form of the model had already inspired the construction and operation of the administrative apparatus of an important absolutist state: Prussia under the Hohenzollern dynasty. I say 'somewhat rudimentary', because of three features of the early Prussian apparatus: the extensive overlap between military and civilian administration; the systematic preference given in the appointment of staff to members of the same privileged estate, the

Junker; the preference for administrative units occupied by more than one individual – so-called colleges – rather than monocratic, that is, operating through the activities of single individuals.

These were indeed archaic features when seen form the vantage point of the mature, self-conscious embodiments of the same model in nineteenth-century liberal states. But on other counts, as seen instead from the perspective of the previous century, eighteenth-century Prussia possessed an administrative system which made it the very model of a more advanced absolutist state.

The advance in question – which many later historians spoke of as 'enlightened absolutism'[20] – was explicitly theorised by its protagonists, in Prussia and in a few other countries, as a transition to a new state form, which expressly emphasised the significance of administrative activities of a non-military nature, and which was labelled 'police state'. This expression – which subsequently developed individious connotations extraneous to the original German notion *Polizeystaat* – deserves some consideration.

The term *Polizeystaat* expressed the commitment of rulers to the development of a country's resources and to the advancement of its population's welfare. In that spirit, the state took it upon itself to promote, steer and regulate a great number of social activities which were previously the exclusive concern of (if anybody) private individuals and social groups. It sought to do so chiefly by means of an open-ended, continuously expanded and revised body of informed and authoritative *Ordnungen*, ordinances, which its functionaries issued and enforced.

Already for centuries the notion of order had been considered as the prime concern of an justification for the exercise of political power. The expression *Ordnungen* validated this earlier meaning of the term; but added to it a further, non-traditional understanding:

> The key criterion by which to judge the goodness of order – the *Wohlfahrt*, the subjects' welfare – is understood in a very different manner from its medieval equivalent, the unchanging *bonum commune* of Scholastic doctrine, to be preserved rather than to be created. Welfare, for the police state, is through and through a mundane, concrete matter of 'material happiness' . . . and as such it is to be produced by means of worldly activity, of political undertakings, of deliberate and demanding decisions . . . 'Police' is defined as the totality of institutions the prince establishes in order to ensure the subject's wellbeing. [my translation][21]

Note that the subjects' wellbeing is not for the ruler an ultimate, self-justifying goal. Rather, political action remains oriented to the by now well-established goals of the state's security and the aggrandisement of its power. In other words, the building up of military might remains (in

Prussia even more than in other European countries) the lodestar of state action; and, of course, in spite of its beneficient interpretation, the term *Polizey* also carries, for the subjects, the familiar connotations of coercion, imperiousness and surveillance. One distinctive aspect of the latter in the new context, however, consists in the effort to systematically collect information on the circumstances of the country's population – beginning with its size and its composition in terms of age, occupation, social and economic status – and on the country's other resources. This shows that 'enlightened' rulers, in Prussia and elsewhere, had become aware of the connection between the traditional concerns of the state – a well-supplied treasury, a well-equipped and effective army and navy – and the social, economic and cultural conditions of the country's population. They had also become convinced that those conditions, once ascertained and monitored, could be purposefully improved and advanced through 'police' activity, as defined above.

For this reason, they undertook to complement the traditional sites and instruments of policy making and administration – the ruler's councils, the courts, the army, estate bodies – with new, expressly designed bodies of personnel and sets of practices, which would advance the country's welfare and thus allow the state to extract more resources from its population. This is a design which Prussia fulfils fairly satisfactorily in the eighteenth century by building up an administrative system at the centre of which stood, characteristically, fiscal and military institutions, and which distinguished itself by the effectiveness of its extractive functions. Another relatively successful exemplar of 'enlightened despotism', in the same century, is represented by the Austrian empire under the rules of Maria Theresa and Joseph II (1740–90).[22]

Neither Prussia nor Austria, however, were to be the setting for the next major phrase in the story of European state-building (if this story is considered, as it is here, as a series of approximations to the conceptual portrait of the state outlined above). That stage is set, instead, in a relatively peripheral, insular polity – England.

4

The Development of the Modern State (2)

I

Beyond absolutism

Once more, this is not the place to attempt a causal account of the development of the constitutional, liberal state, which would have to assign great weight to transformations occurring in the economy and in the stratification system of *ancien régime* European society. At best I can offer the reader a glimpse into the political components and results of those transformations.

One significant implication of the transition from the polity of estates to absolutism, and of the development of the latter, had been the emergence of society as a realm of relatively autonomous, self-sustaining phenomena, involving the activities of private individuals, and centred around the production of wealth and its distribution among the main social strata.

The more the absolute ruler became the sole, unchallengeable holder of political power, the source and referent of all public life, the more the concerns and activities of the major component groups of society, which the ruler had increasingly deprived of their political prerogatives and responsibilities, became focused upon the private aspects of their members' existence.[1] Previously, the arrangements inherited from the polity of estates had given a number of groups (those, of course, existing above the level of the populace, that is of the bulk of the population) frequent opportunities to revisit their collective identity and reassert their collective interests, by performing – within the estate bodies – political and administrative public activities. But now absolutist rulers had denied all groups such opportunities by eliminating or restricting those activities.

Thus, from the standpoint of rulers, society – or, civil society – appeared chiefly as a realm of processes of great political significance, but which on that very account had to be authoritatively disciplined, monitored, administered and policed from above; for, as we have seen, the state's own might depended on the subjects' wellbeing. The political implications of this view, again, amounted to something like a benevolent, enlightened despotism.

But this conception of the relationship between the holders of political power and the environing society, more and more empowered by growing wealth and knowledge, was found less and less acceptable not only by members of groups which had traditionally shared with rulers the privileges and burdens of shaping and executing policy, and were now being excluded from them – the nobility – but also by members of groups whose identity was focused much more on economic activities – the bourgeoisie.

The latter had often in the past willingly surrendered the political prerogatives it had traditionally exercised *qua* third estate, on the understanding that the ruler's judicial and administrative apparatus would politically safeguard its economic interests. But some economic policies of *ancien régime* rulers (particularly those associated with 'mercantilism') placed more and more irksome restraints on property and, especially, on the market – the two chief institutional arrangements by means of which the bourgeoisie pursued their economic interest. Indeed, the very security of bourgeois rights was potentially in jeopardy if a despotic regime, however benevolent, was allowed to act unrestrainedly upon its own understanding of what was good for its subjects. Thus, the economic interests of the bourgeoisie had increasingly political implications incompatible with absolutism, even of the enlightened variety.

Constitutionalism

Those implications, if coherently followed up, amounted to a reversal of the relationship between state and (civil) society as seen from the ruler's standpoint. Far from society being treated as an object of political management by a state operating chiefly in the light of interests exclusive to itself and to which those of society had to be subordinated, the state itself had to become an instrumentality of society's autonomous, self-regulating development. The state's very existence, and its mode of operation, would have to seek justification in the extent to which it allowed that development to unfold according to its own logic, rather than imperiously directing it and bending it to the state's own ends.

This reversed relationship between state and society required in the first place that state power be constrained, rather than absolute. In the eighteenth and nineteenth centuries the notion of constitution was widely used to characterise such a new relationship.[2] This could only be established where society had already experienced, through autonomous economic and cultural growth, its own capacity for development and self-regulation, and where the bourgeoisie – as the main protagonist of that experience, no matter how significantly assisted and occasionally led by members of other, more privileged social groups – was no longer chiefly interested in competing with the nobility for the status advantages and economic privileges dispensed by the ruler. Another condition was that the absolutist project should not have been successful enough to exclude a public, reasoned argument about poltical arrangements and issues.

The English contribution

In the eighteenth century, these conditions were approximated only in England, which accordingly became the main focus of the European discussion about constitutionalism:

> In England all attempts to construct an absolutist state power had failed early on. This failure reflected a combination of many diverse factors, such as: the weakening of feudal forces in suicidal struggles; the peculiar legal status of the nobility, whose strong emphasis on primogeniture created more open boundaries *vis-à-vis* the bourgeoisie; the settlement of the religious question; the early takeoff of modernisation; the insularity of the country, which preserved it from having to manintain a strong standing army as a well as a powerful, centralised administrative apparatus . . . In sum, the forces favouring the advance of modernity were so strong, and those opposing it so weak, that an absolute state towering over society was not needed to counter the latter and favour the former. [my translation][3]

Thanks to these circumstances, by the late seventeenth century England embodied the two main tenets of the ideology of constitutionalism – though here I prefer to draw a sharp definition of both from a much later French source (the Declaration of the Rights of Man and Citizen of 1789): 'A society where the safeguard of rights is not insured and where the separation of powers is not secured has no constitution.' As the English case again shows, these two components are connected. The security of rights requires that law be independent of ands superior to government; but this independence and superiority – itself an essential aspect of the notion of rule of law – can only be guaranteed by a judiciary independent of the executive. More widely, various state powers must operate as checks and balances upon one another, thus directly countering the tendency, characteristic of absolutism, to concentrate all power in the ruler.

By the late eighteenth century, furthermore, England had also become the setting of a momentous new development – the rise of a public. That is, via a number of novel, autonomous institutions – from a network of clubs and coffee houses to newspapers and periodicals – an open-ended, non-corporate set of interested, knowledgeable individuals had learned routinely and peaceably to acquire and exchange information about issues of general significance. These had concerned at first matters of manners, aesthetic taste and culture, but subsequently came to comprise also matters of policy. The individuals in question argued openly about such issues, formed alignments of opinion concerning them, and in the process of so doing informally monitored and censured (or approved) the actions of authorities.

Last but not least, in the English polity an increasingly significant position was held by Parliament, both through legislation, and through its say in the composition of the Cabinet. The English Parliament had arisen in the middle ages, at the same time as a number of other European state bodies, and as an estate body itself – witness the names of its two component chambers, the House of Lords (spiritual and temporal) and the House of Commons. Later, however, while on the Continent absolutist rulers had progressively excluded those other estate bodies from the process of policy formation, the English Commons had successfully resisted such exclusion.[4] It had become a much more permanent assembly than the estate bodies of old had ever been, had taken full control over its own composition, its own agenda, and the conduct of its business, and had assumed extensive powers in the formation of policy. So extensive, in fact, that according to some historians Parliament itself had become, in England, the corporate protagonist of the same kind of absolutist development which on the Continent was finding its protagonist in the person of the monarch.[5]

But the analogy is only partly correct, for by the late eighteenth century the English Parliament had acquired a very distinctive feature, by legitimating opposition. This particular development found expression in, among other things, a distinctive seating arrangement:

> From about 1750 it became customary for the supporters of the government to take their places behind the 'treasury benches', and its opponents theirs in front of those benches – although one must wait until 1783 to see for the first time a total change of cabinet composition accompanied by a change of seats in the House of Commons. In this way the division of the House was institutionalised through parliamentary convention. It was not Parliament as a whole, but the opposition within it, that took up the task of criticising and controlling the government.[6]

Nothing, however, refutes the central inspiration of absolutism as much as the official recognition, made manifest through the institutionalisation of opposition, that policy formation does not express the higher wisdom of an unchallengeable power centre but reflects the open-ended, contingent relationship between two bodies of opinion which, although of unequal strength, legitimately and peaceably contend with one another in order to increase their strength. And indeed a further, significant meaning of 'constitution', still echoed in frequent current uses of the term constitutional, lies in the assumption that contention about the direction of policy is both legitimate and productive, provided it is bounded by the contendents' shared commitment to some 'rules of the game'.

Among the rules of the political game, as played in late eighteenth century Britain, those concerning the election of the members of the House of Commons, and thus indirectly the formation of parliamentary majorities and, even more indirectly, the composition of the Cabinet, occupied a conspicuous but also an ambivalent position. On the one hand, the electoral body was small, its size and composition varied widely between town and country and from borough to borough, and the practices adopted by candidates to secure election were highly corrupt.[7] On the other hand, the electoral process, together with other institutions of the public sphere (rights of assembly, of petition, of association; a free press) did create a link between a small but growing and increasingly informed, critical, self-confident public, and Parliament, which since the Glorious Revolution had come to constitute the seat of sovereignty in the British polity. The relationship between 'ins' and 'outs' within the precincts of Westminster had to reflect that between two bodies of opinion outside those precincts.

On this account, the British polity stood in the imagination of eighteenth century European intellectuals as the embodiment not only of constitutional but also of representative government. Diderot probably had England in mind when, in writing an entry for the *Encyclopédie*, he connected those two features in a general manner, by defining representatives as 'selected citizens, who within a constitutional (*tempéré*) government are charged by society with speaking on its behalf, articulating its interests, preventing oppression, taking part in administration'.

In the last part of the eighteenth century, however, the American and the French revolutions advanced the cause of representative government much more aggressively than did the British constitution of the time (until the electoral reforms of the 1830s). In both cases, the constitutional outcomes of the revolution expressly treated the electoral process as (formally, at any rate) a way of periodically transmitting the political preferences entertained within the broadest constituency (the people of the United States, the French nation) to a legislative body.

Periodical elections were essential to two overlapping purposes. They adjusted the composition of the elective body (and thus, less directly, the direction of policy) to the changes occurring in the distribution of preferences within the constituency. And they allowed that constituency to sanction, by expressing or withdrawing its support, the conduct of representatives with regard to the interests they had been elected to foster.

In both ways, the periodicity of elections acknowledged and strengthened the open-ended, contingent nature of policy, which, as we have seen, was implicit in the institutionalisation of opposition in the British Parliament. For now policy was largely – directly or indirectly – the outcome of deliberations of assemblies with changing compositions, which engaged in a fluid game of competition, contrasting advocacy, mutual adjustment and compromise.

II

The liberal state

Policy, however, was not to be wholly contingent upon the outcomes of that game. The system of representative government which, in its several variants, marked the distinctive nineteenth-century advance in the career of the modern state, deliberately fostered the anti-absolutist legacy of earlier constitutionalism by laying explicit boundaries around the action of state organs, including elective legislatures.

In Britain such action, to be valid, had to observe conditions largely ensconced in broad conventions and traditions. Elsewhere, such conditions were mostly laid down in written constitutional documents; and various 'rights of man and the citizen' were explicitly articulated and proclaimed inviolable. Furthermore, administrative activities were to be authorised by legislative acts.

In this manner, the electoral process, which enabled the citizenry to periodically determine the composition of legislative bodies, enabled it also to affect the content of legislation and, via the latter, the activities of other state authorities. Even agencies such as the army, which had come into being on the initiative of absolutist and semi-absolutist rulers, and traditionally owed their prime allegiance to the Crown, were made to accept, however reluctantly, the supremacy of legislative bodies simply because their expenditures had to be financed from legislatively enacted taxation and authorised through appropriations voted by legislative bodies.

Thus, the whole machinery of the state was supposed to be activated and controlled through law, although some of the acts which set that machinery in motion – particularly those concerning international affairs and most specifically war, and those dealing with urgent threats to internal public order – were acknowledged to be the product of highly discretionary decisions, made unavoidably in a kind of legal vacuum.

The activity of legislation itself, of course, had aspects of utter discretionality, for it expressed the sovereign, and thus unbounded, will of the state. However, as we have seen, it was surrounded by constitutional constraints – both rules of procedure and sets of inviolable rights. In some states, special courts were set up to verify that both kinds of constraits had been observed by a given statute, and to nullify it if they had not.

Historically, the protagonists of this massive process of constitutionalisation of political arrangements, culminating in the liberal states of the middle and late nineteenth century, had been the public, the electorate and the legislative assemblies; these had progressively overcome the resistance of the Crown and of the apparatus of rule originally created by and clustered around it. Yet that apparatus did not in its entirety, and unremittingly, oppose that process in all its aspects. In the Prussian state after its defeat by Napoleon, for instance, some sections of the *Junkertum* manning the upper echelons of the military and fiscal administration, played a decisive role in enacting reforms, some of which had a liberal flavour.

More generally, the constitutionalisation of the state appeared to many administrators as a plausible way of planning and rationalising their activities; and legal speech – as I have already suggested – recommended itself as a technically elaborate, culturally legitimate linguistic medium in which to encode all the diverse components of sophisticated administrative discourse: general directives, consideration of the circumstances, specific decisions, reference to authorities and precedents, instructions to subordinate officials, objections from affected parties, rulings on objections, etc.

Furthermore, modern 'positive' law, issued in the form of statutes and codes, was a marvellously flexible, open-ended instrument of authority, which could – and was likely to – assign to administrators ever new tasks, and entrust them with ever greater faculties and resources. These advantages of the constitutionalisation of administration must have seemed to many officials a good trade-off for the amount of discretionality they might have to surrender, as the justification of their activities ceased to be the will of the ruler, or their superiors' wishes, and became the law.

Furthermore, trained administrators were at first a small and novel social group, somewhat insecure of its standing *vis-à-vis* both the nobility, which had traditionally performed most political and administrative tasks, and the rising entrepreneurial bourgeoisie, which increasingly commanded economic power. It was in their interest to establish themselves as the practitioners of a new profession, and to claim some of the economic and status advantages of the older ones. A reference to the law, both as a body of principles and as a technique of discourse, the knowledge of which had to be gained in the universities (the traditional training ground of the professions) and certified through degrees, suited that interest – as did the principle that administrative activities were to be financed through taxation, rather than by producing goods and services to be sold on the market.

Equally advantageous from the viewpoint of a group which was originally, as I indicated, quite small, was the clear prospect that its numbers whould steadily grow. For on the one hand one could anticipate the expansion of the state's administrative activities; on the other, many individuals were enabled to aspire to office-holding by the demise of patrimonial administration, which had often restricted access to office to people holding certain status qualifications. This latter aspect of the phenomenon is depicted biliously in this passage from Hyppolite Taine's *Le régime moderne*, which saw it as an immediate effect of the French revolution:

> The decrees of the Constituent Assembly throw open to everybody the highest paths, or for that matter all paths. All leading, directive, influential personnel, whether political, administrative, provincial, municipal, ecclesiastical, judicial or financial, are immediately deprived of their positions; to replace them are called all those who aspire to them and who have a good opinion of themselves. All previous qualifications are declared irrelevant, be they birth, wealth, education, seniority, training, morality, or manners, since requiring these might slow down and limit preferment. No one is requested to offer surety or to name guarantors; all Frenchmen become eligible to all employments . . . As a consequence, in all branches of government, in all positions of authority, in all establishments, a new personnel takes over.[8]

These new aspects of the manning and the running of the state, however, should not make us forget that the liberal, constitutional, representative state of the nineteenth century remained very much in the business of rule, no matter how differently it might conduct it from the earlier, absolutist state. Max Weber makes this very clear in his analysis of the modern form of political representation; he labels it 'free' because electors are not allowed to issue binding instructions to representatives (as they could sometimes do in the polity of estates); but the import of it is, he writes, that *vis-à-vis* the elector the typical representative constitutes not a 'servant' (*Diener*) but a 'ruler' (*Herr*).[9]

If the electoral process is thus realistically construed not as a way of abolishing rule or establishing self-rule, but rather as a different (because – once more – open-ended, contingent) way of selecting rulers, this does not make any less significant the questions: who shall have the vote? who can be elected? The prevalent nineteenth-century answer to these questions – the liberal answer – had been foreshadowed by Diderot in the *Encyclopédia* entry mentioned above:

> If the subjects are to make themselves heard without rioting, it is suitable that they should have *representatives*: that is, citizens more enlightened than others, more concerned with the matters at issue, tied to the motherland by their possessions, whose position enables them to perceive the state's needs, the abuses which they occasion, and the remedies to be sought thereto. [my translation]

But Diderot made the same point in even more lapidary fashion elsewhere in the same text: 'C'est la proprieté qui fait le citoyen.' In the European (not the American) liberal state of the nineteenth century, the right to vote and to be elected is typically the prerogative of those adult males who own a required amount of material possessions, or have been educated to a certain stated level (a condition in turn mostly associated with material advantage). As a result, in addition (normally) to all women, a large proportion of the adult male population did not enjoy that right.

What proportion, is a question the answer to which varies historically, but there is clearly a trend toward the progressive lowering of the threshold of the requisite possessions and education, until democracy (in one understanding of the term) is attained with the introduction of universal (male) suffrage.

But up to that point, the differences from country to country, or from period to period, in the size of the enfranchised section of the population, tend to obscure the qualitative significance of the restriction of the suffrage to a section of the population qualified by its position of economic and social superiority. The designation of the resulting political system as a 'mono-class state',[10] while linguistically clumsy, has the advantage of pointing out both the invidiousness and exclusiveness of the arrangements in question, and the fact that the individuals benefiting from them tend to constitute a class.

A class is a collective entity generated across a plurality of individuals by their sharing *de facto* certain resources and interests, not (as the estates of the *ancien régime*) a corporate group with a publicly recognised, juridically distinctive status. The German economic historian Sombart characterised the difference as follows: 'Who are you? one would say previosly. A powerful man. Therefore you will also be rich. Who are you? asks one today. A rich man. Therefore you will also be powerful.' A generation later, the jurist and political scientist Hermann Heller elaborated this difference with reference to the German experience:

> The form of society based on inherited status differences possesed economic, legal and cultural structures which conferred upon it a stable configuration, with well-established, juridically distinctive strata. In spite of all contrasts and of persistent struggles, the political significance of the resulting hierarchy of estates was not in contention. But this ordering of society had long been eroded in Prussia by the time the liberal reforms of Baron van Stein buried it forever.
>
> From this point on anybody, regardless, of status, could take possession of noble, ecclesiastical or peasant landholdings, or start a business. Freedom of the person and of property, freedom of contract, freedom of residence, disposed of the last remnants of the corporate regulation of trades, allowed the cities to grow and laid the juridical foundations of a developed bourgeois society. But the domination of a class, as against that of an estate, presupposes juridical equality: that is, it rests nearly exclusively upon economic inequality, albeit often grounded on inheritance of wealth. A class lacks the closedness of an estate . . . Ultimately class domination tends to rest on the possession of mobile capital, and to that extent its enjoyment by a given set of people is inherently impermanent; for this reason, bourgeois society is characterised by open-ended contrasts and overlaps between constantly changing constellations of economic interests. [my translation][11]

The constitutional, liberal state of the nineteenth-century West was, so to speak, systematically coherent with a capitalist economy. Here, the production and distribution of wealth take place primarily through the market interactions of a plurality of independent, self-regarding units, which seek profit through the productive employment of labour power, itself sold on the market. This system's prime political requirement was a negative one: that public powers should remove all impediments to the autonomous operation of the markets. But meeting this requirement involved the state in a number of positive, forceful activities. These ranged from the development of physical and institutional infrastructures (roads and railways, territory-wide systems of measures, the diffusion of literacy) necessary for industrialisation, to legislative and police measures to tackle the problems posed by a growing, mobilised, increasingly urbanised population, to the promotion of overseas colonisation.[12]

Since most of these activities favoured certain sections of a state's population much more than others, their potential divisive effect was moderated – up to a point – by promoting a more inclusive justification of the burdens of compliance which the state's various activities impose. Established political elites increasingly chose to characterise the state as actively guarding and pursuing the political interests of a wider, comprehensive entity – the nation.[13] This was proclaimed to be the state's ultimate constituency, and was sometimes construed as the holder of sovereignty.

It is plausible to attibute an ideological intent to these intellectual constructions, and to deplore the effects which the related creed of nationalism produced in the course of the nineteenth century (and of the twentieth). But a creed can only produce effects, good or evil, if it is credible; and in turn the credibility of the idea of nation, and of the nationalist creed, in the middle and late nineteenth century, can be seen as an unintended, belated effect of the reversal in the relationship between state and society that I have suggested at the beginning of this chapter.

III

Liberal democracy

The constitutionalisation of politics which had originally been demanded by (sections of) the middle classes, began later to benefit other social groups, by widening and strengthening the public sphere. Urbanisation, industrialisation, the growth of literacy, the increasing ease of comunication beyond the face-to-face range, were allowing increasing numbers of people to establish contact with one another in contexts different from those of work and of domestic life, and to discover what interests they shared with one another. They could, furthermore, make use of the constitutional freedoms of speech, of assembly and of association, to align themselves with like-minded individuals in promoting those interests. Finally, those alignments could legitimately observe and comment on public policies affecting them, decide whether to support the authorities responsible for them or the political groupings opposing them, and thus seek to influence and shape further policy.

In this manner, in the context of constitutional, liberal regimes, advancing economic and social modernisation rendered broader and broader masses politically aware, involved and demanding. These phenomena placed under irresistible pressure the suffrage restrictions characteristic of those regimes, leading to the progressive loosening and eventually to the elimination of those restrictions. We can label this process 'democratisation', and the political arrangements which it puts into place 'liberal-democratic', in so far as it does not wholly displace other features of the liberal, constitutional political order.

Today's Western polities can still be characterised as variant forms of the liberal-democratic state, further discussion of which can be left to other parts of this book. But a few general remarks may be made here.

The progressive universalisation of suffrage so enlarged the electorate that it changed the political process deeply. Schematically, we can distingush three types of change characterising the nature and extent of the transition from the liberal to the democratic phase in the development of the state: changes concerning primarily the composition of the political personnel; those affecting the mode of operation of political institutions, particularly, at first, of elective bodies; and those concerning the agenda of those institutions, the actual repertory of state action. Let us briefly consider such changes in that order.

1 The entry into politics of broader and broader popular masses could only be promoted and managed by new political agencies – organised, mass parties. A new kind of political personnel – political entrepreneurs – created and led those parties, and thanks to their electoral and organisational success gained access to and influence over certain key state institutions (beginning with elective legislatures). They differed from the propertied and (less often) cultured notables who had previously been the protagonists of the political process within representative bodies, if only because, whether or not they lived *for* politics, their economic and status position (their background was sometimes proletarian or plebeian, though more often *petit bourgeois*, as was their occupation) often compelled them to live *off* politics.[14]

On that account, the democratisation process – if considered from the invidious standpoint inspiring Taine's comments reported above – further extended the presumptuous, impatient and greedy search for advantage and influence that in France had been unleashed by the breakdown of the *ancien régime*. That search could now take the form not just of competing for official positions previously reserved for the well-born, but also of promoting, leading or running various kinds of organisations advancing the interests of a given section of the populace. Mainly such organisations agitated for the extension of the suffrage to those sections, and subsequently put forward candidates who would represent them in elected bodies.

But that standpoint is a limited one. It ignores or underestimates the extent to which the new political personnel were inspired, rather than by personal ambition, by ideals of justice and by intellectually articulated critiques of the existent order of things. More importantly, whatever their motivations and their intellectual horizons, the organisational and parliamentary leaders of the parties represented social groups which had been traditionally excluded from the political process, or which the on-going processes of industrialisation, urbanisation and proletarianisation were bringing into being.

2 Thus (the second significant change) the entry of mass parties into the elective, legislative bodies central to the liberal constitution modified their mode of operation. In particular, it partitioned their members into wider, more stable, more persistently and generally contrasting alignments. Thus, legislative bodies progressively ceased to function as settings within which differently minded members would address one another in open discussion, seeking to modify each other's

views or to induce uncommitted members to assent to their own – a process which would sometimes yield new alignments of opinion and produce new lines of policy.

In the changed circumstances, the key protagonists of the policy-making process are organised parties, often committed to pre-established ideologies and platforms, tightly controlled by their leadership, and unwilling to leave much freedom of decision to individual elected representatives. Such parties normally confront one another in the legislative bodies as rigidly formed alignments, and interact on terms imperiously laid down by the respective leaders. Thus the bodies cease to function as autonomous realms within which contingent decisions can be made purely on the basis of their internal processes.

3 Finally, the agenda of the legislative process was progressively modified, by placing upon it new undertakings, new ways for the state to draw upon and expend the society's resources, which expressed the circumstances and the demands of previously unrepresented social groups. Schematically: the political intent of the groups which had previously monopolised representation had been primarily that of limiting state action, in order to increase the scope and the autonomy of market processes. Or – to put it more subtly – they had sought to determine the concrete content of state activities within a stable, relatively restricted range of policies. But the expansion of suffrage begins to offer an increasing amount of legitimate political leverage to groups having no stake in autonomously functioning markets. Mostly, these are either *petit bourgeois* status groups seeking to maintain a precarious economic toehold on the margins of the market. Or they make up a class which owes its very existence to the market but, because it lacks capital, finds that existence uncomfortable to say the least – the industrial working class.

It is not in the interest of groups of either kind simply to influence the choices the state makes from within a limited repertory of policies. Rather, the systematic enlargement of that repertory, and thus the state's progressive encroachment upon the market, is, if not always their express aim, then at least a constant implication of their political preferences.

If this is the extent of the changes associated (more or less directly) with democratisation, why do we speak of *liberal* democracy, to characterise the resulting political environment? Because of two key elements of continuity between that and the earlier, specifically liberal environment. First of all, the parties which organised the entry of the masses into politics respected some significant institutional legacies of liberal politics. They found in place, utilised and preserved the institutions of the public sphere; they assumed the validity of the representative principle, instead of insisting on maximising popular participation in political decision-making; they did not challenge the principle of the division of powers among state organs; and while powerfully enlarging the administrative apparatus of the state, they did not essentially alter the bureaucratic model.

In the second place, all the larger social forces to which democratisation gave political voice, including those based on the working class, basically accepted the centrality of private capital to the evolving industrial economy and the resulting class division, and sought to modify and moderate their effects through political action rather than to suppress them. One reason for this is that doing otherwise would have entailed not only challenging capital and the market, and the related social institutions and cultural values, but also taking on the state itself, which historically (and thus, in my view, contingently)[15] had developed alongside and in alliance with modern capitalism, and whose leading elites had substantial class ties with the entrepreneurial bourgeoisie.

That a thorough socialisation or collectivisation of the economy had never been seriously intended by the working class parties is of course a controversial view, whose validity I do not intend to establish here. It can probably argued, in any case, that whether or not working class demands intended such a socialisation or collectivisation, if such demands had been thoroughly met, they would have profoundly displaced the hold of capitalist interests upon each country's economy, perhaps arrested the course of industrialisation, or at any rate placed it upon very different institutional bases. As it happens, however, this did not occur anywhere in the West. What did occur is that enough demands were met to change considerably the political environment within which industrialisation and the development of capitalism continued. The key change, I repeat, was a drastic widening of the range of social interests on which state action was brought to bear.

While I plan to elaborate this statement somewhat in the second part of the book, it suggests a question from whose vantage point to recapitulate, in the last section of this chapter, the story of the state recapitulated so far. What, as it were, have the European states been *about* in the course of their historical career?

IV

A retrospective

From their beginnings, states were centrally concerned with the practice of two (sometimes overlapping) forms of organised violence: those pertaining to inter-state relations; and those pertaining to keeping control of the population and maintaining order within individual states. Essentially, they developed as ever bigger and more sophisticated machines for building up and deploying armies (and navies) and for policing the territory, preventing and punishing deviant conduct and repressing social unrest. In order to do this, states had to extract from the population a share of the yearly product of its economic activities. To that extent, they were also machines for raising revenue, by means of monopolies, custom duties, the sale of offices, tax farming, imposts and levies of various kinds.

Of all these concerns, the preoccupation with the preparation for and the conduct of warfare remained central throughout the story of the state. But although it constituted a *constant* within that story, at the same time the concern with warfare had also a *variable* aspect to it. For, to begin with, it was a matter of wilful decision (to some extent, at any rate) which state fought which, and the outcome of such fights was intrinsically contingent. More importantly, over the long run, wars came to be fought between larger and larger opponents, and for bigger and bigger stakes. Furthermore, and critically, the technical and organisational ways of waging war changed all the time,[16] and those changes constantly increased the costs of warfare to the states themselves.

It was largely on this account that the absolutist rulers first loosened and then removed the constraints the polity of estates placed upon their extractive activities by obliging them to seek the consent and cooperation of estate bodies every time they sought to increase and improve their military resources and to make war. Also on that account, I suggested, some rulers undertook wider and more penetrating 'police' activities: that is, they established agencies which systematically monitored the changing demographic and occupational composition of the state's population, and sought to improve its health and its education and to promote and regulate economic modernisation. A bigger, busier, more productive, better educated, happier population would yield greater revenues, and thus indirectly increase the state's military might.

From the standpoint of the state, and in particular of its extractive needs, and in view of the persistent priority it attached to building up its potential for violence, external and internal, the gradual (or, sometimes, sudden) abandonment of the absolutist form of the state appeared to be, so to speak, a price worth paying. True, it required some traditional political elites to be set aside (sometimes bloodily); and other political and administrative elites saw new, sometimes vexing constraints imposed by law and by public opinion upon their freedom of operation. But the upsurge of economic rationality associated with the commercialisation and industrialisation of the national economies more than compensated for the state having to dismantle its mercantilist economic policies and other aspects of the *Polizeystaat*.

In particular, the regular, unobtrusive levying of taxes on various phases and aspects of the modernised economic process, steered by the market and chiefly oriented to profit-making, proved a superior extractive device. Furthermore, the progressive generalisation of citizenship meant, among other things, that through conscription the state could field armies of dimensions yet undreamed of. And the nationalist ideals proclaimed by the new political elites provided new justifications for the conduct of traditional power politics, including of course the building up of its chief instrumentality, military might. Finally, as Spencer saw with dismay, and Durkheim with approval, throughout most of the liberal phases of its development the state kept growing, both by extending its web of legislative rules and by adding new agencies to its administrative apparatus.

Thus, the steady trend toward the enlargement of the scope of state action characteristic of the early phases of that development was not substantially interrupted by the advent of constitutionalism and liberalism. During the latter phases, however, a new principle came to determine which old forms of state action were restricted or eliminated, and which new forms were added: state action had to assist as far as possible the special interests of the bourgeoisie – to maximise the impact on social affairs at large of private property, freedom of contract and the autonomy of the market. The predominance of the bourgeois culture in the formation of public opinion, and a highly restrictive electoral system, safeguarded that principle.

However, the principle was placed under severe strain as broader and broader masses became mobilised and organised, developed collective understandings of their circumstances that challenged the cultural hegemony of the bourgeoisie and gained parliamentary representation. Forms of state intervention in the management of social and economic affairs were demanded that opposed the interests of the bourgeoisie by limiting and countering the play of market forces. A new, restricted and negative form of that principle came slowly into operation: the state might, through old and especially new forms of activity, meet those demands, but definitely not to the extent of suppressing market forces, or even seriously hampering their operations.

'Might' does not mean 'would'. It is a contingent matter whether, when, to what extent and in what forms a given state's policies did meet those demands during the latter part of the nineteenth and in the course of the twentieth century. It is a safe generalisation, applying to all Western states, to say that over that period as a whole, the scope of state action increased also in order to further interest *other* than those of the bourgeoisie, without, however, suppressing the operation of market forces and subverting the bourgeois social order. But, as we shall see, the twentieth century witnessed also the formation of new state forms to which this last, critical limitation does not apply.

These and other developments will be discussed more closely in the second part of this book. In the meanwhile, however, the arguments conducted so far about the nature, genesis and development of the state lend themselves to a further set of considerations, addressed in the next two chapters.

5

Controversies about the State:
Attempting an Appraisal

Was the development of the modern state a good thing?

The last three chapters have offered respectively a conceptual (chapter 2) and a schematic narrative account (chapters 2 and 3) of the peculiar ways in which political power has become institutionalised in the modern state. This chapter and the next present some contrasting reflections on those accounts. Chapter 5 seeks to assess the outcome of state-building processes from the standpoint of certain broadly shared human values. In Chapter 6, I shall introduce three different ways of explaining those processes sociologically. These two tasks are connected, and for that reason some arguments will be reviewed in both chapters.

The crudest way of formulating the present chapter's theme – borrowed from a famous semi-spoof history of England, *1066 And All That* – consists in asking: was the development of the modern state A Good Thing? To which the answer must be, at any rate provisionally: it depends. For, in the first place, there are human values in the light of which political power is itself intrinsically evil, no matter whether and how institutionalised; in the second place, even if that answer is discarded, there is no uncontroversially valid, universally shared standpoint from which the matter can be univocally adjudicated.

Granted this, I shall argue below that the modern state constitutes not just a unique, but a markedly superior way of generating and storing political power and of initiating, monitoring and controlling its uses. But I shall not raise the logically prior question of whether political power itself should be seen as a necessary or an optional and thus dispensable, as a deprecable or an admirable, feature of the human condition.

What the state can do: an example from the second world war

I shall exemplify this argument by considering briefly an episode from relatively recent history. On 25 February 1944, a small group of men who collectively bore the title of Combined Chiefs of Staff, addressed to General Eisenhower a brief directive, whose central words were the following: 'You will enter the Continent of Europe and, in conjunction with other United Nations, undertake operations aimed at the heart of Germany and the destruction of her armed forces.' Readers may wonder at various aspects of this remarkable message; for instance, at the fact that in spite of its terseness and the nature of its content, it is loaded with almost poetic metaphor: Germany, it appears, is female, and it has a heart. They may also consider its bearing on the question I put at the end of the last chapter – what have European states been *about*? For the magnitude of the events deriving from the execution of that directive – the invasion of Normandy by the Allies, and the politico-military story that followed it – suggests (to myself, at any rate) that the building of the modern state constituted a tremendous historical success. Let me argue this by considering more closely the follow-up to the directive.

Of course what stands in the foreground is the military achievement represented by the Normandy invasion and the following campaign. Only an extremely large, sophisticated and efficient military organisation could have bridged the gap, as it were, between, on the one hand, those few lines of text addressed to one man, and on the other the gigantic amount of sustained, diverse, murderous effort it brought forth on the part of millions.

At bottom what was involved in carrying out the directive was, of course, innumerable streams of intellectual, physical and moral activity issuing from individuals, each seeking to carry out his or her own assignment resulting from, and implementing, that directive. But all this activity was activated and monitored from a single centre in a relatively efficient and effective manner – relatively, of course, because of the friction unavoidably generated on each side of the struggle by incompetence, misunderstanding, lack or excess of effort, or bad luck (not to mention the other side's determined opposition). This was only possible because that centre could avail itself of a highly sophisticated material technology of command, communication and control, and could thereby set in motion a huge, diverse set of military competences and skills, from those of the boffins and the intelligence experts to those of the sergeant-majors down to the last sapper or artilleryman.

But a military achievement of that magnitude was only possible, in turn, in a certain type of political environment. For all the material and human resources required had been assembled and set into motion by, and for the purposes of, a political entity whose nature and whose modes of operation one can understand only by considering the unique institutional features of the modern state – particularly those envisaged by such notions as sovereignty, law, citizenship, nationality, bureaucratic administration.

Readers particularly disposed to think themselves tough-minded might discount such considerations and suggest instead that *c'est l'argent qui fait la guerre*. Or, to render in modern terms this ancient insight, and focus it on our concern here, they might remind the rest of us that the outcome of the Normandy invasion and of the later Allied operations was determined – in spite of the persistent superiority, in strictly military terms, of the German forces[1] – by the crushing industrial advantage the Allied economy (and of course primarily the American economy) enjoyed over the German. But again one cannot understand how that advantage was mobilised in the context of the war without considering, in the first place, the twin financial devices of taxation and war loans; and in turn how both devices (most particularly the second) were premised on peculiar institutional achievements in the political sphere – from the credit-worthiness of the state to notions of citizenship and patriotism.

To sum up, the massive technological and military feat represented by the successful execution of the directive of 25 February 1944, presupposed a broader, specifically political achievement – the making of the modern state, which had long before laid into place the institutional prerequisites of (among other things) the raising, training, equipping and deploying of a gigantic military force.

I wrote, above, 'among other things'. And indeed I might have discussed a very different exemplar of the wonders the modern state has wrought – say, the landing of a manned spacecraft on the moon, or the attainment of nearly universal adult literacy in many parts of the world, two enterprises which also give ample evidence of what the state can do. I chose instead the directive as my example, in order to remind the reader of three things:

1 the persistent, fateful involvement of the state with 'blood and iron', on which I have already commented at the close of the last chapter;

2 the irreducible element of contingency in the pursuit of the state's larger aims, never more clear and momentous than when states make war on one another;

3 finally, the inescapable moral ambiguity of it all. For although I rather expect most of my readers to agree with me that in the broader scheme of things that directive produced morally valuable, praiseworthy historical results, it is not impossible to think of tenable reasons for opining otherwise, if only because there are different ways of construing that broader scheme of things.

II

The parameters of an appraisal

Looking beyond the above example, I should like to elaborate my own more general appraisal of the peculiar ways in which political power gets accumulated, managed and exercised within the modern state. For reasons indicated above, I do not assume that all readers will necessarily assent to the appraisal I offer. Whether and to what extent they do so will depend in the first place on whether they share the values inspiring it; in the second place on whether they think I am correct in thinking that those values are in fact secured and enhanced by the distinctive features of the modern state.

Let me emphasise that I am not seeking to evaluate the concrete operations 'on the ground' of this or that state, now or in a previous phase of its history, but rather the general institutional features of the State. These are, at bottom, sets of normative expectations, that is, sanctioned understandings concerning (in this case) what political arrangements are *supposed* to be like and how they are *supposed* to operate.

'On the ground', in the time-and space-bound operations of any given state, of course, such arrangements are continually exposed to the wear and tear of unauthorised practice, of interested circumvention, of improvised adjustment, of incompetent performance, of covert and sometimes overt infringement. And it is often correct to impute these phenomena to the ignorant and/or criminal ill will of individual and collective protagonists and beneficiaries of political and administrative processes, to illegitimate interests asserting themselves over the letter and/or the spirit of the law.

But one should not forget an additional, significant source of pressure upon those expectations. By its very nature the modern state seeks to reconcile what are in principle contradictory requirements – to have the cake and eat it too. I am going to suggest that on the whole it does, or at any rate it has historically done, a remarkable job of that impossible assignment; and that a number of disagreeable aspects of its existence and operation arise from its understandable failure to perform the assignment to perfection.

I would claim, then, that the structural design and the operational blueprint of the modern state amount in principle to the albeit imperfect performance of the following institutional feats:

The enhancement and the taming of organised coercive power

Lenin once characterised the state as 'bodies of armed men'; and his contemporary, Max Weber, defined it by reference to its successful claim to the monopoly of legitimate physical force.[2] Indeed each state represents primarily – as it must, it it is to stay in business – an awesome accumulation of organised military might, intended to establish and maintain its status as one sovereign entity among others on the international scene. It must also be able to back up its internal commands, and restrain other subjects from employing violence in their own private dealings. In a passage I quoted in Chapter 1, Peter Berger expresses well the tacit assumption we all make that when the chips are down the state's agents will indeed visit upon us (or, preferably, upon others) that ultimate sanction.

Yet, in its everyday expressions, political experience in contemporary Western states makes relatively little direct reference to its ultimate grounding is organised, military force. The size of the armed forces, the technological and other resources at their disposal, the question of whether and against whom they are to be deployed and committed, depend in principle on decisions taken by civilian politicians an officials. Military personnel normally wear uniforms and carry arms only when they are barracked, on parade, on military exercises or when they guard specifically military facilities. They are, *qua* military, segregated from the rest of social and indeed of political life. They are also highly differentiated from the specialists in civilian violence, the police.

The police often make the modern state's coercive resources and violent disposition well visible in the everyday life of the population. But they are charged also with activities which have no obvious coercive edge to them; the career structure of their profession increasingly places a premium on managerial rather than on command skills; their leaders are in principle responsible to politicians and judges; even their immediately coercive activities (unlike those of the armed forces) are not supposed to be controlled *exclusively* by considerations of effectiveness.

Correspondingly, most aspects of contemporary political experience have become distinctly 'civilianised', and make little direct use of or reference to the ultimate sanction of violence. Those who normally act as the state's agents, in most aspects of its political and administrative activity, are conventionally attired, conventionally mannered people, who operate in a most un-military fashion. Formal laws and explicit terms of appointment, together with well-established conventions, compel them to use highly stylised forms of speech in their activities, to refer to shared information, quote authorities, formulate rationales, cite precedents, acknowledge rules, avoid contradictions and *non sequiturs* and make a case for the actions they are taking or intend to take.

Even in those specifically political aspects and phases of the operation of liberal-democratic states which call for competition between opposing parties and controversies over policy, the opponents normally challenge one another, denounce each other's intentions and wage struggles but avoid taking the short cut through violence in order to hasten and secure the realisation of their interests, or even the enjoyment of their rights.

In his book on Power,[3] Niklas Luhmann comments ironically on Alvin Gouldner's astonishment at the very limited place Talcott Parsons assigned the brute fact of violence in his sociological theory of political power:

> This sociologist's astonishment ought in turn to astonish sociologists . . .
> While undoubtedly sociology can and should take cognisance of the phenomenon of a brutal and self-interested use of power . . . one should not deny, either, that such a phenomenon is surpassed in its significance for society by the institutionalisation of binding legitimate power. A society's day-to-day existence is affected to a much larger extent by reference to power normalised by means of law than by the brutal and self-interested employment of power. [my translation]

In this context, several aspects of contemporary state activity in which coercion rears its ugly head, and breaks through the bonds of rules and conventions intended to restrain it – for example, police brutality, the 'taking of liberties' in the enforcement of public order or in the conduct of criminal investigations – may sometimes be understood as resulting from the serious dilemmas under which state agents labour: for instance the difficulty of maintaining public order or of apprehending culprits while operating exclusively and rigidly by the book.

The enlargement of the scope of political power and the curbing of arbitrium

I have already remarked, and later I shall expand on the point, that many aspects of social life – from health to education, from industrial research and development to sports, from the relief of destitution to the promotion of the arts – are today the object of state policy.

How one explains and evaluates this phenomenon is a question to which we will return. What I should like to emphasise here is that over the whole range of state activities, the same institutional principle applies, the same understanding of the appropriate, defensible way of arranging and conducting those activities. The principle is that such activities are carried out by individuals not *qua* individuals, but in their capacity as holders of offices; such individuals, that is, operate in the light of and on behalf of not their own personal interests, but in those public interests their office has been assigned to guard and pursue.

In so far as this principle is realised, in the modern state political power becomes systematically depersonalised, and the bugbear of the Enlightenment in its political aspects – the *arbitrium* of rulers and their agents – is laid to rest. For the negative rule forbidding state agents to orient the political and administrative powers they exercise to their own personal interests, is complemented by a positive one enjoining them to refer instead to law and to objectively ascertained circumstances and opportunities.

By the same token, those powers are made in principle predictable, at any rate in the modalities of their exercise if not in its concrete outcomes, also for individuals other than those charged with it. Such individuals can then premise their own, private activities on informed, plausible assumptions about the ways in which they will be assisted or hindered by the state's own, public ones. Furthermore, there are arrangements making all political and administrative agents accountable to higher authorities, and intended to deprive *arbitrium* of its ultimate ground – the ability to get away with it.

Once more, it is all too easy to think of instances in which those arrangements have been (and are) circumvented, much to the detriment of the above principle. Yet, in so far as those arrangements remain in place, they do restrain at least the grosser forms of *arbitrium* – lest somebody blow the whistle on them and compel those arrangements to crank themselves into action.

More generally, there are of course a number of reasons why the notion of bureaucracy as constituting an utterly distinctive and superior set of arrangements could be considered implausible. Yet that notion is in no way utterly fallacious. However you qualify it and correct it, it still suggests a mode of administration which differs widely – and, since I am here expressly indulging in evaluation, positively – from those previously encountered in the course of the state's story. If you consider at all closely such practices as tax farming, the purchase of offices and their transmission via inheritance, the role played by court intrigue in the appointment of ministers, the function performed by the lord's judicial prerogatives in the exploitation of his landed estate, the monopoly certain urban estates possessed over some offices, the fiscal and penal immunities enjoyed by aristocrats and ecclesiastics, the system of the advancement of favourites established by many monarchs, the inexistence of formal qualifications for those aspiring to certain charges or of publicly known and sanctioned requirements for their performance, the extent to which the practice of arts and trades was controlled, at the public's expense, by the practitioners, the amount of overlap in the competences assigned different authorities in the control of the same activities, and the resultant confusion and waste; if you consider all this, you will find it difficult not to acknowledge both the considerable factual efficacy and the moral superiority of the principles, however imperfectly implemented, inspiring the construction of modern administrative systems. I am thinking, again, of the notion of conflict of interest as disqualifying office-holders and invalidating their acts; of the practice of competitive examinations for appointment to public office; of the auditing of the expenditure of agencies on the part of a central treasury on the basis of regular budgets; of the equality of citizens before the law; of the expectation that office-holders will operate on the basis of the law, their superiors' directives, and their own 'science and conscience'; of the systematic allocation of competences to offices and of their subordination to ultimate political decision-makers.

In so far as these principles effectively direct and discipline administrative action, the management of political power acquires, besides an unprecedented degree of rationality, two equally rare and closely related characteristics: first, its premises and its purposes achieve a kind of transparency, of public visibility; and second, the cognitive aspect always intrinsic to action comes to depend markedly on the possession and the application of bodies of systematic knowledge, be they as different as juridical knowledge on the one hand, and economic-financial or engineering-logistical knowledge on the other.

Concentration of power and wide social participation

The editors of an Italian collection of essays on the history of the modern state make the following comment in their editorial introduction: 'For all its diversity, the state experience in modern Europe lends itself to be characterised by reference to two central aspects – concentration of power and participation in it. These are undoubtedly two conflicting tendencies . . . but for all that they have coexisted, neither having ever prevailed utterly and definitely over the other.'[4]

Historically, as we have seen, the modern state has been built up within an earlier, loosely constructed system of rule, by gathering at the centre of the polity a number of faculties and facilities of rule previously dispersed over the system's territory among a plurality of local powers. However, as the chief initiator and beneficiary of the process – typically, the king and his court – curtailed the political prerogatives of the privileged local groups, by the same token he reached out directly to wider groups, involving them in a political relationship to himself as his subjects. They became *justiciables* of his courts, paid him tribute and were conscripted in his armies.

The process affected also the rural populace, who had previously been denied any autonomous political significance by their dependence on a thin stratum of politically, economically and socially privileged noblemen and landlords. The king, furthermore, utilised the economic, military, ideological support of new, increasingly important urban elites. In turn the urban elites increasingly favoured new institutions (public freedoms, elections, parties) which allowed the active involvement in politics, first of those elites only, then also of growing sections of the populace, 'mobilised' by urbanisation ad industrialisation, and organised by unions and other associations.

To rephrase the point: the building up of the state progressively suppresses an earlier kind of political process, wherein a plurality of subjects exercised and sought to maintain and enlarge relatively independent faculties of rule. Rule becomes increasingly the exclusive prerogative of a unified, central, paramount political subject. The latter, however, becomes the point of reference of a new kind of political process, resolving around the content and form of policies now exclusively flowing out of the political centre; and this political process involves increasingly numerous actors, who voice (with varying effectiveness) increasingly different claims.

As I pointed out earlier, a key instrumentality of this process is a new type of political relationship – citizenship – directly connecting with the state an increasingly wide portion of the population, which came to constitute a political community. While those individuals holding office from election or appointment gained thereby a privileged access to political power – and could to an extent use that access to their own advantage – all other citizens progressively claimed and attained *some* political significance, however attenuated. In particular, they all could, in principle, aspire to election or appointment as officials – as was individiously pointed out in the quote from Taine in chapter 4. (This is the connection, pointed out by Max Weber, between democracy and bureaucracy.)[5]

This phenomenon of citizenship – as an increasingly general and increasingly comprehensive set of politically significant entitlements and capacities – sharply differentiates the quality of modern political experience, as far as the generality of individuals is concerned, from that of all other large systems of rule. There, typically, at most a small minority of politically significant individuals, closely associated with the ruler, dominate a disenfranchised majority; alternatively, political rights (and duties) are markedly and invidiously different for different groups within the population.

Once more, one could easily point to ways in which the citizenry of contemporary states, even when it formally possesses rights of political participation, is kept from using them effectively to monitor, criticise and intervene in the political process. All too often, the political and administrative elites maximise their own discretion, and secure for themselves the attendant perquisites of power, status and economic advantage by repressing, constraining, manipulating and sometimes even by organising and mobilising popular participation for their own ends. They are best able to do so, of course, in non-competitive, one-party systems; but they also manage to produce similar, if not identical, effects in those we are familiar with.

For all that, again, a potentially participant citizenry imposes powerful constraints on the autonomy of elites; and these constraints are probably all the more significant to the extent that the logic of social, economic and cultural advance calls forth (and calls *for*) an increasingly diversified, informed, sophisticated, demanding citizenry.

It would be possible to list other distinctive achievements of the modern state, and to suggest that they (like those mentioned above) reconcile apparently irreconcilable values and requirements, and moderate (if not triumph over) persistent, momentous contradictions of political experience. It is on this account that clear-sighted philosophers such as Hegel, always on the lookout for the 'reconciliation' of contrasts, saw in the modern state the ultimate attainment of the human spirit. For in his view the development of the modern state had built up political power to an unprecedented extent; and yet it had placed its exercise under constraints which both moderated and rendered its exercise calculable and rational.

Popitz reminds us of what a rare achievement the moderation of political power is:

> Only infrequently in the history of society has it been possible even to entertain in a purposeful and consequential manner the question of how to limit institutionalised violence. Basically, this has only happened in the Greek polis, in republican Rome, in a few other city states, and in the history of the modern constitutional state. And the answers to that question have been astonishingly similar: the postulate of the sovereignty of the law

and of the equality of all before the law ('isonomia'); the notion of placing basic constraints upon the formation of norms ('fundamental right'); distinctive provinces of competence (division of powers, federalism); procedural norms (decisions by collective bodies, publicity, official avenues for redress); norms of occupancy (turn-taking, elections); and norms of the public sphere (freedom of opinion, freedom of assembly). [my translation][6]

III

Yet the diverse and complex sequences of events in the course of which the state form of political organisation originally came into being in Europe, and the later sequences marking its consolidation in Europe and the West, and its extension to other parts of the world, have been counterpointed by redoubtable arguments voicing the concern, and sometimes the revulsion and the despair, of numerous thoughtful observers and critics.

I review very briefly some of those arguments in the remainder of this chapter, to balance out the positive appraisal of the phenomenon I have already offered, and to give readers an opportunity to form their own judgement as to whether, and to what extent, the development of the modern state was A Good Thing. (In fact, as will be noted, some of the arguments in question apply to political power and political activity in general, and they are only brought into sharper focus by referring them specifically to the modern state.)

Contrasting appraisals: conservative

The title of a chapter from a book by Robert Nisbet, 'The State as Revolution',[7] gives the gist of many arguments against the state formulated by conservative European social thinkers. These arguments mostly concern two closely associated aspects of the conceptual portrait of the state offered in chapter 2 above – its nature as an organisation, that is as a purposefully constructed social unit, and the bureaucratic model of its structure and operation. On those two accounts, the state lends itself to the following criticisms:

Artificiality   As we have seen, early state-building was mostly the work of rulers seeking to extend the scope and discretion of their powers beyond those assigned them by tradition. Most of the institutional innovations they introduced had little warrant in the lore and mores of the populations upon which they were imposed. (The replacement of local constabularies by tax-supported police forces, for instances, often occasioned much resentment.)

Later, states often attributed their own existence and configuration to fictional (the social contract) or actual (for example, the American and French constituent assemblies) deliberations, which again superimposed new, artificial arrangements upon existent practices of rule. Many conservative thinkers saw in this a redoubtable preference for contrived and engineered, as opposed to spontaneous and 'organic', arrangements and understandings. This preference they condemned, as expressing a conception of social life at large as something which could be arranged, disarranged and rearranged at will.

Impersonality In the pre-modern European polity, rule was largely structured through interpersonal relations, both between unequals and between peers. It could thus activate sentiments of personal loyalty, of felt commonality, of mutual responsibility. In the ancient German tradition, in particular, an individual's title to rule was made to rest also on the collective acknowledgement (through acclamation by the assembled, armed, free members of the community) of that individual's personal qualities of leadership.

In contrast, we have seen that the attachment to offices of facilities and faculties of rule, which individuals manage and exercise only in their capacity as office-holders, depersonalises the political process. This may constitute a signal achievement from the standpoint of the liberal tradition, but not from a conservative standpoint, concerned that under the new arrangements specifically moral considerations of responsibility and loyalty would cease to motivate respectively the activities of the power-holders and the others' will to obey and to follow.

Enforced uniformity Furthermore, the conservative tradition laments the state's tendency to root out historically grounded differences in the ways in which certain relationships are ordained in different parts of the territory, or by different sections of the population, in order to standardise them and to shape them in a generalised, uniform fashion.

How distasteful such an approach can be to the conservative mind, keen to preserve the irregularities and particularities that testify to the staying power of traditional, unplanned arrangements, is suggested by a sarcastic passage from *Reflections on the revolution in France*, in which Edmund Burke expresses his distaste for the drastic rearrangement of the territorial bases of the French kingdom carried out in the early phases of the revolution:

> The French builders, clearing away as mere rubbish whatever they found, and, like their ornamental gardeners, forming every thing into an exact level, propose to rest the whole local and general legislature on three bases of three different kinds: one geometrical, one arithmetical, and the third financial . . . For the accomplishment of the first of these purposes they

divide the area of their country into eighty-three pieces, regularly square, of eighteen leagues by eighteen. These large divisions are called *Departments*. These they portion, proceeding by square measurement, into seventeen hundred and twenty districts called *Communes*. These again they subdivide, still proceeding by square measurements, into smaller districts called *cantons*, making in all 6,400.

Boundlessness In my first chapter, I mentioned some concerns arising from the fact that, in principle, political power can be brought to bear upon any and all aspects of existence. I mentioned, in particular, the problem of the scope of political power, which has been a recurrent issue in theoretical ad practical arguments about politics, and the tendency for political *pragma* (to use a favourite expression of Weber's, derived from Thucydides) to produce outcomes which are irrational from a moral viewpoint.

These concerns are intensified, particularly (but not exclusively) in the minds of conservative thinkers, when the modern state is under consideration; for the state is so constructed that it can acquire, generate, store and deploy an indefinite quantity of power, turning it to an open-ended plurality of uses. As the last quote from Popitz indicated, most attempts to limit and constrain this open-endedness intrinsic to the state, particularly in the last two centuries, have made use of another of its distinctive features – its close relationship to law. The efficacy of various activities of state organs, in particular, has been made to depend on their legal validity, that is, on their conformity with enacted, general rules which lay substantial or procedural boundaries around those activities.

However, as we have already noted, the production and promulgation of such rules is itself a state activity (and in some constructions, *the* state activity *par excellence*). In other words, laws of the state's own making are expected to lay constraints upon the scope and mode of operation of state power. Conservative critics are, perhaps not unjustifiably, sceptical about the reliability of this arrangement; and they compare it unfavourably with those circumstances, characteristic of some phases of pre-modern political experience, in which political power was seen as compellingly limited by a 'firmament of law'[8] not of its own making, but instead grounded in tradition, sustained by the consensus of the community, possibly divinely inspired, but in any case autonomously, intrinsically valid.

This situation applied in the late-medieval phase of the early development of the state, wherein – according to Gierke – 'law is the result not of a common will that a thing shall be, but of a common conviction that it is.' The poet Browning expressed the same insight (and the same nostalgia) with reference not to the folk envisaged by Gierke, but to the common law which the early European states jointly derived from the rediscovered treasure of Justinian's *Codes Juris Civilis*, and particularly of the *Digest* or *Pandects*: 'Justinian's Pandects only make precise / What simply sparkled in men's eyes before / Twitched in the brow or quivered on their lip / Waited the speech they called but would not come.'[9] Truth to tell, this does not much sound like the *Pandects* as I remember studying them. But in any case, one must see the attraction exercised on minds sensitive to the values of orderliness and of 'the certainty of rights' by a situation where law is not a contingent product of state activity, owing its validity only to the procedure (itself set down by state!) whereby it is produced, but constitutes a pre-established framework, which the state must respect. The alternative (institutionalised in the relation of the state to law) is one which may understandably inspire some disquiet: for a system of entirely state-made law affirms and reinforces the state's intrinsic boundlessness.

Such disquiet was poignantly voiced in the course of an episode recently recounted by a historian of state-making within the Duchy of Württemberg, a region of Germany centred on Stuttgart. In 1692, the duchy's prince regent, Friedrich Karl, tried to obtain the consent of the main estate body, the *Landtag*, to new fiscal and military arrangements not envisaged by the *Tübinger Vertrag* – the Tübinger compact, which back in 1514 had established the reciprocal rights and obligations of the duke himself and of the estates. The prince regent argued that the compact was 'past history' (*alte historie*), and should not stand in the way of innovations required to make the state more powerful and foster the *gloire* of the ducal dynasty. The main spokesman for the estates, Johannes Sturm, replied 'that neither he nor his colleagues could understand how compliance with the law of the land could be construed as unproductive literal mindedness. "If the Law is nothing but past history," he wrote, "then no treaty, no compact, no legislation is valid. The world is ruled only by power." '[10]

Contrasting appraisals: radical

Other powerful critiques of the modern state have been offered from standpoints other than the conservative. The most significant radical critiques are probably those originating from Marx, Engels and their followers. I intend to consider these later on, but here I shall mention two main contentions.

In the first place, the state's claim to concentrate within itself all political power, preventing it from being pre-empted by the holders of other forms of social power – economic in particular – and from being exercised in their interest, is rejected. The class division arising in society from the unequal allocation of economic power is not ignored (much less abolished) by the state. On the contrary, the state tends to reinforce that division and to assist the economically dominant class in exploiting the other(s). The basic import of state-making is to rationalise (and thus to make marginally less savage and unpredictable) the support which political power unavoidably lends to other forms of oppression and exploitation.

In the second place – but this criticism is not easy to accord with the first, and in any case it is common to Marxism and to anarchism – the vesting of all political power in a separate set of institutions alienates it from the collectivity from which all social power emanates and which it is supposed to serve. Set over against society in a sovereign sphere of its own, the state threatens to become utterly self-absorbed and self-regarding, to make the continuous increase of its own power an end in itself, or a means to foster the exclusive interests of its own personnel. State-making disables communities from attaining self-government, and prevents the people from being able to settle their differences among themselves and to lay down and sanction autonomously the ways in which they want to live.

Concerns over the nature of the states system

Further criticisms of the modern state, voiced sometimes from both the conservative and the radical end of the continuum of political and social thought, address not so much the structure and operation of each state taken in itself as the nature of the modern states system.

As we have seen in chapter 2, that system only exists as the product of the self-activating, self-interested interactions of its constituent units. It is not the locus of an overriding, comprehensive political order, culminating in a supreme authority to which the units could appeal in order to secure their existence and assert their interests. Those units are sovereign states, and as such they must themselves provide for their security and advance their interests in open competition with one another.

That competition, furthermore, can always turn into conflict and – in the absence of a paramount power able to settle it authoritatively and to enforce and police that settlement – the conflict can turn into enmity. In order to be able to withstand and to express enmity, each state must acquire as much military might as it can, and – when all is said and done – must be willing to use it.

This essential, constitutive feature of the modern states system – its being composed of units able and willing (ultimately) to pursue their own interests, beginning with the key interest of each in its own security, by making war on one another – imparts to the modern states system a particular turbulence and restlessness, and a potential destructiveness which reaches its ghastly, unsurpassable maximum in the era of nuclear armaments. Now one can perceive more clearly than ever before the dangerousness of a political ordering of humanity where the modern (sovereign, national) state counts as *the* political actor, and which as a consequence can only attain (at best) an unstable, constrained equilibrium, resting purely on relations of power.

Let us reconsider for a moment the issue of *raison d'état* – a notion whose prime reference has always been to the state's external relations, and which shows how the historical development of the state form intensified and dramatised a problematic which in principle concerns also other manifestations of political power.

There is a narrower and a wider way of conceiving the issue of *raison d'état*[11] and the related controversies. On the narrower understanding, *raison d'état* is a conspicuous but not particularly significant theme in early theorising about the state, a sophisticated, largely literary controversy originating from Machiavelli's pronouncements about the nature of state business.[12]

On the broader understanding, the issue is still with us, whether or not in phrasing it one uses the notion of *raison d'état*. It concerns (some of) the consequences of the fact that, by virtue of its sovereignty, each state is expected to look after its own interest, and in doing so must ultimately rely, as I have just indicated, on its own might. One reading of the notion, focused on the term *raison*, seeks to counter the feeling that the state's conduct is guided by a ceaseless, indefinite, relentless striving for power after power, which continuously generates disorder and foments murderous strife. For if the pursuit of power itself is rational, it cannot afford to be utterly unrestrained, to be guided by sheer bellicosity and bloody-mindedness; it will instead seek to avoid, or to make exceptional, the trial of strength represented by armed confrontation, and will normally express itself through diplomacy, and generate relatively stable equilibria between states.

The other reading of the notion emphasises the term *état*, and suggests that the business of politics between sovereign states, being unique in its dangerousness and in the momentousness of the interests to which it is oriented, releases the actor – the state itself – from the constraints that normally apply to moral agents. The state's security is a requirement of such significance that in seeking to guarantee it, rulers may (be compelled to) violate moral and juridical norms, fail to comply with their own agreements with other states, and sometimes override considerations of economic advantage.

Conservative critics lament the fact that this latter interpretation of *raison d'état* generates (or legitimates) a dangerous separation between morality and law on the one hand, and statecraft on the other. They also emphasise that the former interpretation, while it encourages the formation of transitory, mechanical equilibria and adjustments in the relations between sovereign states, does not substantially alter the disorderly nature of the modern states system, and enthrones power as the essential medium and stake of the system's operations.

Radical critics, in turn, remark that often the appeal to the state's external security as the overriding criterion of its activity functions as a cover or a pretext for repressive internal policies intended to uphold and advance the interests of the dominant class(es). Sometimes they also suggest that rationality in human affairs should be conceived in a broader and more substantive sense than in the notion of *raison d'état*, to encompass the realisation of universal human potentialities; they thus reject war as a way of settling conflicts between states.

In this chapter, I have raised the question of how one might appraise the development of the modern state, as a distinctive form of institutionalised political power, from the standpoint of human values. Of course this can only be done by reference to one's own value preferences; and it is in the light of my own that I have advanced a largely positive appraisal of the genesis and development of the state. Subsequently, however, I have complemented that appraisal (and suggested reasons for doubting its validity) by reviewing some considerations, mainly formulated from a conservative standpoint, to the effect that the development of the modern state has no title to being considered a happy episode in human history.

In the next chapter, I shall consider further theories concerning that development, but mainly intended to provide an account, not an evaluation, of it.

6

Controversies about the State: Attempting an Explanation

Below, I select for consideration three significant ways in which students have sought to make sense of the story recounted in chapters 3 and 4, not (as in chapter 5) by evaluating its significance in the light of some values, but by offering accounts of it grounded on some broader principles of social explanation.

I

The evolutionary account

According to one account, the genesis and development of the modern state are best understood as but one aspect, albeit a particularly massive and significant aspect, of an even wider phenomenon, whose main regularities can be stated in general terms. The phenomenon is the broad evolutionary process in the course of which human societies develop from simple to more complex structural and cultural conditions, and thereby establish more stable and secure relations to their environments. In the West, from the end of the middle ages, such development underwent a dramatic acceleration and intensification – a phenomenon often labelled modernisation. In this account, in essence, state-making is seen as the political dimension of modernisation.

The account is, more or less explicitly, predicated on the assumption that there is a fundamental continuity or at any rate a significant analogy between biological and socio-cultural evolution. On this assumption, societal advance can be best understood, *mutatis mutandis*, in the light of a generalisation originally formulated with respect to the biological realm, and which in turn transposes to phylogenesis (that is, the development of a species) a generalisation first derived from ontogenesis (the development of a single organism within that species).

The generalisation is the following: new species evolve inasmuch as life forms in which the several functional requirements for the survival of the organism, met by activities either of that organism as an undifferentiated whole or of a small number of barely distinguishable parts, are succeeded (and to a certain extent supplanted) by new life forms, which have evolved organs, that is, anatomically differentiated structures, each specialised in performing *one* of those activities.

Thus understood, the evolutionary process yields a plurality of species, whose relations to their environment increasingly rest on a close correspondence between, on the one hand, each of their functional requirements, and, on the other, each one of their differentiated structural features. By and large, it is this correspondence that secures each species' survival, among other reasons because it allows the organism to register more discriminatingly a greater range of different signals from its environment, and to exploit more efficiently a larger variety of resources. This also makes it possible for a given species to undergo further modifications in the same sense, which produce of course new species. These tend in turn to be more and more differentiated, both in the sense that each has increasingly specialised organs, and in the sense that a greater variety of species develops, each adapted to and making use of a specific part or aspect of the environment.

Transposed to the realm of history, this view emphasises the advantage a given society gains, in dealing with its natural environment or with other societies, from becoming more and more complex, by developing increasingly differentiated arrangements for attending to different aspects of social existence.

In the historical realm, of course, the process of specialisation, or of division of labour, through which that advantage is gained, proceeds in a much more contingent, discontinuous and unpredictable manner than in the biological realm. For on the one hand human beings sustain their relations to their environments (natural and social) largely through *minded* processes of cultural invention, imitation and adaptation, which can produce and diffuse much more varied arrangements much more rapidly than is normally possible to other beings through blind natural processes of variation and selection. On the other hand, in human societies any given set of arrangements, once in place, tends to become an object of contention between groups interested in maintaining and strengthening those arrangements and groups interested in modifying and eliminating them. The relations between these contrasting groups involve, again, distinctly human determinants (such as social power, in its various forms) and processes (such as conflict). These produce, as I have indicated, highly contingent outcomes, including sometimes the conscious intensification and acceleration, and sometimes the stagnation, suppression or reversal of the differentiation process itself.[1]

Open-ended, desultory, and 'wobbly' as that process may be, given episodes of it can sometimes, over a given period and within a certain regional locale of human history, acquire such momentum, continuity and visibility, that their analogy with the biological evolutionary process, if discriminatingly used, becomes particularly compelling and convincing. As I have indicated, the notion of modernisation has been widely used to characterise one major episode of this kind, and the genesis and development of the (modern) state constitutes a particularly momentous and explicit aspect of that episode.

State-making as modernisation

Social structures – in human societies, at any rate – are much more subtle and abstract matters than biological ones. To give a crude instance, human queens are not as innately, materially and thoroughly different in their bodily configuration from their subjects as queen bees are from worker bees. The social structure 'queen-hood' exists only to the extent that the flow of reciprocal conduct between human queens and their subjects is patterned by certain normative and cognitive expectations – as Durkheim puts it, by particular *manières d'agir et de penser*. In other words, human structures are *institutional* in nature – a word which points both to the fact that they are historically produced and to the fact that pluralities of expectations form ordered complexes, each focused on one particular type of social business. The formation of organs in nature life forms finds a parallel within the social realm in the way in which such ordered complexes multiply, and each specialises in structuring a flow of social activity which makes different demands on actors, produces and consumes different kinds of social and natural resources and attends to different social requirements.

The rationality gain

In this perspective, the superiority of modern over pre-modern societies lies in the fact that in the former evolution has advanced far beyond the level attained in the latter, and has attained to a much greater extent the advantages of matching structural arrangements to functional requirements. Most structural arrangements, furthermore, are increasingly constituted by cognitive and normative expectations which make possible and reward rational conduct, that is, deliberate choice among alternative courses of action, in the light of their relative conduciveness to a given aim.

In the same perspective, modernisation appears to have yielded an unmistakable, massive rationality gain for society at large, whose business comes to be transacted in increasingly diverse, specialised ways, each aspect of it under the auspices of different institutional arrangements, no longer constrained by considerations seen as extraneous to the matter in hand. For instance, the modern economy arose as productive establishments became differentiated from households, adopted profit (a purely economic datum) as the key consideration orienting their practices, and began to operate on markets, which among other things allowed the formation of prices no longer constrained by moral assumptions about their justness or lack of it. And the rise of the modern economy, in turn, has been associated with a veritable explosion of productive powers and with a historically unique expansion of consumption possibilities for broad masses of the population.

Similarly, in the political sphere, the modern state was built up as a machine for performing (to repeat a previous phrasing) *all* and *only* the political tasks pertaining to a given territory. I have already mentioned the secularisation of the state as an early and particularly significant aspect of the larger process of differentiation of political from other social activities. The state progressively frees itself from constraints and burdens of a religious nature, and thus from its dependency and obligations toward ecclesiastical authorities. It proclaims its indifference to the religious affiliations and concerns of its subjects/citizens, who are free to cultivate them in the separate sphere of a religion understood as a private matter, and as a matter for one's conscience.

Similarly – at any rate up to a certain point in its development – the state tends to divest itself of all direct productive tasks and of responsibility for the allocation of economic facilities and rewards, leaving such matters to the market transactions of producers and consumers, which it regulates in a general and abstract manner via its private law, without taking an interest in the specific outcomes of those transactions. It can thus devote itself, via a growing body of public law, to promoting, so to speak, a division of political labour, by differentiating itself into a plurality of purposefully organised and rationally operating agencies, each specialising in one kind of political or administrative activity.

Considering the latter in particular, I gave already suggested that bureaucratisation constitutes in principle a particularly effective way of discharging complex and changing administrative tasks. And the 'positivisation of law' can be seen as a way of securing the population's compliance with a certain set of normative expectations, by making the validity of laws depend exclusively on their being produced by following given procedural rules, rather than on their perceived accord with ideological conceptions of justice and fairness.

The Victorian sociologist Herbert Spencer gave the first extensive presentation of the conception of social change summarised above, characteristically inscribing it within a broader view of the evolutionary process as a whole. His view of the modernisation process is also echoed above; but his own formulation of it did not find a place for (and indeed tended to treat as a perverse nuisance) the fact that with the advance of modernity political power and the state did not lose significance and indeed their scope seemed to be increasing.

This is a major respect in which Durkheim considerably qualified and corrected Spencer's views about social change and modernisation. According to Durkheim, Spencer had failed to see that the process of differentiation could have aberrant, maladaptive effects (for biological organisms as well as for societies) unless it was accompanied and counter-balanced by a process of integration – that is, by arrangements that kept the differentiated structures from becoming excessively autonomous, not to say contentious, with respect to one another, and ensured their cooperation in the interest of society as a whole.

What arrangements could perform this function in modern society, is a question to which in my view Durkheim gave, as it were, two primary and one subsidiary answers. One primary answer saw modern society as attaining integration (or, in Durkheim's own phrasing, solidarity) chiefly by the extent to which its differentiated structures depend on one another, treat each other's outputs as their own inputs. Another primary answer emphasised instead the necessity of a normative and cognitive consensus among individuals which would override the diverse and potentially conflicting interests generated by structural differentiation. The subsidiary answer (which curiously enough can be treated as an elaboration of both the primary ones) considered the key integrative mechanism of modern societies to be exactly the phenomenon that so bothered Spencer – the persistent presence and the widening scope of state action.

As I see the matter, what I call Durkheim's subsidiary answer is an essential component of the first account of the genesis and development of the modern state I have chosen for consideration, and it has been increasingly emphasised (not necessarily with reference to Durkheim himself) in contemporary readings of that account.[2] Basically, the argument is that while all parts of society are equal in being functionally specialised and thus mutually interdependent, one part is more equal than the others in that it expressly attends to the need for social integration; it is, as it were, the part that specialised in acting self-consciously and expressly on behalf of the whole. The state is that part; and on that account state-making has constituted an absolutely critical component of the advance of modernisation.

Although they cannot be elaborated here, there are significant connections between this line of reasoning and a number of traditional political views about the state: for instance, its necessary territorial reference, its sovereignty, and its tendency to widen the generality and the significance of the bond of citizenship.[3] But the basic point is sociological: a society where, so to speak, the state has taken charge of political experience, is thereby strongly empowered, made capable of more satisfactory – because more deliberate, variable, selective, effective – relations to its natural and social environments.

Some critical remarks

I find quite compelling the basic imagery underlying this version of our theme – the view of society as constituting a more and more advanced and sophisticated division of labour, where a lot of different things go on under the auspices of distinctive arrangements, and yet *tout se tient* (everything hangs together). And in chapter 5 I have already argued that such a society is particularly empowered by state-making. The following statement by a contemporary political scientist, Samuel P. Huntington, expresses this point particularly well, although it does not use the expression 'state':

> The most important distinction between countries concerns not their form of government but their degree of government. The differences between democracy and dictatorship are less than the differences between those countries whose politics embodies consensus, community, legitimation, stability, and those countries whose politics is deficient in those qualities . . . The United States, Great Britain, and the Soviet Union have different forms of government, but in all three systems the government governs . . . All three countries have strong, adaptable, coherent political institutions: effective bureaucracies, well-organized political parties, a high degree of popular participation in public affairs, working systems of civilian control over the military, extensive activity by the government in the economy, and reasonably effective procedures for regulating succession and controlling political conflict. These governments command the loyalties of their citizens and thus have the capacity to conscript manpower, and to innovate and to execute policy. If the Politburo, the cabinet, or the President makes a decision, the probability is high that it will be implemented through the government machinery.[4]

Yet there is a significant difference between pointing out the advantageous consequences of certain political features of a society and explaining the genesis and development of those features – as has been pointed out by the critics of so-called structural-functional theory. The analogy between biological and social evolution is potentially enlightening, but it becomes misleading if one does not acknowledge the differences between the realms of nature and the realm of history.

Within the former one can give a cogent account both of how variant structural arrangements emerge, and of how selection operates among them; and this, among other reasons, because it is generally possible both to identify precisely the units involved – individual organisms, populations, species – and to specify how the process affects them by the (relatively) simple test of survival or extinction. In the realm of history that test is straightforwardly applicable only to individual human beings, not to the collective units to which the structural functional argument seeks to refer, and which are very difficult to identify empirically in the first place. (Exactly what, or perhaps who, was the Roman empire, and exactly when did it decline and fall?) In any case, in that realm it has not been possible to discover mechanisms of variation and selection of structural features which are closely, operationally analogous to those known to operate in the realm of nature.

Besides these and other generic reasons for doubting the claim that one can construct a valid theory of social change on the basis of its analogy with biological evolution, the following objections can be posed to the account presented above:

1 The account, as we have seen, argues that as the structurally differentiated parts of society become more numerous, their functional interdependence also increases. But it looks as if some parts do not, as it were, know their script too well. They appear intent upon not only establishing their own autonomy, but also asserting their own priority over all others, each attempting to maximise the share of society's resources that it controls and consumes at the expense of the other.[5] In particular, it is very difficult for the structural-functional approach to make sense of the several weighty indications that during their genesis and much of their development many states have had an essentially predatory or racketeering relation to the rest of society.[6]

2 Currently, the outcome of some of the conflicts occasioned by the rivalry between parts of society seems to be not just a momentary arrest or reversion of differentiation, but something of a trend toward the de-differentiation of society. For some of its parts gain enough power over others and the whole to impose upon them their own distinctive rationality. Also, structures fashioned to perform certain tasks involve themselves in rather different ones.

3 The above account assumes that the phenomena it emphasises have adaptive significance, increase the society's stability and improve its relation to its several environments. This assumption certainly deserves to be revised, since numerous

contemporary social trends – the nuclear arms race, for instance, or the damages wrought upon the natural environment by unrestrained technological development – appear to threaten the survival of mankind. And at least the first trend is definitely driven by the state.

4 Further, the evolutionary approach has difficulty accounting for the known historical particulars of the genesis and development of the modern state, beginning with the location and timing of that genesis. If the state is to be primarily understood and explained as the issue of general evolutionary processes which fashion in it a superior device for securing politically the relationship between a society and its environments, why should it not have evolved independently in a number of places and at different times? And how can one account in evolutionary terms for the fact that, as I have already suggested and as I shall argue below, the ideal-typical state depicted in chapter 2 is demonstrably cobbled together from a variety of unrelated, and often contrasting, institutional arrangements?[7]

5 Finally, the basic imagery of the evolutionary account is, so to speak, centripetal, inward-bound; both differentiation and integration are processes predicted to take place within pre-constituted social entities. How can one reconcile this with the fact that state-making processes, as I have repeatedly emphasised, concern and reflect the characteristics of the relations between political entities – primarily warfare, whose outcome is (particularly in the pre-industrial era) intrinsically unpredictable?[8]

These are intended as rhetorical questions; for, as I have already suggested, the evolutionary account, enlightening as it may be as a statement of some of the consequences of state-making strikes me as providing a much less forceful and tenable argument about its causes, and its concrete historical course.

The marxist account(s)

A different – though perhaps not so radically different – account of the genesis and development of the modern state is offered by Marx (and Engels), and by students who approach the phenomenon in the light of Marx's own insights into it. Those insights are multiple, diverse, and not always compatible, and have thus inspired different, indeed sometimes contrasting interpretations.[9] Most versions, however, share a broad perspective, which is all that need be stated here. It is possible, from that perspective, to perform two tasks to which in my view the evolutionary account proves unequal. It is possible, that is, both to account for where and when the modern state emerged and underwent its early development; and to acknowledge the critical role played in that process not by the presumed requirements of society as a whole, but by distinctive, sectional forces contending with one another within the same society.

The first task is performed by viewing state-making as an aspect not of a generic process of societal evolution, but of a more narrowly identified phenomenon – the rise and advance of the capitalist mode of production. Implicitly, this view addresses also the second task: the sectional interests directly or indirectly driving the state-making enterprise are seen to be those of the collective protagonist of the genesis and development of that mode of production, that is, the bourgeoisie – although by its very nature this class does not claim political leadership openly and exclusively for itself.

The nature of political institutions

To understand and evaluate this Marxist argument concerning the genesis and development of the modern state, it is necessary to see it as part of a broader argument, which can be phrased as follows.

All political institutions – not just those of the modern state – are made necessary by one critical feature of historical societies. These are all fissured through and through by a fundamental division between a minority enjoying privileged access to and control over the means of material production, and the majority who, denied such privilege, obtain access to those means only on terms laid down by the minority, and make use of them only under the control and largely to the benefit of the latter.

Being thus exploited and oppressed, the majority has interests inherently opposed to those of the minority, which it can only realise by modifying or indeed subverting the existing arrangements of production and the resultant dominance of the minority. Thus, the majority can only advance those interests by engaging in conflict with the latter.

From this perspective, political institutions appear essentially as devices whereby the minority, availing itself of its control over the fundamental processes of production and reproduction of material existence, suppresses, deflects, contains or moderates that conflict, thus securing its own advantage over the majority. Most importantly, such institutions organise and deploy the ultimate social resource, organised coercion, in order to secure the minority's privileged position, often enshrined into legal right and as such dependent on enforcement.

Being essentially geared to maintaining and servicing a society's primary structures of exploitation and oppression, that is, those directly related to production, political institutions change historically with those structures, and with the attendant charges in the nature and the distinctive interests and preoccupations of the dominant minority. Thus, to the epochal change constituted by the transition from the feudal to the capitalist mode of production, there corresponds a derivative, but none the less necessary and significant change in the political institutions of the societies harbouring that transition.

The genesis and development of the modern state are thus understood primarily as processes whereby the political environment of society was restructured in order to make it (and then to keep it) compatible with, and indeed as far as possible conducive to, the orderly functioning of the capitalist machinery of exploitation and accumulation.

Let me exemplify. As a political centre engaged in state-making extends the reach of its facilities and faculties of rule, by the same token it widens and secures the boundaries within which markets become established and operate routinely. Or – with 'right' replacing 'duty' as the elementary institutional basis of the performance of tasks of rule, the political, administrative and judicial machinery becomes more sophisticated and predictable in its functioning; and this again assists the formation and operation of those myriad relations of self-interested exchange which constitute the molecular components of a capitalist economy. Thus, two critical aspects of the genesis and development of the modern state (the consolidation and the rationalisation of rule, as I have called them elsewhere)[10] were indispensable to the accumulation and reproduction of private capital, on which is in turn based the dominant position of the bourgeois class.

In the more recent phases of its development, the state undertakes new, wider responsibilities of societal and economic management. This allows it to sustain the accumulation process in the changing circumstances of capitalist development, which have made it more difficult for markets to stabilise that process, and to moderate and institutionalise social conflict, rather than directly repressing it.

Some criticisms

Taking this as the barest outline of the core argument shared by most, if not all, versions of a Marxist perspective on our theme, let us seek to evaluate it. To begin with, it is clear to me that this approach deserves to be taken seriously, and on a number of counts appears superior to the previous one. Basically, it articulates the obvious insight that, as it were, it is no coincidence that the modern state and modern capitalism developed, by and large, side by side, at any rate from the seventeenth century, in Western Europe. However, the Marxist account emphasises only some of the historically significant correlations between those two orders of phenomena, and neglects others. Furthermore, it probably overstates the extent to which the two developments were synchronous and functionally correlated.

There is little doubt that modern capitalism arose and developed, as Max Weber once phrased it, 'in alliance with the emergent power of the modern state'. But the alliance in question involved, in my view (to be elaborated below) two autonomous forces, neither of which was originally and inescapably dominant over the other.

The alliance was based on a convergence of interests, between on the one hand the thrusting power of capital seeking to eliminate the restraints imposed upon the scope and autonomy of market relations by the vested interests of the landowning class and of town-based trading and productive estates, and on the other hand the drive by energetic and enterprising rulers to centralise political power by confiscating those fragments of it still vested in estate bodies and in aristocratic dynasties. The alliance continued into the era of expanding commercialisation and early industrialisation of the economy, when both these processes became critical to the state's own concern to establish a new tax base and lay new financial foundations for its war-making capacity.

By the middle of the nineteenth century, something more than an alliance seemed in evidence in a number of Western countries – something like an outright takeover of the political sphere by the dominant capitalist class. If one considers the workings of nineteenth-century political institutions – the kinds of political personnel, policies and judicial and administrative practices they generated – Marx's notorious characterisation of government as 'the executive committee of the bourgeoisie' would have appeared, at that time, much more plausible than it had before.

Or since! For, by the end of the century, in a number of Western countries the establishment of liberal-democratic institutions had led to the formation of socialist and labour parties and of other working-class organisations. These had begun to constitute a significant political counterweight to the continuing economic predominance of the bourgeoisie, and demanded and supported the continuing expansion of the state's own power to oversee and control the social process at large, countering and limiting the sway of market forces upon it. The continuation and intensification of these trends in the twentieth century has made the relationship between the social power vested in capital and that vested in the state highly contentious, among other reasons because of the growing internationalisation of capital.

Whether the Weberian expression 'alliance' remains appropriate today to characterise that relationship, has become a contingent question, whose answer varies from place to place (not to mention, of course, according to what one understands by 'alliance'). In liberal-democratic states, what can always be said is that the social power of capital represents an abiding, high-priority constraint upon state policies, which must to some extent preserve and/or foster the requirements of profit-making and of continuing capital accumulation.

To what extent they do so, however, varies considerably from state to state, or indeed with changes in the governing majorities within a given state. Besides, as is being learned in some Western countries today, there is no guarantee that even policies which obligingly attach the highest priority to the requirements of capital will generate political support from the capitalist element, or for that matter will actually satisfy those requirements and generate investments, and strengthen and diversify a country's industrial base.

In sum, neither historical nor contemporary evidence suggests that the story of the state can be satisfactorily accounted for by viewing the state as standing in a position of constant and narrow subordination to the social power of capital. Even the rudimentary account of that story offered in chapters 3 and 4 shows that much of it has revolved around war, territorial aggrandisement and a concern with making state revenues larger and more secure, rather than around activities intended to generate and maintain the material and institutional premises for the economic advance and the wider dominance of the bourgeoisie. Furthermore, major turning points in that story have resulted from developments and contingencies pertaining strictly to the strategic-military sphere,[11] the significance of which Marxism constitutionally underrates. The import of all these themes (and related ones) cannot be taken on board by a Marxist understanding of the state that actually bases itself on Marx's (and Engels's) own original and distinctive views of the matter.

III

An alternative approach

For all their differences, the two accounts examined so far share two related features, and, in my view of the matter, two related flaws. In the first place, they are both, to use a recent, striking phrasing of this point, society-centred rather than state-centred. That is, they account for the state's existence and its dynamic by referring primarily to social processes which are not themselves of a political nature, and which political developments such as state-making are seen to complement, assist and secure. In the second place, both accounts present the genesis and development of the state as highly determined phenomena. According to both accounts, that is, the genesis and development of the state have of course shown considerable diversity, from place to place, in their timing and in their detailed institutional expression; but their broad course has obeyed a single, compelling logic, which each account, in its own distinctive way, seeks to identify and elucidate.

In a sense, all of this book seeks to present an alternative approach. In the remainder of this chapter I shall both reflect on previous chapters, and foreshadow those to follow, by suggesting the merest outline of such an alternative, which finds its inspiration chiefly in insights drawn from the work of Max Weber. However, some of those insights had been formulated by earlier writers (from Tocqueville to Burckhardt); and of course many other writers subsequently complemented, qualified or revised them.

A state-centred understanding of the state

The alternative approach is characterised in the first place by its rejection of the society-centredness and of the deterministic orientation shared by both the previous accounts. This characterisation, however, should not be misunderstood. It does not entail making the state into *the* dominant force in modern history, thus opposing to a society-centred view of the state a state-centred view of society. What is sought is, rather, a state-centred view of the state itself. In a previous book I have sought to convey this aspiration in a footnote commenting on divergent Marxist interpretations of the class significance of French absolutism:

> Apparently, from a Marxist viewpoint one can argue either that the [French] monarchy 'worked for' the bourgeoisie or that it 'worked for' the nobility; what, for some reason or other, appears out of the question is that the monarchy may have 'worked for' itself, meaning of course not the monarch and its dynasty alone but the whole apparatus of rule that surrounded him.[12]

The position implied in the above quote does not in the least deny that in many cases the arrangements and policies of states are best understood as constituting, or resulting from, the resolution of contrasts between social forces, each deriving its particular interests primarily from the possession of, or exclusion from, forms of social power other than political, and each seeking sanction and support for those interests from the state. However, this line of interpretation should be systematically juxtaposed to, and compared with, one that sees the state – a set of institutions specifically concerned with accumulating and exercising political power – as itself constituting a distinctive social force, vested with interests of its own, which affect autonomously, and sometimes decisively, the state's own arrangements and policies.

While directed primarily against the Marxist view, incidentally, this position differs also from the functionalist view, which sees the state not as committed by its very nature to pursue the interests of one part of society, but as a differentiated, specialised organ serving the needs of the whole society, preserving its integration and guiding its unitary development.

I would contend that this state-centred position, when properly developed, yields a better understanding of the phenomena with which we are concerned than is possible from the society-centred viewpoint. This book as a whole, again, should exhibit the grounds for that contention.

An emphasis on contingency

As I have indicated, both previous accounts construe the genesis and development of the modern state in a deterministic manner. The evolutionist account sees them as an aspect of modernisation, which it considers in turn as intensifying a broader trend toward greater and greater societal differentiation and complexity (and the attendant need for societal organs specialising in integrative functions). The Marxist account (in most of its variants, at any rate) sees the state emerge and develop in response to the specific form assumed under capitalism by the dominant class's need to have its economy-based dominance politically secured and fostered.

Rejecting the deterministic orientation common to those two accounts does not entail discarding the insights one can derive from them. As I have shown both in this chapter and elsewhere, it is enlightening to consider the state's story as constituting (among other things) a sustained process of institutional differentiation; to acknowledge the empowering effect a society may derive from making its political arrangements more state-like; or to point out the very different extent to which the interests of the dominant and of the subaltern classes have dictated the agenda and the mode of operation of the liberal (or liberal-democratic) states.

Nor does one have to construe the state's story deterministically in order to acknowledge the compulsive consistency and continuity with which that story has unfolded in its various locales. There is little question that, in response chiefly to the continually increasing costs of warfare, each major European centre of rule, decade after decade, century after century, has had to extract more resources from the society over which it ruled, thus to establish more and more elaborate fiscal arrangements, and to gather to itself more and more extensive faculties of rule.

However, these undertakings of rulers were necessary but not sufficient conditions for success in the increasingly competitive European states system (and in the drive for colonial expansion around which the rivalry of European states largely revolved). In particular, which of two states at war with one another would win was ever an intrinsically open question – no matter how precisely later chroniclers and historians might identify in retrospect the makings of the victory of one of the contendents.

In due course, furthermore, the outcome of a given confrontation would affect a further question – which particular military, fiscal and administrative arrangements would serve as a model for other states, and thus bias their political development toward one kind or another of political development. Many of the uniformities and similarities which one can observe in the political development of states, and which society-centred accounts treat as evidence of a systemic logic at work – be it the evolutionary logic of differentiation, or that of capital expansion and bourgeois dominance – issued in fact from self-conscious processes of selective imitation by one polity of the arrangements and policies of the other.

Those processes were contingent both because they were deliberate – that is, they took into account alternative possibilities – and because such deliberation considered, among other matters, how things had turned out the last time a given country, under consideration as a possible model, had gone to war, or, more generally, how that country rated in the current power stakes. For instance, it was largely the unique standing of Britain as an imperial power in the eighteenth and nineteenth centuries that made its peculiar political institutions the object of a great deal of attention and respect in other countries, and the source of much influence upon the design or reform of their political institutions. And the Japanese officials who had for years been preparing law reforms after the French model, were suddenly told to change course and look to Prussia, when that state led other German states to victory over the Second Empire in 1870–1.

If the vicissitudes of the relationships between states thus impinged upon various aspects of the genesis and development of 'the State', its development was also affected by the varying relationships between political power and the other two forms of social power mentioned in our first chapter – economic and normative power – but most particularly, in the last few centuries, between political and economic power.

The issue – to what extent one of these two forms of power imposed its own superiority over the other – was settled in different ways from place to place and from time to time. The settlement of it found expression in a variety of institutional arrangements, concerning such things as taxation, the degree of autonomy of the central bank *vis-à-vis* government, the regulation of union activity or the extent to which public authorities owned or controlled industrial assets.

I think that today, more than ever, and all over the world, the relationship between political and economic power remains at issue. This is so because that issue has been settled according to widely different patterns in various parts of the world, which often seek to impose their own pattern of settlement upon other parts, and because, at the same time, each pattern finds itself confronted with new circumstances and possibilities which tend to destabilise it.

Necessity and contingency in the genesis of liberal democracy

Let me restate a few points made so far. The dynamic of the genesis and development of the modern state resulted largely from the strenuous efforts made by rulers, each by means of his/her apparatus of rule, to widen and secure their power base and to increase their own effectiveness and discretion in managing and mobilising societal resources. The continuity and earnestness of such efforts – comprehensible if one reflects what was at stake in them – accounts for the fact that as one surveys the state's story as a whole, one is likely to perceive in it a compelling tendency for political power to build up.

This tendency, however, acts upon each of a number of autonomous and mutually competing subjects. Territorial rulers, as we have seen, have to compete with magnates and with estate bodies, and even when they overcome their resistance, the manner of their doing so affects the further build-up of their power. Furthermore, each territorially (more or less) unified power actor must engage in the restless power struggle characteristic of the states system. Finally, institutions and groups deriving their identity and their interests from their control over non-political resources also seek to enlarge and secure each their own power base, and to that end seek to maintain their autonomy of the political power centre, and/or to affect its structure and its operations.

The outcomes of these diverse but intersecting power struggles are intrinsically open-ended and unpredictable. Yet from time to time, in a given locale those struggles attain a decisive outcome, which embodies itself in distinctive, particularly effective arrangements.[13] These, once in place, undergo further institutional elaboration – which imparts continuity to the process and gives it a semblance of irreversibility – and may exercise a kind of lateral influence upon institution-building elsewhere, engendering a belief that state-making in general is driven by a kind of necessity and possesses universal significance.

And indeed universality and necessity are involved; for the emergence in Europe of the early states system powerfully modified the environment in which all other systems of rule existed, and in the long run compelled all parts of the world to try and adopt state-like political institutions. But to an extent the universality is misleading, because that process of adoption, even when successful (and it was not, and is not, always successful) always bears some trace of local institutional legacies. And the necessity with which at a given time certain arrangements seem to impose themselves and remain in place, is largely the outcome of past choices – the kind of necessity of which Mephistopheles speaks to Faust: 'For devils and for spectres this is law: / Where they have entered in, there also they withdraw; / The first is free to us: in the second, we are slaves.' To illustrate this point, let us reconsider some aspects of my previous narratives of the state's story and of my own evaluation of it in the light of the question: what gave liberal democracy a chance? After all, one might have expected the process of state-making, once started in earnest, to build up continuously into some kind of large-scale, rationalized despotism. And, indeed, some people would claim that it did.[14] But this view, I submit, does not adequately recognise the distinctiveness and the significance of some political institutions which developed and established themselves in the West over the last two centuries. Now – why did they so develop and establish themselves? What set the West on this particular course?

Any tenable answer to these questions would obviously have to list a great number of factors, the convergence of which toward that result was decisive precisely because it was inherently improbable. Consider just the following components of such an answer, most of them pertaining to the earlier phases of our story.

In the homeland of the modern state, Western Europe, the efforts of early state-makers found already in place certain institutional legacies, certain principles concerning the exercise of rule, which constrained and influenced those efforts. In particular:

1 Germanic legacies, such as the preference for the election of leaders by acclamation, and those leaders' dependence on a retinue of persons of equal dignity and standing, though not of the same rank, with whom they entertained mutually binding relations. It was even understood that, if a ruler failed to live up to his own obligations toward such peers, or advanced unwarranted claims toward them, they could legitimately offer armed resistance and opposition.

2 Roman legacies, such as the notion of a *res publica*, that is, a set of concerns shared by all members of the polity, and to which equally shared resources should be committed; or the idea of office, that is, a set of honourable but also onerous prerogatives and responsibilities which remained invariant as a succession of people assumed them.

3 Ecclesiastical components, such as the principle, most clearly articulated in the context of the Conciliar movement, that 'what concerns all must be considered by all'; or the Christian elaborations (via the institution of chivalry) of feudal notions concerning the obligations of the powerful toward the powerless.

Furthermore, early state-makers seeking to unify politically even relatively small territories often had to deal with a variety of distinct regional and local communities, differing in ethnic background, language, custom, productive practices, settlement patterns and historical experience.[15]

This variety, originally generated – one may suppose – by the number and variety of physically distinct habitats characteristic of Europe (compared with the great plains that had been the primary locales of Near and Far Eastern empires) was further increased by the intensive development (or redevelopment) of towns beginning in the second millennium AD. What town and rural (or fishing, or sailing, or mining, or pastoral) communities had in common, as far as the territorial rulers were concerned, was a fierce attachment to their local traditions, and a disposition to preserve, in their dealings with trans-local powers, the degree of autonomy necessary to protect and advance those traditions. In the towns, furthermore, the advances in the division of labour and more generally in social differentiation generated further, occupationally based communal groupings, some of which opposed the rulers' preference for uniform arrangements and policies throughout the wider territory.

The upshot of all these considerations is that it simply was not given to most European rulers, most of the time, simply to grab from the population all the powers and resources which they needed and which their apparatus of rule could manage. They operated in an environment marked by traditions, however dimly apprehended, on which a variety of collective and individual subjects grounded their diverse claims. Simply to ignore these would have been seen (and as far as possible resisted) as usurpation; instead, the rulers themselves had to appeal to the existent traditions (including of course those relating to their own prerogatives) in order to advance their own claims. Thus, at any rate to some extent, early European state-making proceeded not as a straightforward process of power accumulation through trials of strength, but as a sequence of mutual adjustments between the competing claims of protagonists who acknowledged one another and one another's claims.

Of course throughout this process it was also vital that rulers should be able *de facto* to enforce their claims, and overcome other parties' opposition to that enforcement. But in order to be able to do so they generally had to marshal their resources; and their resulting preoccupation with increasing and securing their revenues led rulers on the one hand, once more, to acknowledge the claims of others and modify their own claims accordingly, and on the other, to accept different, non-normative, non-traditional constraints upon their action.

For example, recent research[16] has emphasised the following circumstances. Because of the variety of distinct habitats (mentioned above), the pedlars and merchants of late-medieval, early-modern Europe undertook to transport from land to land, on a regular basis, fairly large amounts of diverse goods, many of which were relatively bulky and of low value – unlike the exotic, luxury goods exclusively transported in other parts of the world. Even assuming that European rulers felt the same predatory instincts as their counterparts elsewhere, it was in their long-term interest not to swoop in and simply confiscate the goods crossing their territories, but rather to encourage their continuing flow, in order to exploit it via relatively low and predictable tolls and levies. Equally latter-of-fact considerations – essentially, don't kill the goose that lays the golden eggs – placed some restraints, in the long run, on the rulers' tendency to default their payments to moneylenders, especially when these had become large, internationally established banks.

More generally, as has been pointed out long ago,[17] as the European economy progressed, the increasing significance of mobile as against landed wealth considerably restrained what had long been the most typical form of usurpation by rulers – the forcible takeover of other people's assets. For these could now take the form of small, easily concealed and transportable amounts of bullion or coin, or even of a piece of paper recognised as a negotiable instrument by the international banking network, with which their possessors could easily flee abroad – as could the possessors of the increasingly sophisticated productive skills which economic advance made increasingly valuable.

Besides, wealth was not the only resource that mattered in the state-building enterprise; another one was qualified personnel. Rulers who sought to diminish their dependence on noblemen and clerics had no alternative but to involve in that enterprise members of the burgher estate, and subsequently of the bourgeois class, particularly those bourgeois trained in law by the universities.[18] Such people, one may presume, unavoidably imported into the political, administrative and judicial decision-making processes, preoccupations characteristic of the strata from which they originated. Some of those preoccupations, in turn, favoured what I have called the jurisdicisation of politics: in particular, the formation of a body of public law inconsistent with a ruthless and arbitrary use of discretion on the part of the ruler.

There are other ways in which the broad social and cultural environment of European state-making biased its course away from an out-and-out despotic direction. I have just said that more and more members of the apparatus of rule had acquired their qualifications in the universities. But the universities diffused their intellectual skills and cultural preferences also into other contexts, within which state-making had to proceed and to which it had to adapt to some extent. Or think of the potential significance of the diffusion of printing and of literacy. These on the one hand favoured the bureaucratisation of rule, the management of political affairs in a more and more uniform and potentially levelling, despotic manner; on the other hand, they led literate individuals to consider themselves as the protagonists of a distinctive set of processes, the 'public sphere',[19] which in turn constituted a vital setting for the articulation of liberal demands. They also assisted mightily in the formation of nationhood, and thus fostered a sense of the unity and uniqueness of a population, which could view itself as the ultimate constituency of the political order.[20]

The point of this review of some (mostly remote) 'makings' of liberal democracy, was to emphasise how varied they were, how far back into the European experience they reached, and how improbable was their convergence. The basic implication of this argument – that the particular course taken by the making of the Western state was a highly contingent affair – will be strengthened, in the second part of this book, by considering more closely a set of twentieth-century experiences which have extensively modified and differentiated the basic structures inherited by the state from its past, as well as the circumstances it confronts today and some resultant contingencies of its near future.

Part II

7

Liberal Democracy in the Twentieth Century (1)

I

The expansion of state activity

This second part of the book deals with the most significant changes in the structural design and the mode of operation of the state in twentieth-century industrialised societies.

In this chapter and the next I will discuss what seem to me the most massive and wide-ranging of these changes, as far as liberal-democratic systems are concerned: the growing size and diversity of the institutions making up the state, and their active involvement in a much expanded and differentiated range of social activities.

My chief concern will be to identify the causes and the consequences of this phenomenon. But it may be useful in the first place to give the reader some idea of its dimensions.

Consider, for instance, the following scattered indications of the validity of the so-called Wagner's Law[1], which states that government spending tends to rise faster than the growth of the national economy as a whole. In the United Kingdom government spending accounted for the following percentages of the gross national product in the following years:

1890—8.9%
1920—20.2%
1938—30.0%
1960—36.4%
1970—43.0%

1981—50.3%

1983—53.3%

Or, in the USA the amount of government (federal, state and local) spending as a proportion of the net national product almost tripled in the period between 1926 and 1979.

Or, for all OECD countries over the period 1953–73 the average percentage of the national product accounted for by government spending rose from 34 per cent to 49 per cent.[2]

Another set of indicators concerns public employment. It is often difficult to obtain precise information on the numbers involved, and it is a controversial matter how their significance should be assessed. At any rate, Richard Rose produces a time series (see table 1), dealing with five selected Western countries, and showing what percentage of the labour force was employed by public bodies at various points in time.

TABLE 1   *Percentage of labour force employed in public sector*

	Date			
Country	*pre-1914*	*pre-1939*	*1951*	*1981*
Britain	7.1	10.8	26.6	31.4
France	7.1	8.9	16.0	32.6
Germany	10.6	12.9	11.9	25.8
Italy	4.7	7.8	11.4	24.4
USA	1.5	7.7	11.8	18.3

Source: R. Rose, 'The significance of public employment', in *Public employment in Western Europe*, ed. R. Rose (Cambridge, Cambridge University Press, 1987).

The differentiation of state activity

As to the growing internal differentiation of the state, and the growing diversity of its activities, I will refer in the first place to a classification proposed by a German sociologist. According to Renate Mayntz the tasks to which state activities attend fall within five main categories:

1 Regulation of the relations between a given national society and other ones;

2 regulation of the relations obtaining between individual or collective subjects within the society;

3 provisioning of the political-administrative system with resources;

4 supply of services intended to satisfy collective needs other than those envisaged under the first two headings;

5 steering of social development toward specific objectives, such as increasing national integration, social equality, economic growth, improved public health or better education.[3]

The first three sets of concerns are those which define the state itself[4], and the 'classical' ministries of the European state became established in order to attend systematically to them. Respectively, the ministries of war and of foreign affairs dealt with the first class of tasks, the ministries of justice and of the interior with the second, and the ministry of finance with the third.

On the other hand, most of the growth in personnel and expenditure in the latter part of the nineteenth century and in the twentieth century, and most of the further development of ministries and of other units, reflected the state's involvement in the other two sets of concerns, which it had not previously made its own.[5] If broadly interpreted, the notion of welfare state – which I do not intend to discuss expressly in this book because it has been amply analysed in recent literature[6] – encompasses many of the activities falling under these two clusters. This has been established with reference to the French case by scholars who have classified state expenditure as being connected with the development of the national economy (for example, expenditure on public works, education, social security, etc.) or *not* being so connected (for example, expenditure on defence, foreign affairs, justice, etc.). Their data suggest that over the period from 1815–19 to 1965–9 the proportion of the national product spent on the first kind of state expenditure has gone from 2.43 per cent to 24.25 per cent; that of the second kind of expenditure from 9.49 per cent to 12.53 per cent.[7]

The unique significance of total war

In seeking to identify some major causes of this complex development I turn in the first place to a phenomenon which time and again, in the previous chapters, has reasserted its central significance for political experience in general, and thus for the nature of the state itself – the phenomenon of war. While, as I have already suggested in chapter 4, the relationship to that phenomenon is a constant aspect of the existence of the state (war is a continuous possibility if not a continuous experience), war has been historically a highly variable matter; and major changes in the modalities of warfare, and in the structure of military forces, have from time to time induced equally significant changes in political arrangements.[8]

In keeping with this generalisation, one can plausibly connect many aspects of state growth in our century with the phenomenon of total war, which – although envisaged earlier by military experts and by visionaries – dramatically entered the continuum of history with the First World War.

By total war I mean a military conflict which a national society can only enter and sustain with some hope of success if it commits, and exposes to the risks of wear, waste and destruction characteristic of war, a very high proportion of all its material and human resources.

Among the causes of this phenomenon stand two closely connected changes in the properly military aspects of war: its 'massification', that is, the fact that it involves larger and larger sections of the population; and the use of industrial and technological processes in warfare, enabling a warring country to attack from a distance, via artillery and the air force, not only an opposing country's troops but also its demographic and productive centres. Among its consequences are the unprecedentedly diverse, rapid and intense effects which the conflict has on all aspects of the life (and death!) of the populations it involves.

The state stands, as it were, between these two clusters of variables. Throughout is historical career it had always been the protagonist of the phenomenon of war; but in the twentieth century total war compelled it to undertake to an unprecedented extent the production and the extraction of the resources required to sustain the war effort, and to manage (as far as possible) the impact of those processes (and of the opponent's activities) on its own population.

In my view, one can reasonably impute to total war, or to the awareness of its possibility and of its burdens, many significant developments in the institutional shape of the state and its relationship to society. In the course of the First World War, for instance, various belligerent states set up tripartite arrangements for adjusting the contrasting interests of businessmen and workers, whereby the state played the role of mediator and sometimes of arbitrator.[9] During the Second World War the state experienced the formidable enhancement of the nation's industrial capacity made possible, say, by rapidly and extensively mobilising women into the industrial workforce, or by coupling the industrial apparatus with the scientific resources guarded in academic and research institutions.[10] In both cases, the new arrangements were only partly dismantled after the war; at any rate, they remained in a country's collective memory as reminders of unprecedentedly far-reaching and effective ways of involving the state in the management of social affairs. And the attendant public expenditures regressed very markedly at the end of each conflict – but never all the way to the point they had started from.[11]

Yet even a phenomenon as compelling and wide-ranging as the advent of total war (or as the Great Depression, to give another example) essentially intensifies and accelerates the effects of even broader and more continuously operating causes at work in the constitution of Western society and inherent in its political institutions. To simplify my account of these causes, I will assign them to two main categories, concerning respectively the demand for state action and the supply of state action.[12]

That is: on the one side – demand – various component groups of society find it in their interest for the state to monitor, control and take charge of features of their own existence previously determined wholly by other, non-political aspects of the social process. They thus seek (more or less successfully) to induce the authorities to undertake new policies affecting those features. On the other side – supply – such undertakings primarily express the interest the authorities themselves have in increasing the social resources they can consume and allocate, in widening the discretionality of their operations. In order for the state to take on new commitments, it is often necessary to assign new facilities and new faculties to existent state units, to increase their personnel or to constitute new units.

The terms demand and supply are meant to suggest that the two categories of causes interact with and condition one another in producing determinate effects. However, it is plausible and (I hope) enlightening to distinguish between primarily demand-induced and primarily supply-induced effects.

II

On the demand side: economically weaker groups

Here I am trying to identify collective actors, other than those directly involved in policy making and public administration, who, in the course of the twentieth century, found it in their own interest to promote a wider involvement of state institutions in the management of social affairs, and to shape and orient the resulting policies.

I have already suggested, toward the close of chapter 4, that groups at a disadvantage on the capitalist market – chiefly, employees – found, in the widening suffrage and in the related processes of representation and legislation, a means to temper that disadvantage. One may make sense of this by referring to the distinction between forms of social power introduced at the very beginning of this book. Schematically, *economic* power belonged to the bourgeoisie, sections of which also shared *normative* power with the remnants of earlier dominant groups. Thus, those in a position of economic inferiority used the quantum of *political* power acquired through electoral participation to widen the scope and increase the penetration of state action, in order to restrict and moderate the impact of that economic inferiority on their total life circumstances. Through legislation, for instance, the state would limit the duration of the working day, establish minimum salaries, impose and monitor safety standards for industrial operations and encourage the formation of unions qualified to represent the workers' interests in collective bargaining negotiations with employers.

Although socialist and other working class parties provide the most significant examples of this kind of strategy,[13] it is important not to see a unified working class as the sole protagonist and beneficiary of it. Such a view would be wrong in three respects. First, the working class itself is not always unified: often, it expresses itself politically through more than one party, because it is divided on ethnic or religions grounds, or because ideologically different parties contend for its support. Second, the game of mobilising state activity as a remedy to economic weakness is often played at least as successfully by lower middle-class, *petit bourgeois* groups seeking to protect their economic niche – for instance by slowing down the advance of large-scale department stores and supermarkets – as by the working class.[14] Finally, to attribute solely to the strategy in question the improvements which both the working class and those other groups experienced in the course of the century, might mean to commit the *post hoc, ergo propter hoc* fallacy. Those improvements probably resulted also from other factors, ranging from the colossal gains in productivity associated with advancing industrialism, to the increasing use of contraception by the populace.[15]

It is also important to recognise that although the working people generally had to struggle in order to acquire the quantum of political power with which to prime their promotion of greater state activity, their success in that struggle was made possible by a number of pre-existent and environing conditions not of their own making.

Earlier, I stressed the conditions constituted by the legacies of constitutionalism, by the existence of the liberal public sphere, and by the presence of political entrepreneurs capable of mobilising and organising the disenfranchised strata. Here, I might add two other, overlapping political circumstances. First, the prevailing legitimating myth of the state – the idea of nation – projected the image of a more and more comprehensive political community as the constituent basis of the state, and morally validated the trend toward universal suffrage. Second, beginning with the French revolutionary and then the Napoleonic wars, warfare had also, as it were, opened itself to the masses and inspired them to seek and match the inclusiveness of fighting with the inclusiveness of voting. After both world wars, both in victorious and (to a lesser extent) in vanquished countries, established elites seem to have felt that the toll of death and suffering exacted from the masses had to be compensated for, however partially, by public policies remedying some of the disadvantages which they suffered in peacetime. (An example of this was the British idea of 'houses fit for heroes'.)

However it might have become established, the link between the (broader and broader) masses and the representative, legislative institutions at the centre of the political system, once in place, served increasingly as a conduit for diverse demands. Many of these went unattended, of course, because they were raised by parties too small or too radical to enter or influence the parliamentary majorities, and/or because they clashed with the centrality of the market to the economic process and the resultant limitations on political action.

But even some of the demands that were unsuccessful at first had their chance later, as the electoral fortunes of parties or their degree of radicalism changed, and this led to the formation of new majorities or new coalitions. Furthermore, market forces turned out to be capable of adjusting to, or indeed making positive use of, more extensive and penetrating forms of state intervention.

Economically stronger groups

This second is the critical consideration; for it points to the fact that, increasingly, demands for state action came also from socio-economic groups in possession of economic power, who raised such demands in order to further strengthen their market position, or indeed to allow the market to continue functioning. This strategy makes sense in a number of different circumstances, which obtain more and more as the twentieth century advances.

I have already suggested that in order to become established and to function, the market had always imposed on the state its own political requirements, ranging from the provision of judicial and police services, to the management of the currency, to the containment and, if necessary, the repression of the more threatening challenges from the working class. A national bourgeoisie, furthermore, has never hesitated to put pressure on its state to conduct trade and colonial policies which would assist it in securing domestic and outside markets where it might buy cheap and sell dear.

Furthermore, there had long been, in the modern capitalist environment, privileged economic groups who depended for their fortunes not on entrepreneurial prowess but on state favour. Although Max Weber considered these groups a throwback to a pre-modern, specifically politically oriented form of capitalism, he well knew that they still prospered in his own time; and Pareto was led to despair and to self-inflicted exile by the success of such groups (in particular, industrialists who insisted on high tariff walls to defend them against foreign competition) in early twentieth-century Italy.

But in the course of the century the dependency of private economic forces on positive state action ceased to be a significant, but nevertheless deviant phenomenon. It became a systemic feature of industrial capitalism, associated with the most advanced and important, not the weakest or most backward-looking units of the system.

The requirements of advanced industrial capitalism

To understand why, consider in the first place that as industrialism advances, enterprises wishing to enter the market, or to maintain their own position within it, have to mobilise larger and larger inputs of capital and of scientific, technological and managerial know-how. The first wave of industrialisation had had as its protagonists, in mid-to-late eighteenth century England, a large number of relatively small textile firms, each using small amounts of capital, employing a small workforce, and utilising widely available or easily acquired technical and managerial skills. A century later, the second major wave, centred in Germany, was focused first on heavy metallurgical and chemical, and later on electrical industry. Its capital requirements could only be met by a large investing public operating via a powerful network of banks; the leading firms had to be much larger and organisationally more complex; and their production processes involved more advanced machinery and much more sophisticated scientific knowledge.

These trends have continued through successive waves of industrialisation in the West and elsewhere; and their implications have been, on the one hand, to assign the leadership in the respective industrial environments to larger and larger firms, on the other to tie those (as well as the smaller ones) into more and more complex systems, needing in turn to be at least partly established, financed, regulated and sometimes managed by public authorities.

Consider for instance the difference between the early provision of industrial power to factories, via the factories' own independently built and operated steam-driven power plants, and its later provision via an electric grid, distributing the energy produced by a relatively small number of standardised, carefully coordinated, unitarily managed power stations, possibly fuelled by nuclear reactors. Or, consider the difference between deriving the know-how on which an industry runs from the operating skills and the technical lore independently developed by craftsmen, and deriving it from a massive research effort, coordinating the inquiries of a number of academic laboratories. Or, consider the difference between a market on which the throughputs of people and goods travel on a system of roads, highways and canals erected over the centuries on the initiative of a plurality of local trade centres, and a situation in which they have to rely to a large extent on purpose-designed, centrally coordinated railway, motorway or airway systems.

Each of the contemporary alternatives requires a much greater involvement, direct or indirect, of public powers. At the very least these will intervene, for example, to confer corporate status on the large private enterprises which might undertake to build and operate railways, to assign to them the required rights of way, to validate juridically the unprecedented kind of standardised contracts they enter with travellers and shippers.

The increasing size of the strategically significant industrial units, the increasing complexity of the systems into which they are tied, and the increasing cost of building and operating those systems, have further, important (though sometimes indirect) political consequences. For instance, the self-equilibrating mechanism of the market is less likely to work well when the market is dominated by a few large corporations. These are more likely to enter cartel agreements to share out the market among themselves or to limit technological innovation to the detriment of the public. Furthermore, if these arrangements do not work – say, in the face of a world recession, as in the thirties – the prospect of a number of these industrial giants going to the wall poses a grave threat to a given country's level of employment or standard of living. Thus, they have to be supported through increased public expenditure and regulation, or even through the state investing in them.

More generally, larger firms constitute larger accumulations of economic power; their operations and particularly their investments, being less the product of competitive processes and more of strategic choices, are a more suitable matter for negotiation with public authorities.

Increasingly, under advanced capitalism, the operation and development of a country's industrial system depends on complex and expensive infrastructures – for instance, schools, universities, research establishments – which are mostly provided for and maintained by the state.[16] Furthermore, at the very centre of the system are often found whole industrial sectors – typically, those associated with the so-called military-industrial complex, or with space exploration and other high-tech ventures – which depend on state contracts for the majority of their financial needs. Finally, a high level of aggregate demand, resulting from the spending choices of buyers of both intermediate and finished products, is indispensable both to the health of the industrial system at large (the absorption of whose output depends on large sections of the public having considerable disposable income) and to that of the political system itself. For the latter, as I have already suggested in chapter 2, relies for its legitimation – and thus for its relatively smooth functioning – on the citizenry enjoying a relatively high and possibly rising standard of living.

Thus, while it remains as mandatory for advanced as for earlier capitalism that the state should allow the market to function as an autonomous realm, today that very requirement commits the state itself to more activity, and to more expensive and varied activity, than it did in the past. Furthermore, state activities not themselves intended to satisfy that requirement must not interfere too heavily with the freedom of action of private economic power.[17] Either way, the processes of policy formation and implementation of contemporary states are systematically open to inputs originating also (and sometimes primarily) from the holders of that power; and the effect of those inputs is often to make state action more extensive and penetrating.

Social claims for regulation

This is also the upshot of (successful) demands originating from groupings which share interests other than economic ones, or reflecting general societal requirements. Recently, for instance, growing concerns about the conditions of the natural environment have found expression in political demands which can only be satisfied if the state confers new faculties and facilities upon its agencies, allowing them to monitor the environment, to identify the processes which threaten it and to halt or moderate that threat. Equally, new forms of state action – and new public expenditures – are sometimes necessary to remedy or eliminate conditions which offend the evolving sense of what is fair or unfair in dealing with people of different gender, colour, religion, sexual preference and so on, or of what the entitlements are, of, for example, groups of people suffering from various kinds of handicap.

More generally, much state activity, past and current, can be seen to arise in response to a fundamental query, which can be starkly formulated as follows: how do people know how to act? For centuries, now, economic and technological development has generated ever new ways for people to feed, clothe, house, present, entertain and employ themselves, and to communicate with, associate with, divert, support, assist, vex, hurt and kill one another. At the same time, such development has often weakened or displaced some of the contexts and processes from which and through which people used to derive norms orienting and constraining their conduct – the local community, the neighbourhood, the nuclear family, religious communities, occupational collectivities, stable, well-defined circles of associates, established conventions on matters of conduct and taste and clearly defined and accepted social hierarchies.

A concept frequently used by sociologists to charaterise the resulting situation is that of anomie or normlessness; a less common, less pathos-laden characterisation – prefigured in Henry Maine's famous contrast between 'status and contract' – sees instead a transition from a situation in which norms tightly prescribe the individual's conduct to one in which norms allow (or indeed compel) the individuals to engage in 'elective', choice-making conduct.[18]

In this latter situation the function of norms is that of laying down frameworks within which that conduct may proceed autonomously. That is, norms do not specify what the individual is to do, as much as they indicate how he or she is to make his/her choices, and exclude certain possible choices which he or she might otherwise make. The question then becomes: what are the sources of such norms? how are those frameworks laid down?

One should not underestimate the extent to which people in new circumstances can and do work out by themselves, for themselves, and for others, new frameworks for their reciprocal choices, sanctioning them through gossip, the conferral or withdrawal of reputation, the formation of public opinion, or the exercise of normative power and economic power.[19] The latter, in particular, asserts itself imperiously in the employment situation of the newly proletarianised masses, through the 'dull compulsion' of the market, and by requiring human beings to allow themselves to be treated as resources.

But these spontaneous processes of adjustment may take a long time, during which a normative vacuum obtains; they often affect relatively small numbers of people, operating within narrow spaces (say, in the factory); and often, because the phenomenon needing regulation is novel, confusing and contentious, they do not yield comprehensive, decisive, binding indications as to how, after all, people are to act.

This is where the state may step in, armed with two exclusive, over-lapping resources: positive law, that is, a set of purpose-made, binding, potentially durable and yet changeable norms; and an ensemble of agencies specialised in producing, implementing and enforcing such norms.[20] At first these are, typically, general and abstract commands, whose business it is to transcend the boundaries of locality and of narrowly defined memberships, and to lay down frameworks within which a multiplicity of open-ended, contingent choices may be made by individuals acting on their own behalf. Increasingly, however, the commands in question empower and commit state agencies to themselves undertake public tasks beyond the reach of single or associated individuals (or concerning which the latter have incompatible preferences), and to confer upon individuals resources and capacities allowing them in turn to act on their own behalf.

The production of norms of both kinds is preceded and followed by the state's effort to ascertain the circumstances within which and upon which it seeks to act. As a counterpart to this, the population must submit itself, willy-nilly, to the state's monitoring and surveillance activities.[21] Once more, to conduct those activities the state both establishes new agencies of its own and interacts with other groups and organisations which can provide it with the appropriate know-how and information.

III

On the supply side: the invasive state

To summarise the argument just made, the state expands and diversifies its activity to fill a vacuum of regulation and to remedy a shortage or a maldistribution of resources engendered by spontaneous socio-economic change and by the lag in the development of the attendant norms. We may label this as the *serviceable state* argument, for it envisages the state as acting obligingly in response to increasing social demands. Previously, I had sketched what could be labelled the *partisan state* argument, which attributed the same phenomena chiefly to the interested pressures of (in one version) strata disadvantaged by the capitalist order or (in another version) of dominant economic forces which receive the state's assistance in exercising that dominance.

In my view, there is no reason to choose once and for all between these interpretations, to assume that in all cases the burden of explanation fails on one of them to the exclusion of the other. Both the notions of the serviceable state and of the partisan state (the latter in two versions) point to potentially enlightening hypotheses. Although probably any close, historically grounded account of a particular instance of the diversification and expansion of state activity would give priority to the one or the other interpretation, taken as a whole the phenomenon in question appears (to use fashionable language) as overdetermined. That is, it stands at the point of convergence of more than one in principle mutually independent (or even, on other issues, contrasting) causal processes. In fact, in this section I will consider a further set of such processes, emphasised by what one might label the *invasive state* argument.

The argument is as follows: besides responding, however selectively, to the pull of interests emanating from the outlying society, the dynamic of the expansion and diversification of state activity expresses the push of interests lodged inside the state itself, whether as a whole or in its parts. The shared intent of these interests, I have already suggested, consists in maximising the scope and discretionality of political and administrative arrangements, and in increasing the share of the society's resources produced and managed by means of those arrangements.

What accounts for this dynamic? Various elements of an answer have been given at previous points in this book. At the very beginning, for instance, I imputed to all forms of social power a tendency to increase their own autonomy at the expense of one another, and for each to try and secure for itself some portion of the other powers. I also suggested some grounds for expecting political power to exhibit that tendency in a particularly imperious and impatient manner.

Differentiation and self-referentiality

A further, again rather abstract and generic, argument can be derived from two features of the modern state, already considered in chapter 2. First, the state constitutes a functionally differentiated system of society; second, it is composed in turn of functionally differentiated arrangements, attending to different aspects of the management and exercise of political power.

As it can be said that the larger society generally attains a rationality gain by having its political affairs attended to by a state, as against other kinds of political arrangements, so it is often the case that a state partitioned into an orderly plurality of differentiated agencies enjoys the advantages of purposefully divided, specialised labour. At both levels, however, both as a whole and in its part, the state is liable to a general tendency which applies to all differentiated systems. They tend to become locked each into its own specific concerns, to view the larger reality each from its own perspective, to become self-referential.[22]

This tendency is particularly strong in the specifically modern, functional form of differentiation. This is more abstract than other forms, for here the diverse systems do not consist in discrete groups of people, but in sets of differentiated roles and activities, possibly carried out, in *each* system, by the *same* people.[23] For this reason the distinctiveness of each set must be maintained by emphasising the institutional autonomy of the criteria presiding over its activities, assigning to each a standard of its own (profit to the enterprise, *raison d'état* to the state) and possibly a differentiated medium of operation (truth to the system of science, money to the economic system). 'Thus the processes internal to those system are released from immediate control on the part of the larger society, and higher risks are accepted by that society and by the various partial systems, which become mutually unaccountable.'[24]

A further phenomenon enhancing the self-referentiality of differentiated systems is their recourse to what are sometimes called reflexive mechanisms, that is, those applying their activities to themselves.[25] For instance, in a modern economy there are markets where money itself is bought and sold; in universities, there are departments or faculties which teach how to teach; in a modern legal system there are laws according to which further laws can be produced. A consequence of this enhanced self-referentiality is that each system tends to over-produce its own output. The production department of a firm is typically capable of producing more goods than its marketing system can distribute or the market can absorb. Similarly, a legislative body is typically so set up that it can – and often does – pass more laws than even lawyers can comprehend, police bodies can enforce, and judges can apply.

As mentioned above, these generic processes apply both to the state as a whole and to its constituent parts. At each level, they induce the system in question to become over-involved in itself. The specialised part, in the end, conducts its relations to the whole which had instituted it as a means to the more effective pursuit of its interests, less in the light of those interests than of others specific to itself. Or, rather, it views the interests of the more comprehensive system from the vantage point of its own.

Normally the pursuit of interests – whatever they are – requires the expenditure of resources. Thus to command resources becomes a prime commitment of all units, inducing competition among them. If the resources are a fixed quantity, the competition is a zero-sum game – that is, each side can only gain to the extent that the other loses – and may become very sharp, until higher authority settles it by its decisions; hence the great expectancy surrounding, for instance, the periodic ritual of the British budget, never as great as when the total sums to be allocated are fixed or even diminishing, cuts are the name of the game, and the question is who is to be cut more and who will be cut less. But the budget itself is typically the final product of a great deal of infighting between the greater administrative units, each pushing its case and defending its turf via the minister nominally intended to lead it but largely compelled to represent it. And the budget's larger decisions are in turn followed by other rounds of infighting, involving this time smaller administrative units among which the cuts have to be apportioned.

However, liberal-democratic states mostly operate in economic environments which typically, thanks to the high productivity of the industrial system, generate a recurrent surplus output, part of which can be added to the resources extracted by the state in the first place, and subsequently allocated by the state to its constituent parts.[26] Besides, additions to those resources can also come, in principle (as they regularly do in wartime), from more extensive and effective extractive activities, for example, from increased fiscal pressure, or from incurring public debts, or from the government taking over and managing on its own behalf the production or the distribution of certain goods and services. Once more, larger and smaller administrative units become involved, each mainly on behalf of interests specific to itself, in contentions around the question of how to generate and allocate additional resources.

Another relevant characteristic of states in general, implicit in much that I have said so far, is that they treat policy formation as a contingent process, as the product of purposefully deliberated decisions. The formation of those decisions is expressly treated as a matter for public controversy in liberal-democratic states, where – in principle – *politics is the matrix of policy*. Parties, as the typical protagonists of politics – or at any rate, as we shall see in the next chapter, of one kind of politics – on the one hand function, as we have seen, on the demand side, as formulators and proponents of policy alternatives; on the other hand, when and in so far as they are successful in the political game, they get a chance to operate on the supply side, to orient and direct (up to a point) the activities of state organs.[27] They thus add to the dynamic toward expansion built into those organs (according to the previous argument) the peculiar push of their attempts to implement the policies they stand for, as well as of their leaders' yearnings for the experience of power and patronage.

The acceleration of supply

The reader will have noted that so far my arguments about the invasive state, or (otherwise phrased) about the supply-side components of the expansion and differentiation of state activities, have mostly been formulated in generic terms. I have referred successively to the tendencies built into political power as such, into (functionally) differentiated systems, into politics-driven policy making . . . What – the reader may wonder – is the specific twentieth century story concerning these phenomena?

My own feeling is that the more historically specific aspects of the phenomena we are interested in operate chiefly on the other, the demand side of the account, and have to do principally with the overlapping development of capitalism and industrialism.[28] It is largely from these that there flow such historical factors as changes in the demographic structure and in the structure of social inequality, the rise of mass consumerism, the increasing economic significance of science and technology and the need for state intervention in the economy.

There is indeed one massive, historically located set of causal processes which could be classified among those we are now considering – the processes associated with the phenomenon of total war. I have chosen to mention these in the opening section of the chapter, because in my view they cut across the distinction between demand and supply factors. In considering the acceleration in the supply of state activity undoubtedly undergone in the twentieth century, nothing of comparable significance to the First and Second World Wars comes to mind. Yet a few additional considerations may account for that acceleration.

New personnel involved on the supply side: at the top

In the first place, in the course of the twentieth century, and particularly since the Second World War, the state, in liberal-democratic countries, increasingly mobilises (and to an extent is mobilised by) new forms of knowledge and expertise cultivated by disciplines and practiced by professions previously inexistent or excluded from the context of policy formation.

Traditionally, that context saw a complex process of confrontation, mutual adjustment and cooperation, between on the one hand the political will represented by the elected leadership and on the other hand the political-administrative know-how embodied in the top administrative personnel, which had its main sources in juridical and financial knowledge. From mid-century on, the composition of key parts of the state apparatus and the modes of speech and argument typical of their personnel, come to reflect the aspiration to a new kind of consciously rational policy-making process, where the actual choice of political targets, not just the ways and means thereto, is the product of sophisticated, scientifically controlled, empirically and theoretically grounded reasoning.[29]

The expansion and differentiation of the state come to be pushed not only be the generic processes mentioned above, but also be the intent of putting to use newly developed (or at any rate claimed) capacities for monitoring and guiding the social process from above. Those capacities are supposed to be based on the distinctive cognitive resources of the regional planner, the policy analyst, the economic forecaster, the systems engineer, the organisation and management specialist, the pollster, the public relations expert. All these new specialists – and the expensive, new-fangled gadgetry they often require – must somehow become lodged in the various branches of the administration, and it the traditional offices cannot accommodate them, new staff staff organs must be created, or new arrangements for consultation put in place.

Different as they are from one another, most of the forms of knowledge cultivated and applied by this new personnel have in common a strong orientation to the production of effects. They differ in this from legal knowledge, which ultimately pertains to the qualification of past facts and the imputation of responsibility for them. On this count alone, as the new personnel found its way into the top levels of the policy-making and policy-implementing machinery of the state, it felt under a compulsion to promote new state activities and to experiment with new ways of carrying out the state's established activities. Whether or not it was ultimately successful in proving the value of its new approaches, in the process of introducing them into the machinery the new personnel imparted a new dynamic to it.

New personnel on the supply side: at the bottom

The same thing can probably be said, but for somewhat different reasons, of the lower levels of the state apparatus, and particularly of parts of it associated with the expansion of the welfare state, especially at the local level – from the state-funded school to the social security office. One reason is that each of these parts became the niche of a sometimes (more or less) new, but in any case much expanded occupation,[30] the practitioners of which are naturally interested in continued employment, better working conditions and improved career prospects.

Another reason for the dynamic tendencies of this layer of the state apparatus lies in the availability of a cognitively tenable and morally strong rationale for its expansion. This consists in pointing to an open-ended multiplicity of needs, of forms of deprivation, exclusion and human misery, afflicting large numbers of people and in asserting the responsibility of society for remedying or assuaging those afflictions.

The strength of the assertion rests, in turn, on two grounds. First, the afflictions themselves are often socially caused, if only in the sense of reflecting more and more demanding social definitions of who is a fit and useful member of society. Second, the increasing diffuse affluence of advanced industrial societies makes morally intolerable their disregard for the needy conditions of parts of their populations. An explicit or implicit corollary of this argument considers state action as the chief if not the exclusive medium through which such societies should discharge their obligation.

IV

To sum up, a distinctive supply-side dynamic was imparted to liberal-democratic states, beginning around the middle of the twentieth century, by the extent to which the respective societies experimented with two different yet compatible visions of themselves: the vision of the managed society and the vision of the caring society. Each experiment found expression chiefly in (partly) new ways of institutionalising and exercising political power, and thus in (partly) new arrangements and practices of the state. Thus, each became to an extent an expression and a vehicle of tendencies toward expansion and differentiation built into the state itself. (This coupling of conjunctural trends with structural tendencies may help explain the fact that even where and when – say, in Reagan's America or Thatcher's Britain – serious attempts were made to unhitch the wagon from the stars of those two visions, the wagon kept on rolling.)[31]

One may wonder, at this point, why those two visions of society should become embodied, as I have just suggested, in new arrangements and policies of the state. The reason is probably that the dominant social force in liberal-democratic societies, industrial capitalism, is intrinsically at loggerheads with both the vision of the managed and the vision of the caring society.[32] Its institutional core, the market, precludes the management of society as a unitary entity. It is also 'the most impersonal relationship of practical life into which humans can enter with one another' because of 'its matter-of-factness, its orientation to the commodity and only that'; and on that account it knows nothing about caring.[33] This, in itself, may justify the recourse to the state as a counter balancing force.

But does it? Needless to say, this is a difficult question. To begin with, the relationship between, in particular, industrial capitalism and the caring vision is more complex than I have indicated. The market, as has just been remarked, knows nothing about caring, yet it compels upon the units operating on it a degree of economic rationality and an openness to technological innovation whose (however unintended) by-product in the contemporary West has been a vast, unprecedented bounty of productivity – vast enough to, as it were, bankroll the very notion of a caring society which the market, again, knows nothing about.

In the second place, it has been persuasively suggested, advanced industrial capitalism needs, and indeed engenders, a number of disparate, even contradictory, developments which together have the effect of moderating or modifying the centrality of the market to society.[34] First, the tertiary sector of the economy, that is, the provision of services (as against the production of objects), tends to become dominant, and in the larger economic units the handling of social relations – the management of human resources, as it is sometimes called – becomes a major concern: in both ways, the central economic processes themselves become, as it were, people-centred. Second, in order to dispose of its product (be they goods or services) the economic system relies on the prevalence within populations of constantly changing consumption practices, more and more detached from primary needs for shelter, clothing and nutrition; but such practices can only be sustained if a growing number of people are motivated to consume goods and services by a concern with their image, a commitment to fulfil their fantasies, a basically playful attitude toward existence. Third, the idea – and/or the rhetoric – of planned management of social affairs may originate within a corporate environment and then become extended to the society as a whole, at which point it inevitably fastens on the state as the locus and medium of its realisation. At this point, as it were, Mr McNamara goes to Washington.[35]

Other aspects of that difficult question concern the qualifications the state possesses as the key protagonist of the search for both a managed and a caring society. There is little question, on the face of it, of the state's calling on the first count: it has always represented itself as the locus of a comprehensive outlook on society, transcending sectionalism, addressing all individuals, building up power from and with respect to all parts of society. If anything can manage society as a whole, one might say, the state can.

Yet, that 'if anything can' is a big 'if'. In any case, the state's qualifications for *caring* seem rather more doubtful, considering the centrality of organised violence to its very identity, the steely edges of the notion of *raison d'état*, the strong emphasis on impersonality in its administrative operations. All the same, one may remark that in the historical career of the modern state, a positive concern, however motivated, with the welfare of individuals, goes at least as far back as the eighteenth-century *Polizey-staat*, that the notion of citizenship is essential to the liberal-democratic state, and it is a dynamic, expansive notion, capable of encompassing ever more extensive and intensive forms of assistance to individuals.[36]

In this chapter, I have considered some explanations of what I consider the central development in the structure and activity of the state in the twentieth century. The next considers some of its consequences.

8

Liberal Democracy in the
Twentieth Century (2)

The main consequence of the developments we have discussed in the last chapter consists, in my view, in the tension they engender between two tendencies coexisting in contemporary liberal democracies.

On the one hand, policy comes to play a larger and larger role in the management of the social process at large, and thereby in the circumstances and opportunities of individuals. For instance, the life chances of the members of a given family are only partly determined by the market value of the labour of its breadwinner(s); other significant determinants are the amount of tax paid on the wages corresponding to that value, the entitlements of family members, *qua* citizens, to certain publicly provided services (say, free education or free medical care) and possibly some transfer payments from public funds to the family (say, child allowances). Furthermore, even the size of the breadwinner's wage often results from negotiation processes in which some state organs have played a role, and/or from the more or less privileged relationship between the firm paying them and some state agency.[1]

On the other hand, although it remains largely true that, to phrase the point again as in the last chapter, *politics is the matrix of policy*, the politics in question more and more rarely consist in the open confrontation in the public sphere between organised bodies of opinion, competing for public support for alternative policy proposals on the part of the citizenry. Those outputs of public money and binding regulations through which different authorities initiate, control and constrain an increasing number and variety of aspects of the social process are less and less decisively and transparently determined, in turn, by inputs of political preferences originating from the society at large and assessed and balanced against one another according to the rules of the public sphere.

In this sense, and to this extent, an increasingly politically managed society is at the same time, paradoxically, progressively depoliticised. The chief task of this chapter is to explore this paradox.

I

Why did the administration expand so much?

One key to this question is provided, in my view, by the obvious consideration that as the administrative apparatus of the state acquired greater and greater significance in the course of the century, it underwent important qualitative changes in its configuration and in the nature of its tasks.

The expansion and diversification of state activities on which I commented in the previous chapter had their chief locus in the administrative branch. This seems obvious and unavoidable, yet consider for a moment what alternative solutions were excluded. They might have consisted in abolishing or weakening the powers of legislative, judicial and administrative bodies, perhaps by opening all of them to the electoral process, or otherwise involving the citizenry more frequently and intensively. Such solutions, however, had been tried out – with no great success, it must be said – in the context of revolutionary experiences (for instance, the Paris Commune of 1870–1, or the short-lived *Soviet-*, that is 'council'-based phase of the Russian revolution). This probably made their adoption unlikely during the more peaceable, protracted and deliberate processes of institution-making characteristic of liberal democracies.

In principle another possible alternative might have been to consider, instead, assigning the new tasks to the legislative or the judicial branches without merging them with one another or altering too fundamentally their composition and their mode of operation. But that mode precluded such solutions. Judicial and legislative bodies, as normally constituted, operate through people talking to one another. They are thus subject to the one at-a-time rule, that is the various contributions to the agency's operation cannot be simultaneous but must follow one another. On this account, the scarcity of time comes to constitute a tremendous bottleneck for their activities. (Hence the great significance of control over the agenda, especially over that of legislative bodies, for these, unlike courts, often cannot *take their time* in producing their decisions.) However, administrative agencies can circumvent that bottleneck by differentiating themselves into parts that operate simultaneously, because typically they transact their business in writing and not through talk. Thus, other things being equal, it is generally easier for the state to respond to increasing demands by directing them toward organs which multiply the uses of a given unit of time rather than by organs incapable of doing so.

Further resistances to the increase and growth of legislative and judicial bodies may have arisen from the constitutional theories which had originally inspired their establishment. Parliaments built upon the English model, in particular, still have difficulty dividing themselves into functional committees charged with legislative powers of their own, probably because according to that model Parliament is the seat of sovereignty, and must exercise it as a whole, for sovereignty is considered indivisible. Similarly, the ideal of the 'unity of jurisdiction' which in the course of state-building had inspired the replacement of independent, locally based judicial bodies with a nationwide judicial system culminating in a single supreme court, made unacceptable the idea of building up a set of differentiated, highly autonomous subsystems, and of encouraging judges to specialise in order to match the increasing diversity, and the increasing technical nature, of matters for decision.

To these negative reasons for making the administration the main locus of expansion and differentiation, we must add positive ones. As societies become more complex, and the interdependencies between their parts more numerous and opaque, the state must equip itself to respond to and act upon its several demands in a more prompt, informed and knowledgeable manner. In other words, the cognitive aspect of state action must become more and more significant.

But the various state institutions differ in their ability to acknowledge and emphasise that requirement. On the one hand, legislative bodies are the locus for the formation and expression of what might be called political will, that is of consciously partisan resolutions of conflicts and commitments of resources. On the other hand, once formed, such will mostly expresses itself in the form of juridical commands, some of which are in turn (in principle) the chief referent of the activities of judicial bodies. Thus, both kinds of bodies are mainly oriented, respectively, to the production and interpretation of normative expectations: that is, of expectations focused on how people ought to behave, and which for that very reason can be entertained even contrafactually, that is in the face of people behaving in fact otherwise.[2] Cognitive expectations, on the other hand, are focused on the way people (or things) do in fact behave, and for that reason must change in response to what is actually the case.

I have repeatedly emphasised that, particularly on the Continent, administrative bodies have traditionally been constituted and operated (and have selected their personnel) with an eye to the law as the main source of guidance. As I have already remarked, however, such bodies have always been concerned also with ascertaining what is the case and with taking charge of its maintenance or modification. To that extent, they have always had to gather factual information and to apply non juridical knowledge to their activities. In any case, administrative agencies can be run with an eye mainly to cognitive expectations; and, as I have already suggested, they can variously mobilise the activities of personnel specifically trained to produce and apply such expectations in the pursuit of intended effects. Thus in so far as the changing conditions of society require that the cognitive components of state action be emphasised and strengthened, that intelligence on those conditions be routinely collected and acted upon, agencies can be set up or restructured to act accordingly.

The broad philosophy of the division of powers which liberal democracies have inherited from classical constitutionalism also favours an expansion of the state's administrative branch. It assumes that the legislature functions as the 'cybernetic governor' of the state machine. That is, by making even small changes in the law (or in the budget) it can activate and control much greater changes in the activities of other parts of the machine. Parliament can always do things – once the talking stops – at a stroke. It is afterwards, downstream from the legislature, that the hard slog begins, and the administration takes charge. Often, however, it can only do so by absorbing and deploying new resources, hiring new personnel, establishing new units, laying down new arrangements. It is primarily in these activities, then, that what I have called the supply factors in the expansion and differentiation of state action find expression.

The loosening of political control over administration

Whatever the reasons for it, this fact alters profoundly – and, in my view of the matter, negatively – the interaction between politics and policy and the functioning of the public sphere. To see why, we may begin with the elementary consideration that the chief institutional link between the citizenry and the state is the electoral process. This in turn controls the composition of representative, legislative bodies, but does not directly affect the sphere of administration. It is true that in most liberal-democratic systems those bodies determine, through their own majorities, the composition of the executive, the content of legislation and budgetary decisions. But the resulting, indirect connection between on the one hand the citizenry and on the other the administrative machinery of the state is weakened by several intervening processes.

First, for a number of significant reasons that machinery, in all liberal democracies, has long enjoyed a great deal of autonomy with respect to what its components teasingly call their political masters. Those components make up a large, self-confident body of professional administrators who, in the declared intent of protecting their own impartiality and avoiding partisan abuse of administrative facilities, have secured massive guarantees of their tenure, their career prospects, their pension rights and the autonomy of their professional judgement. The actual running of the machinery rests with the elite members of that body; those members and the others enjoy monopoly control over the knowledge and information indispensable to its functioning. All this reduces the significance of the inputs of specifically political vision and commitment the ministers and their direct associates might try to make into the conduct of administrative affairs. (The BBC television programme 'Yes, Minister' constituted a sustained illustration of this phenomenon which was not only very witty, but also uncannily knowledgeable and insightful.)

In the second place, the leverage which a parliamentary majority can gain upon those affairs via the content of legislation and the voting of budgets is also not very significant. Essentially, because of their very complexity, both statutes and budgets have to be themselves pre-arranged by professional administrators, and the related text and documents are often so lengthy, complex and opaque that only the administrators themselves can in fact determine (in two senses of determining-declaring and causing to be) their operative meaning.

Furthermore, as I have already remarked, the administrative machinery of contemporary states makes increasing use not just of legal and financial-fiscal knowledge, but of other, novel and particularly arduous and sophisticated forms of knowledge. Here lies the technocratic challenge to the idea of policy as an expression of political will, as embodying reasoned but ultimately self-determining – and thus responsible – choice. Basically this deprives the politician him/herself of authority – and leaves the mere citizen nowhere.

To sum up these points: the more administrative activity becomes the very substance of policy, the more the link between politics and policy is loosened and weakened. As a recent essay puts it:

> Modern bureaucratic states typically distinguish a technical, professional or administrative sphere in government, which they hold separate from politics. Indeed, the military, civil service, scientific agencies and public health services are generally not only thought but legally required to be divorced from politics in the restricted but important sense of being nonpartisan and professional.[3]

II

Bureaucratic politics

This, however, is not the end of the story. For the much increased, differentiated and increasingly autonomous administrative apparatus becomes in turn the site of a different kind of politics. This is less and less connected with, more and more sheltered from, the visible politics of the public sphere, but by the same token constitutes an increasingly significant component of the political process in its entirely – bureaucratic politics. This expression, as I employ it, does not signify only that it has the administrative action of the state as its object, but also that it finds its protagonists in the increasingly numerous and diversified units responsible for that action. These have become the bearers of distinctive, self-regarding interests, and it is the power relations between those units and the interactions and adjustments between the irrespective interests, which to a growing extent set the actual course of state policy – for instance, by determining the content of legislation, or of the budget, or of critical decisions taken within the executive.[4] (In the United States, for instance, the content of each yearly military budget is the outcome of protracted, fierce infighting between the armed services.)

Bureaucratic politics expresses in the first place the tendency for all units resulting from a process of differentiation to become increasingly self-referential (as phrased in the last chapter). They operate, that is, primarily in the light of concerns exclusive to themselves, which constitute also the vantage point from which they view their relations with one another and with the larger whole.

However, there is more than this to bureaucratic politics, for the units in question are not, in fact, entirely locked each into itself. Although one may assume that their ultimate objective is their own self-preservation and aggrandisement, each shares with many similar units an interest in autonomy and security, and in pursuing its own interests it must seek allies from among those units. Above all, the larger administrative units, those directly in touch with non-state environments (business, the professions) must, within those environments, find partners with whom to exchange services and favours and to share information and other resources, and whose support they can bring to bear on the making of decisions that affect them. Thus, to give another contemporary American example, a federal agency set up to promote the building of houses for people on low incomes may end up expending its funds on contracts and consultancy fees to fat cats and building very few homes for its supposed beneficiaries.

In this fashion, on the one hand the diverse and conflicting interests of an increasingly complex society map themselves onto the state's administrative system; the system, on the other hand, plays an increasingly significant role in defining those interests and determining their strategies. To this extent, bureaucratic politics affects state policy not only at the output end, by determining through what agencies and practices it is going to be implemented; but also at the input end, by selecting the interests which affect its making.

This selection process is often highly biased. It favours organised as against non-organised interests; organisations which can as against organisations which cannot advance the cause of the administrative units with which they deal; organisations led by people who share the social background, the language, the cognitive assumptions, the moral and political preferences of administrative elites, as against those led by other kinds of people.

Thus, bureaucratic politics, even though it does (among other things) transmit to the loci of state policy-making political demands originating within society, is likely to attach to those demands different weights, and to order them accordingly to different priorities, than would the politics of the public sphere.

III

Invisible government

But bureaucratic politics is not the only aspect of the political process which, although it is sometimes known to journalist and scholars,[5] is largely shielded from public monitoring and criticism. Students and critics often apply the expression 'invisible government' to this or that specific aspect of the political process, say the role of security agencies. However, it can also be treated as a generic reference to all aspects which have in common the fact that they are placed outside the scrutiny of the public sphere; in this sense, it denotes a very high proportion of the actual makings of policy in liberal democracies. Here, I will discuss very briefly two such aspects and barely mention a third.

First, high-placed policy makers are more and more often assisted in their activities by staffers and consultants. The rules according to which these are recruited, assigned to tasks, expected to operate, promoted, rewarded and fired, differ from those applying to standard civil service positions, in which to an extent those processes are open, visible and accountable. They recall patrimonial, rather than properly bureaucratic practices;[6] they place a huge premium on the staffer's or consultant's unquestioning personal loyalty to and ideological affinity with the policy-maker and on his/her absolute discretion, rather than on his/her trained capacity for professional judgement or commitment to objective criteria of decision. Furthermore, sometimes the individuals in question effectively take the place of the policy-makers themselves in day-to-day affairs, and in this capacity they monitor and override the decisions taken in their official capacity by top personnel in the agencies they deal with. At the very least, when they yield to the temptation of flaunting their influence, they may gravely embarrass the politicians officially in charge of those agencies – as in the British case in October 1989 leading to the resignation both of the chancellor and of the premier's economic adviser. In any case, for a number of reasons, access to the individuals in question often constitutes a privileged channel for outside interests seeking to exercise covert influence on policy.

Second, in common with all other states, liberal-democratic ones must equip themselves with appropriate machinery for detecting and neutralising hidden threats to their external security (espionage, for instance) or their internal public order (terrorist conspiracies, for instance). By their very nature, the agencies establised to that end must often operate covertly, be financed from *black funds*, circumvent the official norms regulating the handling of foreign affairs, the policing of domestic ones, and particularly the acquisition and storage of information. Whether and how they can do so without totally violating the principles of accountability applicable to all public bodies is a difficult question for all liberal democracies. But if the agencies violate those principles grossly and with impunity, this makes them into 'a state within the state'. They absorb growing amounts of resources; they can use the information they possess (or claim to possess) to bias policy decisions toward the outcomes preferred by one party, or by a given set of sectional interests, even outside their own direct province of competence; they can conspire against their own political masters and subvert wider constitutional principles; they can, literally, get away with murder.

It is in fact claimed that they not only *can* but frequently *do* do such things; and, given the nature of the question, it is practically impossible, except in very limited cases, to assess both those claims and the related counterclaims. But on the whole it does not seem unwarranted to assume that this particular invisible component of policy making has become disturbingly significant, often with the complicity of visible policy-makers, in many liberal democracies since the Second World War. In particular, the story of the relationship between the CIA and the United States Congress provides plenty of examples of this phenomenon; at the end of the Reagan presidency, the so-called Contragate scandal constituted, so to speak, the joint effect of that phenomenon and of the previous one, the excessive decisional autonomy of powerful

House staffers such as Col. Oliver North.

A final component, which I mention because although it is extremely difficult to assess, it is probably on the rise (certainly so in Italy), is constituted by the extent to which the protagonists of various forms of illegal business and of organised crime systematically affect certain aspects and phases of policy making. They can do so because they have infiltrated the policy making circles or coopted some of their members or can systematically thwart and distort the processes of policy implementation (for instance, those intended to control drug traffic or to monitor the stock market or the banking business).

IV

The conditions of the public sphere

From what has been said so far, the reader may have derived a notion that in liberal-democratic societies there exists a public sphere institutionally intended as the potential locus of politics, and indeed capable in principle of operating as such; but that that sphere is increasingly shunted out of the actual policy-making process, since the settings, the protagonists and the distinctive practices of that process increasingly distance it from the public sphere and protect if from its scrutiny.

This notion must now be corrected somewhat, because it is in a sense too optimistic. For if we consider the actual workings of the public sphere, we realise to what extent the depoliticisation I have attributed to liberal democracies is caused by phenomena internal to that sphere, not just by the increasingly remoteness and invisibility of policy making.

The public sphere was originally conceived as the site where the citizenry engages in a certain kind of discourse, which produces and diffuses information about public issues, assesses the merits of alternative lines of policy on such issues in the light of articulated moral preferences and ideological principles and thereby shapes opinion. Competing bodies of opinion would then, via the electoral process and otherwise, make their respective inputs into the policy making process. This conception has been made less and less plausible by many phenomena, three of which I discuss below.

The first concerns the channels through which such discourse actually goes on in contemporary democratic societies, and the nature, quality and quantity of the information and argument they convey. Essentially, as television has supplanted the press and radio as the main mass medium, establishing and maintaining these channels of communication has become more and more expensive, and requires more and more sophisticated skills; besides, the press itself has become bigger and bigger business. This has decreased the number and variety (and possibly the reliability) of information sources; has conferred upon those sources, wedded as they are to the socio-economic and political status quo a disproportionate ability to effectively address large audiences; and has sharply narrowed the range of widely voiced judgements and seriously entertained policy options. In fact, the information at the disposal of the public, the definition of the issues it concerns, and the criteria by which it is evaluated, are largely produced by the very forces which have a stake in increasing the significance of bureaucratic and other forms of invisible policy making.

The second, overlapping phenomenon consists in what might be called the privatisation of concerns. The increased consumption opportunities (and needs!) and the wide-ranging supply of goods and services characteristic of advanced industrialism, have motivated people to give a higher and higher priority to increasing their disposable income. The chief means of doing this still lies in improving their market position, and although in order to do this people may engage in collective action – say, strikes – such action is generally sustained by a narrow definition of the identity they share, and rarely concerns broader, specifically public concerns. The same thing applies to collective strategies intended to increase, relatively or absolutely, those aspects of the individual's life circumstances determined by the action of authorities. Finally, while advanced industrialism tends to increase people's leisure time, most of it is expended on privately enjoyed entertainments and pastimes, and catered to by the media.

Hence the overlap with the previous phenomenon. From the standpoint supplied by the conception of an informed, argumentative, critical citizenry forming competing bodies of opinion, what issues from the media is mostly not signal but noise, which on the one hand responds to people's search for entertainment and on the other generates it. The circumstances of public life, domestic and (to a much lesser extent) foreign, still constitute many of the themes raised by the media. But their treatment is increasingly shallow and perfunctory, and dominated by the search for sensational news; so that it ceases when a given theme no longer occasions dramatic, newsworthy events. The related problems may go on simmering away, but once neglected by the media they turn, in the minds of people at large, into another component of a larger public life perceived as remote, baffling and intractable. Rarely invited by the media to attend to a serious argument about political issues, the public normally focuses its attention (if at all) on the personalities involved and on the slogans they voice, or simply turns away toward an unending flow of politically insignificant news and diversions with which to relieve the ennui besetting private individuals.

The third phenomenon is really a corollary of the previous two. Contemporary publics have fewer and fewer opportunities and incentives for mobilising around public issues and for experiencing the attendant heightened feeling of widely shared involvement in and concern with public issues. The pressure of jobs, the pull of family concerns and the attraction of media entertainment drastically reduce the time and energy people can devote to expressing their wider collective identities outside the contexts of their routine existence, to openly and loudly voicing their feelings and preferences about the public affairs confronting the authorities.

Those who can still be mobilised to that effect belong mostly to relatively marginal and generally ineffectual groups – students, drop-outs, (sometimes) the unemployed, certain sections of the under-class. The manifestations of their displeasure and concern are generally so staged as to become media news, and by the same token offer the larger public an opportunity to convert their own solidarity or opposition into the same attitude of vicarious, passive participation through television viewing. For most people, turning out at election times constitutes practically the only regular expression of partisanship – and for that matter of active citizenship. But such times are few and far between, preceded by prolonged but confusing and hollow campaigns, and elections are widely perceived to make little difference to anything of great significance; so little that in many countries electoral turnout is decreasing, in spite of the fact that in practically all of them state policy continues to impinge widely (and indeed increasingly) on the life circumstances of the citizenry.

V

The role of parties

One might object, at this point, that these critical comments about the public sphere are off the mark. For we have barely mentioned so far the existence of a plurality of parties, which constitute themselves in the public sphere and specialise in gathering and selecting social demands for state action, which they then bring to bear, either in government or from the opposition, on the making and execution of policy. A somewhat similar function is performed by a variety of interest groups and occasionally of social movements; but these encompass narrower interests or single issues, and their impact on policy is less visible and institutionally legitimate. Parties on the one hand periodically measure via elections their respective standing with the citizenry at large, and on the other – in parliamentary systems, at any rate – take specific responsibility for policy (or the critique of policy) through the formation of majorities and oppositions. It is on them that the task of properly political as against interest representation falls. By the same token the role they play in liberal democracies may reduce the force of the comments above about the reduced liveliness and efficacy of the public sphere.

And indeed party pluralism is a most significant and worthwhile aspect of the liberal-democratic constitution, as we shall see a *contrario* when we consider, in the next chapter, states where there is only one party. At the same time, one should not overestimate the parties' effectiveness in remedying the progressive depoliticisation of liberal-democratic societies.

If, as I have suggested above, the actual site of policy formation has moved away from elective, representative institutions, in itself the fact that parties control the composition and the operation of those institutions does not make them into effective instruments of the public's political efficacy. Furthermore, if my earlier argument has any merit, policy formation and implementation are to a large extent the product of bureaucratic politics, and this form of politics largely processes inputs from administrative agencies and from the organised interests enjoying privileged access to and influence upon those agencies. But to that extent, not even the party or party coalition which controls the composition of the cabinet and its programme of government thereby becomes *the* maker of policy. In sum, even though the expansion and diversification of state activity have been, to an extent, the product of party policies,[7] the associated structural modifications in the democratic polity have considerably diminished the significance of parties.

The economicisation of politics

That significance has been similarly affected by a distinct though related phenomenon. Namely, in all Western industrial societies, since the Second World War, the political process has come to revolve chiefly around economic issues – primarily, *which* state policies can best promote industrial growth, and how the attendant burdens and the resulting advantages should be distributed within the population.

In this context, all parties – or at any rate all constitutional parties enjoying or aspiring to the status of mass and of potentially governing parties – came to underwrite, more or less expressly, the following set of assumptions, which together amount to a kind of economistic sublimation of politics:

1 Industrial growth (including, in some versions, a successful transition to a post-industrial society) is definitely worth having, and indeed constitutes the dominant societal goal.

2 All significant aspects of the social process, including politics and state action, justify themselves if and to the extent that they contribute to industrial growth.

3 The traditional concern of politics and state action with the allocation of burdens and advantages among major social groups must itself be subordinated to and made compatible with the promotion of industrial growth.

4 Scientific and technological development, including the development of managerial and economic know-how, holds the key to industrial growth; and to identify the optimal way of promoting that growth, and distributing the related burdens and advantages, has become to a large extent a technical task, to be performed according to relevant, objective knowledge.

Most parties, it seems to me, have ceased to contend over these matters, and redefined implicity or explicitly their traditional policy preferences and their distinctive standards of political action as just so many pieces of cumbersome ideological baggage. They make use of it only occasionally, mostly in order to assert a party's continuity with its own past so that its traditional social base would not become disaffected and and disorientated. In this manner, Western political parties have narrowed down the range of political issues defined as meaningful and political options defined as acceptable. As a consequence, they have come to resemble one another, in their actual policy orientations, much more closely than they had previously (and, possibly, more closely than the constitutional theory of liberal democracy had assumed them to be).

This development has had a number of consequences for the standing of political parties within the polity and indeed within the larger society. In the first place, it has fallen upon non-party (and sometimes anti-party) social movements to raise broader issues[8] – such as those concerning the natural environment or gender inequalities – and to propose options which the parties had defined out of the political agenda. Secondly, parties have made it very difficult for themselves, when they come to power, to insist on their constitutional prerogative of politically monitoring administrative processes (no matter how loaded with policy implications) since those had been defined as essentially technical concerns, and entrusted to the professional rationality of this or that set of experts. Finally, all parties have come increasingly to consider and to recognise the competition over the occupancy of governmental posts and the allocation of other political spoils as their sole effective concern.

The real role of parties

This latter development – theorised, incidentally, in the definition of democracy by Schumpeter and his followers[9] – has become so visible, in spite of the parties' reluctance to acknowledge it fully, that it has caused parties, and other aspects of political conflict, to lose moral standing in the eyes the public. The public have found themselves increasingly unable to view the parties as credible, effective tools for the political guidance of the social process, and for the formulation of binding targets and boundaries of state action. To put it in Italian, parties are increasingly seen as contending not so much over the *governo* of the polity, as over its *sottogoverno*.

The result of this is not that all citizens become estranged from parties. On the contrary, some seem to say to themselves, 'if you can't lick 'em, join 'em'. That is, they seek to use to their own private advantage the parties' ability, if not to shape policy, then to influence a number of narrower, day-to-day political and administrative processes. Having, as it were, given up on parties as channels of their own participation in the input side of politics, they make use of them to obtain advantages on the output side: the appointment to a post on the board of a publicly owned enterprise; the speedier handling and more favourable disposition of an application for a building permit or a subsidy or even of a pending judicial controversy; the chance of a hearing from a minister or a high-ranking bureaucrat.

In contemporary Italian practice (particularly rich in examples of this kind) individuals often negotiate for such favours not just with a given party but with a given faction of one, or even with the personal following of a given leader. In return, they commit themselves to delivering their own vote and those of their associates to the party, faction or leader in question; or they promise that, once appointed, say, to the board of a public enterprise, they will favour other supporters when choosing a contractor on behalf of that public enterprise. Thus, the loss of standing with the larger public suffered by a party, or even by parties in general, may well be compensated – as far as concerns their ability to stay in the political business – by the fact that they can still make themselves useful, particularly when in power.

Parties thus attract the negotiated loyalty (to use an intentionally contradictory expression) of considerable numbers of individuals, tying them together into clientele networks, which mainly, I repeat, converge around factions or leaders. But this does not make them into suitable settings for the formation, or channels for the transmission, of policy demands arising from the public sphere.

VI

The significance of citizenship

These, then, are some of the manifestations of and reasons for the paradoxical coincidence of an increase in the political management of Western societies with their depoliticisation. The paradox in fact disappears if, simplifying the matter enormously, we suggest that, essentially, a huge growth in the output of state action has not been accompanied by a proportionate growth in the structures processing the public's decisional inputs into state activity. This means that many such inputs have had to originate either from within the state itself, via bureaucratic politics, or from arrangements and understandings between parts of the state apparatus and privileged parts of society, a phenomenon at the centre of some versions of the so-called neo-corporatist thesis.[10]

Let me stress that I am speaking of decisional inputs; it is as the source of these that the Western public has lost significance. It has not lost it to the same extent as regards other inputs; it has, in particular, borne (however reluctantly) the growing burden of an entirely different input, that of monetary resources.[11] For, of course, the fiscal take – in its several forms – has had to grow enough to finance (wholly or in part) the huge expansion in state activity.[12] But the fact that we speak of a fiscal *take* rather than *give*, suggests that this input has grown very much on the state's own initiative, and the public has related only passively to it, through its compliance. More generally, although the citizenry by and large has gained, as a whole or in its several sections,[13] from the increased size and range of state activity, it has not found in the public sphere proportionally greater opportunities to control that activity politically. Thus by and large citizens as such, even when they benefit from state activity, stand today to a growing extent in a passive and dependent relationship to the state.

To support this view, I will reconsider briefly the earlier argument that over the last 150 years the content of citizenship has increased through the expansion of rights. Individuals, that is, have had given to them, on the basis of abstract and general legal commands, more and more capacities and entitlements *vis-à-vis* the state. This, it can be argued, has had an equalising effect, for it has tempered the inequalities resulting from market relations.

The significance of this development, however, should not be overstated. The historically more recent rights, and particularly those affecting a person's social standing, economic security, cultural competence and sense of worth, can only become effective to the extent that public authorities provide facilities in the form of, say, hospitals, trained nurses, schools, leisure centres, or whatever. But citizens as such have very little hope of redress if this provision is not adequately made. Furthermore, even when facilities are provided, citizens wanting to make use of such services are all too often put through the hoops of the indifference, inertia, niggardliness and incompetence of those operating them supposedly on their behalf, and the simple appeal to their rights often does little to overcome those obstacles. But then, one might argue, if my enjoyment of a right depends largely on somebody else's activity, how much of a right is it, really? Ultimately, the less I am able to initiate, orient, control those activities, the less that right looks like a right to me – in spite of the fact that in the end the activities are performed anyway and I benefit from them.[14]

Besides, in so far as the substance of the rights of citizenship depends on policies implementing them, it is sometimes doubtful that their enjoyment compensates for the inequalities created among citizens by the fact that they reside in different localities, are of different gender or belong to different socio economic strata. Far from eliminating or restricting those inequalities, the variable extent to which those rights are actually enjoyed may possibly strengthen them. In any case, the actual enjoyment of those rights may depend on the individual's ability to influence the practices of the authorities; and, in turn, this ability is generally unequally distributed. (Even in highly inclusive, wholly publicly funded health systems, for instance, middle-class patients generally manage to secure more and better health care from the system than working-class patients suffering from the same illness.) To that extent, a distinctive, political dimension of inequality may either add itself to the status and economic dimensions or cut across those, but in either case leave little of the original promise of citizens' equality fulfilled.

VII

A personal note

The tone and content of this chapter and the last have been prevalently critical, and may suggest to the reader that I hold a largely negative view of the situation and trends of contemporary liberal-democratic states.

In fact, I consider myself lucky in that, having been born in fascist Italy, and having watched the death throes of that regime while barely into my teens, I have lived the rest of my life in a liberal-democratic political environment, in Italy and elsewhere. All the same, I am aware both that there are certain painful tensions intrinsic to that environment – one might argue that liberalism and democracy can only make up an unstable, perhaps incoherent compound[15] – and that some of its contemporary developments make it both less liberal and less democratic. But the emphasis placed on those developments in the last two chapters should be balanced but against my expressly – though not unreservedly – positive assessment of the state's story in chapter 5. For most of the aspects of 'The State' emphasised in that assessment are in fact unique properties of its embodiment in Western liberal democracies. In the next chapter, my all too brief account of a way of institutionalising political power that is expressly at variance with the liberal-democratic tradition, may suggest *a contrario* how many virtues I see even in the inadequate and perhaps faltering embodiment of that tradition in the contemporary West.

In particular – to maintain the emphasis placed in this chapter on the public sphere, and to balance out the critical overtones of my treatment of it – there still is a public sphere in the contemporary West. And party pluralism, even if in Western countries it does not constitute a particularly effective instrument through which the citizenry can determine the political agenda, opt among alternative policies and hold accountable the political elite, is yet the product of intrinsically valuable arrangements, which to some extent still allow autonomous power centres to emerge within society, to address and compete with one another and to set constraints around the action of political power. In other words, one might say that party pluralism is significant and worthwhile not so much in view of its consequences as on account of its causes.

As I write, furthermore, in one Eastern European country after another the citizenry, suddenly mobilised in relatively great numbers, are both celebrating the beginnings of a re-establishment of the public sphere, and agitating for a further extension of that process. It is clear to them (and to the established political elites now threatened by them) that the process must culminate in elections in which a plurality of parties compete for public support. In an sense to be clarified in the next chapter, those countries are currently rediscovering politics, and in doing so they affirm the unique virtues of arrangements about which sizeable sections of the Western publics had become somewhat disenchanted.

9

A New Type of State

I

Having explored some major changes occurring in the twentieth century in the structure and operation of liberal-democratic states, in the modalities of their political process and in, as it were, the texture of their public life, I shall again remind the reader (see the end of chapter 4) that those changes took place against the background of two considerable elements of continuity.

First, in contemporary Western states some significant features of the liberal constitution remain in place, in however modified and attenuated a form. State action is still to some extent constrained by rights of citizenship, including those of the public sphere; by the division of powers; and by the persistent significance of the bureaucratic model of administration. Also, much of the process of policy formation involves conflict and accommodation between more and less powerful sets of interests, which to a considerable extent still express themselves via a number of political parties competing for votes.

Second, the political realm remains complementary, and for certain purposes subordinated, to a set of non-political processes, primary among which are those concerning the production and distribution of wealth. And these processes still reflect on the one hand the dispersal of social capital into a plurality of discrete 'packets' under private control competing on the market, and on the other the control of capital over labour.

The twentieth century, however, has witnessed the development of state forms to which these two generalisations do not apply. Their most visible common trait consists in the fact that, paradoxically, one distinctive feature of the liberal-democratic constitution, the organised mass party, is alive and well in the states in question, *but* there is only *one* such party, and the basic condition for the existence and operation of others, the existence of a public sphere, has been suppressed, together with most other features of that constitution.

Thus, what I have signalled above as the first element of continuity between contemporary liberal democracies and the liberal state does not apply to these states. The peculiarly close relationship obtaining there between one party and the state modifies the nature of both entities, the party and the state, and is so distinctive, that one may designate the resulting political environment as a party-state.

There are, and there have been, a number of different types of party-state. Disregarding those characteristic of Third World countries, two varieties have operated in the twentieth century within industrial societies – the fascist variety and the communist variety. They differ, essentially, in that only communist party-states also reject the second element of continuity with their past which characterises liberal-democratic systems, that is, the existence of a capitalist economic order and the associated form of class division. This chapter discusses only communist party-states and does so in a highly general manner. However, to the extent that it has a concrete referent, this is constituted exclusively by the Soviet Union.[1]

II

Origins of the Soviet party-state

When I first conceived of this discussion in the mid eighties, and indeed also when I first drafted this chapter, in 1988, my paying special attention to the Soviet Union was still a matter of choice, for at the time relatively similarly constituted communist party-states were well-established in other East European countries. Since then, things have changed at an astonishing pace. Those other countries have undergone changes which, if consequently enacted and thoroughly institutionalised, could alter their political environments profoundly and irreversibly, in the direction of the same values which have inspired my positive assessment of the development of the modern state in Chapter 5.

As to the Soviet Union itself, so far its political structure has not been changed to anything like the same extent. Of Gorbachov's two felicitous and promise-laden slogans – *perestroika* (restructuring) and *glasnost* (openness) – only the second seems to have already made a sizeable impact on the current circumstances of Soviet public life. But *glasnost*, as

I interpret it, was never meant to make that much of a difference to the institutional features of the Soviet state, as against the cultural climate of Soviet society.

Thus, not enough *perestroika* has actually taken place, in the Soviet Union, to deprive the argument that follows of whatever validity it might have had when I began to formulate it to myself – before Gorbachov. In any case the argument is meant primarily as a reflection on the past experience of the Soviet system, rather than as an assessment of the directions it is currently taking or that it might take in the future.

Let us, then, begin at the beginning: for the makings and the course of the Russian revolution of October 1917 already reveal to what extent the nascent Soviet state was committed to repudiating the two elements of continuity between today's liberal democracies and their liberal origins.

Let us begin with the *second* element. Lenin's party was always committed to destroying private capital and the market, and as it took over state power it sought to use it immediately in that destruction. Once it accomplished that, the state was originally meant to wither away, both because its supposed *raison d'être* – the political maintenance of exploitation and class division – had disappeared, and because the first socialist revolution in Russia was expected to be followed by others in the more advanced Western countries, making their states dispensable and eliminating the necessity for one in Russia.

However, once they had taken control of the machinery of the Imperial Russian state, and modified it to suit their purposes and circumstances, the Bolsheviks never found it convenient to steer that machinery toward its own extinction. Rather, they employed the state's unique resources (beginning with its command over organised coercion) in a particularly unrestrained and ruthless manner, in order to monopolise that control and make it last. They did so by (among other things) progressively eliminating any competitors for that power. In doing so, they thoroughly disassociated their state also from the *first* liberal legacy – the existence of a public sphere within which the composition of the political leadership and, less directly, the content of policy, would be at issue in a legitimate and orderly contest for public support among competing parties.

There were basically two reasons why Lenin's party was able (or indeed was compelled) to act in such a radically innovative manner in the political realm. In the first place, the Tsarist autocracy, which had been in the process of destroying itself in the course of the First World War, had never previously allowed a public sphere and a constitutional order to come into being. And the provisional government, which in the February revolution had gathered the *damnosa hereditas* of Tsarism, had only been able to take the first few steps, under war conditions, toward establishing such a sphere. Furthermore, the Bolshevik party, which had operated through its brief historical career as a conspiratorial, underground or exiled party, had never been allowed to engage in constitutional politics. In this sense, we might say, Bolshevik rule was forced upon a novel and (from the Western standpoint) abhorrent path to the exercise of state power because of *where it came from.*

But also – in the second place – because of *where it was going.* For, as I have indicated, the Bolsheviks intended to use state power as their prime tool in a wholly new tasks – first to destroy the power of private capital and the market, and then to manage the economy and control society without either capital or the market.

Although many of the Bolshevik policies in question were undertaken under the urgent pressure of threatening circumstances, their long-term effect, modified and elaborated of course by many later developments, was that of creating a new form of state, which has proven durable, and which after the Second World War was imposed as a model upon the political reordering of all East European societies.

In the next three sections of this chapter I shall distinguish, somewhat artificially, three main aspects of that form – the state's structure, the scope of its operations, and the mode of those operations. Under each heading, I shall discuss exclusively the most visible, distinctive and persistent features characterising this new state form. I refer to it as the Soviet-type state, for those features have originated in the Soviet Union and are still reflected with particular clarity in its political system, while they presented considerably different variants in other countries within the Soviet orbit.

In the concluding section of the chapter I will attempt a comprehensive characterisation of the Soviet-type state, and consider briefly its current circumstances.

III

Structure of the Soviet-type state

To begin with, I should like to suggest that the political environment in question has something in common, as far as the visible structures and the day-to-day practices of rule are concerned, with (at any rate, some) liberal democracies. In both, the most obvious, routine aspect of the citizen's political experience consists in dealing with (and being dealt with by) large numbers of functionaries, manning a series of offices grouped into ministries and other larger units. In both systems, these offices differ greatly in the kinds of practical activities they conduct (from policing public spaces to running hospitals and research establishments), but all are hierarchically organised, all exercise faculties backed by coercive powers, all run on public money, all operate by reference to general rules, many of which set them tasks to be discharged in the interest of the citizens themselves. In other words, in both types of system the central fact of everyday political life is the existence of a set of continuously operating, specialised agencies manned by professional officials and engaged in administration.

In both, furthermore, this administrative aspect of political experience is complemented by a properly political one, which in principle activates and controls the former; and, again in both, a very important role as far as this political aspects is concerned is played by one or more entities called political parties. On the face of it, a Communist, ruling party in a Soviet-type state is again similar to the more extensively and elaborately organised mass parties of liberal-democratic states. It is a voluntary association, which does not possess means of coercion of its own, which comprises individuals who subscribe to its political programme, and which seeks to confer upon its own leaders the commanding roles within state institutions. It operates according to its own constitution; and it is internally differentiated, so that, for instance, among its members one can easily distinguish, at one end, the purely rank and file element to whom party membership is a relatively minor aspect of existence, and at the other end the members of the top party elite, whose lives revolve around their party roles and those they play (or hope to play) within state organs. True, the constitutional principles of so-called democratic centralism shared by Communist parties (in or out of power) differ somewhat from those proclaimed by other parties, but they do not differ so markedly from them in their practical significance, which is largely that of preventing dissenting factions from challenging the party elite's control over the policy and the resources of the party.[2]

In other words, on the face of it, Soviet-type systems have a state recognisably similar to those of liberal democracies, and their ruling Communist parties, in turn, look fairly much like the parties active in those democracies. Yet these analogies are profoundly misleading if they lead one to disregard the overriding significance of one distinctive structural feature exclusive to party/state relations in the Soviet model. As I said, the Soviet-type state is a party-state. That is, within a Soviet-type state, the Communist party of the country in question has permanently and exclusively vested in it, either expressly or by well-established, unchallengeable convention, constitutional powers of decisive significance. It exercises these powers through its own organs, but in doing so it routinely and bindingly sets the policies, directs the activities, commits the resources of the state.

This is not just a matter of a party which happens to be more or less constantly in the majority and whose leaders thus regularly occupy key positions in state organs, and in that capacity exercise the organs' faculties. This sometimes happens in liberal democracies, when large majorities favour, election after election, the same party, placing it in a secure hegemonic position. In such circumstances, there may come into being a close identification between that party and the state, and consequently a *de facto* erosion of the distinction between party leadership and state leadership, between party ideology and state policy. But in the Soviet Union that distinction does not even exist *de jure*, particularly at the higher constitutional level. Organs whose composition and whose decisional faculties are determined by party rules, and which respond, if at all, only to other party organs, are thereby empowered to directly, officially and legitimately determine state policy and supervise its execution by state organs.

The 1977 constitution of the Soviet Union stated this quite explicitly in Article 6 (which at the beginning of 1990, was being revised):

> *The leading and guiding force of Soviet society and the nucleus of its political system, of all state organisations and public organisations, is the Communist Party of the Soviet Union. The CPSU exists for the people and serves the people. The Communist Party, armed with Marxism-Leninism, determines the general perspectives of the development of society and the course of home and foreign policy of USSR, directs the great constructive work of the Soviet people, and imparts a planned, systematic and theoretically substantiated character to their struggle for the victory of communism.*

To this effect, the leaderships respectively of the state and of the party are (again, officially and bindingly) overlapped, either through express constitutional arrangements, or through well-established practices, which empower the party to select, or at least to verify the eligibility of, the appointees to a large number of significant offices in – among other organisations – state organs (the so-called *nomenklatura*). Furthermore, all significant ramifications of the state apparatus, including those concerned with production, are closely monitored by party organs operating at the same level, which are empowered to criticise their activities and enjoin their modification.

What accounts for this structural peculiarity of the Soviet-type state? The simplest answer, as I have already suggested, can be given in historical terms. The utterly privileged constitutional position of Communist parties in the Soviet Union and in other East European countries is a direct legacy of the impatience with opposition and competition which the Bolshevik party, under Lenin's leadership, manifested very soon after its takeover of state power in October 1917.[3] As we have seen, once established in a position of unassailable power in Soviet Russia, the

Bolsheviks never let go of it. They strengthened it further and further in the twenties and thirties, and in the late forties they imposed the same model of party/state relations on other East European countries.

Or one may seek an answer in an analysis of the limits and the liabilities of Lenin's political thought, its totally inadequate sense of the significance of institutional arrangements shaping and binding power, its lack of awareness of the possibility of what in chapter 1 I have called the horizontal dimension of the political experience, of politics as the possible matrix of policy.[4] (Even when, toward the end of his life, Lenin became uneasily aware of the danger that after his death Stalin would use and abuse the powers of the party-state in a particularly ruthless and destructive manner, he attributed that danger chiefly to Stalin's *nyekulturny* (uncivilised) personality, rather than to the dictatorial nature of the powers in question, and to the fact that society as a whole was defenceless against them.)

Personally, I would emphasise a different way of making sense of the peculiar relationship binding party and state in the party-state. A necessary, though perhaps not sufficient, condition for the open, official transformation of a party into the stable, visible, dominant component of the state's very structure, is that it should effectively be the *only* party active within the state. Conversely, in liberal democracies the arm's-length relationship between the various parties and the state is a product of party pluralism (in the sense of the existence of two or more parties).

But party pluralism is in turn an aspect (both a cause and a product) of a wider phenomenon, the existence of a public sphere – a set of arrangements allowing people freely and openly to address one another concerning public matters, to judge, support or criticise the policies of authorities and to organise themselves into groups in order to shape public opinion and promote alternative policies. The Soviet-type state is not, as it were, surrounded, complemented and monitored by such a sphere. In fact, if by politics we understand a process whereby within the public sphere multiple, autonomous collective actors openly and legitimately compete with one another, each on behalf of special interests, to limit, influence and determine policy, we might go as far as saying that *there is no politics in the Soviet-type state.*

Lately, it seems, *glasnost* has been making this statement a great deal less tenable. Nevertheless, it is important not to misunderstand it. It does not assert that there is no debate, in the societies ruled by Soviet-type states, on the appropriate goals of policy, on the nature and content of collective interests, or other such issues. Nor does it assert that debates on such matters only involve tiny, utterly privileged and exclusive minorities. The point is rather that such debates, no matter how many people they involve, are normally initiated at the behest of a higher authority, who can establish their themes, determine the range of options to be examined, decide how long the debate can go on, and above all determine in advance to what conclusions it can lead. Normally, under these conditions what is missing is not discussion, the raising and weighing of alternative definitions of issues and of views about their solutions. What is missing is the *public, open-ended confrontation* between in principle equally legitimate readings of the environing circumstances, and formulations of the appropriate policy for dealing with those circumstances. This results directly, on the one hand, from the exclusive, totally privileged constitutional position of the Communist party; on the other, from the inexistence of other collective entities, organising and expressing different and conflicting interests, and autonomous with respect to the party-state, which might in some way threaten that position.

But why, one might ask, is it not possible, in the Soviet Union and in similarly constituted societies, for social interests to organise themselves autonomously in the public sphere? Why, as a consequence, does the latter simply not exist as an institutionally autonomous social realm?

Here I must refer again to the communist system's express intent to manage and control society without recourse to private capital and the market. This entails by definition the suppression of the right of private individuals to own productive material resources and to exploit them to their own advantage through strategies of their own choice, including the employment of other people, or the formation of corporations or other private partnerships.

But again, why should the existence of this particular right be a necessary (but not a sufficient) condition of the existence of a public sphere? Why should it be more significant than other rights of individuals, such as the ownership of non-productive possessions, or access to collectively provided education and medical care, or the right to worship according to one's conscience, which to some extent obtain in a number of East European countries.

The reason is simple, and is suggested by an argument developed at the very beginning of this book. The right of private property in the means of production is the basis of a distinctive form of social power, economic power. For by vesting in some subjects the faculty of excluding others from access to and fruition of a portion of the society's productive resources, it allows the former to set the terms under which the latter will gain conditional access and fruition. Furthermore, it entitles the property owners to mobilise the state's own power on their own behalf.[5] Finally, it splits society into two groupings, marked respectively by the possession or lack of possession of such right, and tends to place the majority within the latter grouping in a position of systematic inferiority and dependency toward those in possession. (Note that this holds irrespective of whether one does or does not accept the Marxian view that the employment relationship entails exploitation. The systematic inferiority of non-property owners on the market for labour *vis-à-vis* property owners has been recognised also by Durkheim and by Weber. The latter, in particular, emphasised the subordination of employees within the employment relationship.)

By constituting a set of power relations which in principle the state respects (and indeed sanctions and enforces), private property in the means of production generates over the surface of society a number of loci of privileged autonomy, of immunity from direct state interference, of capacity to exercise control over the circumstances of oneself and of others. If other suitable institutional conditions are present, between these points there may flow also the currents of controversy and consensus concerning matters of policy characteristic of the public sphere.

This may be one reason why, in fascist party-states, the exclusion of those other conditions has been more radical and explicit than in Soviet-type party-states. Unlike the latter, fascist party-states are not by their very nature committed to abolishing private property in the means of production, the capitalist employment relationship, market power, etc. To this extent, they allow some premises of a public sphere to stand, and in order to prevent its emergence they must explicitly exclude other premises. For instance they openly suppress the freedom of the press and of association, and proclaim out-and-out anti-democratic principles such as the Nazi *Führerprinzip*. In so far as they operate in societies where no other forms of social power exist, communist party-states, instead, may sometimes pay lip service to democratic principles and institutionalise practices such as periodic elections – in which, however, no serious competition for votes takes place.

The validity of this view may be suggested by the following consideration. The East European country where the communist party-state was first forced to allow an approximation to a public sphere and to acknowledge the existence and the legitimacy of an organised opposition was Poland. But Poland was also the country where, for complex reasons, the regime had previously allowed the Catholic Church to operate as an independent centre of social power – in this case, of normative power, to use the terminology of chapter 1. Furthermore, that power centre had played a key role in the formation of Solidarity, which in turn at one point controlled *de facto* the working masses to a sufficient extent to render it an independent centre of economic power. On both counts, then, the Polish party-state found itself confronting a society where, like it or not, some centres of independent social power did exist. This was a highly anomalous condition for a Soviet-type state, and it compelled the Polish

Communist party to consent to highly unusual (and eventually untenable) arrangements, involving some power sharing between itself and Solidarity, as well as a relatively extensive and far-reaching reactivation of the public sphere.

In normal conditions, however, there are – to summarise my argument – two chief reasons why no public sphere (and thus no politics) exists, or can exist, in such a state. On the one hand, because private individuals, singly or in association, do not possess the right to appropriate and manage on their own behalf productive resources. On the other, because an essential aspect of the public sphere, the emergence of party pluralism, would destroy the privileged, exclusive position occupied by the Communist party in the constitutional order. Put otherwise, the premises of a public sphere are lacking, and its potential consequences are inadmissible.

IV

Scope of operation of the Soviet-type state

Again, the inexistence of private property in the means of production accounts for what I consider the single most significant aspect of the operations of the state under the Soviet model – the enormous extension of their scope. The range of social concerns on which the party-state's activities are routinely and directly brought to bear is hugely increased in comparison with liberal-democratic systems.

Why so? Both systems with and systems without private property in the means of production must find answers to a set of very significant economic questions: which goods shall be produced and which services rendered, by whom, where, at what cost, through what processes? who shall be employed, on what terms? But the systems differ greatly in the way they answer those and related questions.

In systems acknowledging private property in the means of production those answers are the (largely unplanned) by-product of the self-regarding market operations of a plurality of discrete, mutually independent and competing (individual and corporate) units, each operating on behalf of its own interests, largely in the light of the information encoded in the prices of the various factors of production; those prices, in turn, result chiefly from the interactions taking place between those units. Thus, since it itself produces the data it needs to function, the market constitutes a distinctive, autonomous realm, following and imposing a logic of its own: for the activities of the several units generate, via the market, most of the essential constraints under which they operate; they bring about an equilibrium which their operations in turn presuppose.

But where private property in the means of production does not exist, productive units do not to the same extent stand in relation to one another as discrete, competing units, each activated by the pursuit of its own advantage and all interacting with all others via the market. Thus those questions about the economy have to be answered otherwise than as a result of the autonomous, self-seeking interactions of such units. It is probably not the case, in principle, that they *must* be resolved by means of an enormous extension of the scope of state activities.[6] That this has been the case in Eastern Europe, however, is a matter of historical record; and once more, perforce, the record begins with the experience of the Soviet Union.

As I have insisted, the abolition of private property in the means of production was the main plank in the Bolshevik revolutionary programme. Its realisation was in practice a fairly protracted and tortuous process, among other reasons because the first stab in this direction – the appropriation and management of industrial assets by workers' councils – led to distressing results from the standpoint of production (not to mention productivity). Also, one particular means of production – agricultural land – had to be dealt with on rather special terms, from the standpoint of Bolshevik ideology, since its treatment directly affected the delicate relationship between the party, which defined itself as the political vanguard of the industrial working class, and that *awkward class*, the Russian peasantry.

In any case, it was not until the late twenties, with the end of the New Economic Policy (which had made substantial concessions to the stronger elements within the peasantry, in the direction of 're-marketising' the economy) and the beginning of agricultural collectivisation and of forced-draft industrialisation, that the Soviet system began to draw the implications for the scope of its own activities of the complete abolition of private property in the means of production. There was no longer, I repeat, a plurality of discrete, competing units based on private property, whose autonomous, profit-oriented operations could generate a framework of data on economic variables on which the productive units would base their activities.

Put otherwise, no private enterprise, no market, no proper, information-laden prices, no effective constraints to induce rational allocations of resources and optimal organisation of processes either for the single enterprise (now collectively owned) or for the system comprising all such enterprises, no intrinsic inducements to produce (and thus to industrialise). What, then?

The answer was central planning. That is, not only would all enterprises be owned by the state and managed on its behalf; but a new set of specially constituted state organs would make all the basic productive decisions, and assign their fulfilment to enterprises. These would function not as independent units seeking to maximise their profits, but merely as technical agencies for the implementation of their authoritative assigned targets. To be sure the central planning organs were to be guided by sophisticated economic calculations in setting production targets, specifying production processes, assigning prices to the inputs and outputs of enterprises and to their final products. However, upstream of such calculations stood expressly political decisions concerning the pace and direction of the industrialising processe; and, downstream, the calculated directives of the planning organs were to be treated as authoritative commands of higher to lower administrative units.

To this model of the relationship between productive enterprises and the party-state the Soviet Union has essentially remained faithful to this day, although from the sixties on several attempts have been made not only to modify its implementation (for instance, concerning the relations between central and regional planning organs) but also to introduce into it more or less substantial aspects of the contrasting, market model. Such attempts were also made, sometimes more successfully, in other East European countries. But the overall lesson of these attempted reforms is that it is basically impossible to carry them far enough to remove the model's flaws (to be discussed below) without introducing new proprietary arrangements. These, however – it is feared – would in turn destabilise the basic structural design of Soviet-type societies.

In that design, as it now stands at any rate, the party-state, as we have seen, involves itself in the management of economic processes to an extend and in a manner which finds only distant parallels in liberal-democratic systems, however *dirigiste* they may be. (Closer parallels may perhaps be found in wartime capitalist economies, but even there the planning arrangements do not substantially after the principle that large *quantums* of productive resources are privately owned).

Naturally, the fact that the Soviet party-state adds very substantially to the range of activities it shares with liberal-democratic states has considerable structural consequences. To begin with, to the organisational layout of the state must be added all those agencies involved in the elaboration of more and more specific and detailed plans, and in supervising their execution by individual enterprises. Furthermore, many of these agencies are shadowed by party organs, which intervene in the selection of their higher personnel and monitor their performance. In particular, enterprises find themselves at the receiving end of two sets of controls: on the one hand, the controls exercised by the state's planning organs in charge of a given enterprise's branch of production; on the other, those exercised by the party authorities dealing with the affairs of the territory in which that enterprise is located. (The territorial coordination of productive activities is the chief economic function of regional party organs, and on that account it makes sense to think of regional party secretaries as 'the Soviet prefects'[7], that is, as the Soviet equivalents of French and Italian state officials operating in various parts of the country, and charged among other things with coordinating the activities of the local offices of different central ministries.)

Furthermore, one might perhaps consider enterprises and other productive establishments as themselves parts of the state proper, and their employees as state employees. On the one hand, such units are recognised to have a distinctive purpose (production of goods and services) and a distinctive mode of operation (focused on the technical division of labour and on accounting) with respect to more conventional parts of the state. On the other hand, their autonomy is severely limited, for enterprises are not considered to own their means of production, depend financially on budgetary allocations from the state, and operate largely by carrying out higher directives, just as any lower-level administrative units of the state's would.

As to their workers, they are considered employees of the firm, rather than to the state. However, as normally workers can only leave employment with one enterprise by obtaining employment with another, standing in the same relationship to the state, it does not seem implausible to consider the state as the universal employer.

Besides carrying out a range of vital economic functions via planning organs and local party offices (not to mention the enterprises themselves), Soviet-type state involve themselves in shaping and controlling aspects of people's life chances that in liberal-democratic systems are instead largely determined by market forces. Of course, even in liberal-democratic systems, the market is far from being the exclusive determinant of life chances; but, when all is said and done, it remains the dominant one in comparison with citizenship rights and other aspects of the political circumstances of most individuals and groups.

It might be noted that also in Soviet-type systems, there is a sense in which the individual's market position remains critical, for people's jobs determine to a considerable extent their incomes (and that of their family) and most jobs are acquired by the individual choosing to join a particular enterprise or other employer. Also, individuals expend much of the income accruing from such employment on products and services in their capacity as consumers supplied (well or, more often, badly) by the existent market. In this sense, and to that extent, it must be recognised that also in Soviet-type systems the life situation of individuals largely reflects choices made, respectively, on a labour and on a commodity market.[8]

However, this analogy with liberal-democratic societies is potentially misleading. As far as the labour market is concerned, the analogy conceals, in the first place, the restriction placed on people's occupational choices by the fact that, as we have noted, the state is the (nearly) universal employer. Second, it conceals more specific restrictions on those choices. Consider, for example, those firms associated in the Soviet Union with the particular status of certain 'closed enterprises'. Citizens can only get jobs with these firms, which have a (sometimes very remote) relationship to the defence system, if they obtain an administrative permit. If they do not obtain it, they are thereby excluded from the often very considerable and invidious advantages enjoyed by the employees of closed enterprises – better pay, better working conditions, better equipment and higher occupational status than those enjoyed by similarly qualified employees holding similar jobs in 'open' ones.[9] Third, the analogy ignores all those occupational positions which, according to the *nomenklatura* principle, are reserved to party members or at any rate to applicants in good standing with the party.

Also, as far as the commodity market is concerned, the analogy conceals various facts. First, the prices of many commodities (including services) are not, in turn, market prices, but most emphatically political ones, mostly set by the state in order to secure near-universal access to certain basic necessities (fuel, basic foodstuffs, housing). Second, the general, open-to-all-comers market for commodities is, in all Soviet-type societies, notoriously beset by chronic shortages, and the quality of the goods available is often very poor. This means that often people with disposable incomes literally have nothing on which to spend their money, for the objects and services they want are simply not available in the amounts and the quality they want, where and when they want them.

Access to such commodities, further, is sometimes open to politically privileged categories of people, through a system of special shops which do not, however, constitute a market in the sense of acknowledging and sanctioning only the purchasing power of would-be buyers. It is true that buyers sometimes have access to a number of coloured markets (so designated because too diverse and specialised to be convered by the term black market). But again that access is politically controlled (for example, by concessions regarding the holding of foreign currency), and in any case such clandestine or semi-clandestine arrangements do not provide a legitimate, public remedy to the deficiencies of the official distribution system.

Thus, as can be seen, even in so far as people apparently manage their life circumstances through market-like operations, the settings in which these are conducted are not proper markets, for political decisions impinge on them very widely (and, from the economic standpoint, arbitrarily). Besides, over such decisions exercise even wider leverage over many aspects of people's lives. For instance, arrangements similar to those controlling employment in 'closed enterprises' restrict the Soviet citizens' choice of residence. Many of the Union's larger cities, those providing residents with better medical, educational, cultural and shopping facilities, are officially decreed to be 'closed cities', meaning that citizens need to apply to police authorities for a permit in order to settle there.[10] And qualified students applying for admission to the more prestigious higher education institutions are filtered through processes which allow a great deal of discretion – mostly guided by political considerations – to be exercised by the gatekeepers.

In sum, besides taking charge of the processes presiding over the production of wealth through planning, the state also controls those concerning its distribution.[11] A British Sovietologist, Neil Harding, has emphasised this aspect:

> The overwhelming majority of the inhabitants . . . are reliant upon [the state] for employment, promotion and pensions. The state is, effectively, the sole distributor of social welfare benefits in the realms of health, eduction, housing, culture and recreation . . . Citizenship is conditional upon socially useful work, and political and social preferment is based upon its exemplary fulfilment. Citizens' rights are expressly confined in their exercise to those activities that serve to strengthen the social system of production superintended by the State. They may not be exercised to challenge or limits its prerogatives nor to canvass alternative formulations of its proper objectives.[12]

By speaking of culture and recreation, this passage points to a final sphere of social life in which Soviet-type states play a much larger role than liberal-democratic ones: the sphere encompassing the production and distribution of knowledge, intellectual and artistic life, and mass information and entertainment. The party-state devotes much organised effort to shaping and determining the things people carry around in their heads, particularly as regards larger questions potentially of great public significance, such as those concerning the causes and consequences of existing social arrangements, the resulting social divisions and the associated interests, the nature and intent of the larger social forces at work in the contemporary world, the broad course of past history and the future direction of the socio-historical process, the definition of what is true, good and beautiful.

Optimally, the party-state expects such matters to be expressly entertained and discussed by people, if at all, only in the light of the official ideology (Marxism-Leninism), as interpreted by the Communist party itself. Thus, it seeks to prevent individuals from working out alternative understandings of those matters and communicating them to one another outside of narrow private circles, and above all from acting collectively upon those understandings. To this end, the party-state jealously guards its own monopolistic control over the sources and media of public discourse; and exercises such monopoly in order to broadcast only ideologically correct understandings of such matters, or arguments concerning them carried out within the framework of the official ideology.

There are two compatible ways of explaining such concerns of the Soviet-type state and appreciating their seriousness. In the first place, they are intended to prevent the emergence within society of autonomous centres of (in the terminology of chapter 1) normative power that would affect the social process by elaborating and putting abroad values and beliefs which people might find authoritative and on the basis of which they might act. Secondly, they are intended to sustain the impression that the Communist party posseses a uniquely meaningful and correct view of the world, validated by the party's past successes in governing the society in question, and is thus entitled to guide its future progress toward greater and greater justice, equality, freedom, peace and wellbeing.

On both counts, it is vital that the essentials of Marxism-Leninism, an account of the party's historic achievements, and a view of its current goals and strategies, should have no rivals as themes, or – even better – as assumptions of public discourse. It is also vital that the party itself should consistently act as an unchallengeable, infallible organ for the authoritative restatement and interpretation of the body of thinking in question, and its leadership should be able to settle decisively, at any given time, controversies concerning the application of that body of thinking to contemporary issues.

Note that this construction of the massive amount of ideological work constantly carried out by the party-state (via the educational system, publishing, the media, the propaganda agencies and ideological activities of the party, etc.) does not assume that all, or even the majority of, individuals find its products meaningful, credible, or for that matter understandable. Much of the point of that work lies, rather, in excluding alternative understandings, accounts and renderings from a public hearing, restricting their elaboration and circulation to the relatively insignificant medium of private conversation, the code of veiled allusion in artistic work, or the precarious channels of joke, gossip or *samizdat*. (As I write, thanks to Soviet *glasnost*, the imbalance between official and unofficial inputs into the opinion-making process seems to be a great deal less sharp than it has been for decades. But a considerable degree of imbalance persists; and, of course, one cannot feel assured that it will not increase again in the near future.)

V

Mode of operation of the party-state

This third theme is more difficult to address than the two previous ones, having to do not with the design of the institutionalised arrangements for exercising political power, nor with the flows of activity originating from that exercise, but with (one might say) more cultural aspects of political experience. For instance, how visible are the agents of the party-state in everyday life? how do they normally deal with the citizenry, with what mixture of imperiousness and respect? how frequently do they threaten or practice violence in those dealings?

Clearly, the answer to these and similar questions is the product, in a given system, of innumerable factors, including some strictly of a historical nature, not directly relevant to the present consideration of the contrast between the liberal-democratic and the Soviet model. To maintain this emphasis, I shall mention only two aspects of my theme, both of which relate directly to points already made above – the close interpenetration between party and state, and the inexistence of a public sphere in Soviet-type systems.

The first point concerns what I would call the attenuated significance of law as a constraint upon state activity. As I have repeatedly emphasised, law – understood as a set of enforceable general commands – is an indispensable technique for organising, directing and controlling state activity. Laws addressed to state organs, however, can leave a greater or lesser margin for discretionary action on the part of individuals manning those organs, or devolve the control over their discretionality more or less widely to technical, as against legal, considerations. And the point is that, when contrasted with liberal-democratic systems, laws in Soviet-type party-states allow much greater discretion to state agents, or more freely refer to non-legal considerations. Another way of phrasing this point utilises a distinction, proposed by an Italian administrative lawyer,[13] between two kinds of legal norms addressed to state organs: 'norms of relation', those acknowledging the legitimate interests of subjects other than the state itself and its organs, and setting boundaries on the activities of the latter in order to safeguard those interests; and 'norms of action', which simply mandate those activities and standardise them in the interest of effectiveness, economy or whatever.

Basically, then, norms can chiefly constrain or chiefly empower state action. In Soviet-type systems, I suggest, they mostly do the latter rather than the former. Even the laws intended to recognise and favour the interests of citizens do not vest these into rights, the violation of which might vitiate the action of authorities; for the latter, rather, they constitute *interna corporis*, internal arrangements, of which citizens have no official cognizance and to which they cannot appeal.

A similar, overlapping characterisation of the significance of law within communist party-states has been proposed by an eminent Australian Sovietologist, T. H. Rigby.[14] Laws, he suggests, may be used to establish two different kinds of state agencies: those intended to apply rules in regulating other subject's activities (a homely example would be a policeman directing traffic) and those directed by law to perform tasks (for example, a detective instructed to identify the perpetrators of a crime). Again, Soviet-type state agencies are primarily of the latter kind.

This may seem a rather too mild way of characterising the relation to law of systems which, chiefly but not exclusively in their Stalinist phases, have often been characterised by massive, brutal, murderous illegality. But it is important to identify those features of party-states which, in my view, are built into their very nature, and are likely to persist even if, and as long as, they seriously pursue the course of socialist legality. For ultimately what, if anything, gives bite to the legal restraints upon state action in liberal-democratic systems, is once more the existence in them of a public sphere, of an actual or virtual plurality of subjects who can legitimately organise to monitor, denounce and oppose authorities which play fast and loose with laws protecting their interests. But – once more – a public sphere does not exist in Soviet-type systems, and it is not at all clear that even a sincere commitment to socialist legality might in itself compensate for that inexistence.

The second aspect of the mode of operation of Soviet-type states I would mention, consists in the constant and overwhelming pressure of political considerations upon administrative activity. This aspect directly reflects the very nature of those states *qua* party-states.

As we have seen, the Communist party – an organisation inherently committed to the formulation and pursuit of political goals – is thoroughly overlapped with the state, which is largely a complex of administrative agencies. This allows the party to shadow those agencies, to remind them forcefully and pressingly (among other things, by intervening in the selection and advancement of their top personnel) of political considerations which they might otherwise lose sight of. Left to themselves, all administrative bodies have characteristic inertial tendencies – respect for precedent, attachment to established working procedures and well-demarcated competences, preference for due deliberation, careful husbanding of resources (beginning with one's energies), avoidance of initiative, buck-passing, red tape, etc. The party systematically counters such tendencies by stressing the urgency of given tasks, by demanding administrators to be flexible in reassessing their priorities, by urging them to confront squarely and energetically unsatisfactory circumstances, by emphasising ideological as against managerial criteria of action.

The party – as administrators are compellingly reminded – embodies a higher order of reason than administrative convenience and continuity. The party's organisational links with the masses, its glorious history, its guardianship of Marxist-Leninist doctrine, the very fact that its highest organs coincide with those of the state, entitle it to bypass and short-circuit, in the name of political commitments, the state's carefully constructed hierarchical arrangements. It can authorise (nay, demand) functionaries to disregard the later consequences of attaching at a moment's notice an absolute priority to certain tasks over all others, of throwing all resources into their pursuit.

It should be noted that productive enterprises, in particular, are politically monitored and goaded not only (as I have already noted) by territorial party authorities, but also by the party units operating within each enterprise – the cells – whose members and leaders are entitled to exercise a kind of guardianship of the party's ultimate sovereignty and of the supremacy of political over all other considerations.

This insistence on political priorities and rationales reflects the peculiar Leninist understanding of politics, with its emphasis on power, on the political elite mobilising and committing the energies of the political rank and file, on the necessity of eliminating or neutralising opposition, foot-dragging and back-talk. It has distinctive, threatening overtones of impatience and imperiousness, of getting things done at all costs. Witness the prevalence in the Soviet Union, in particular, of what is called 'storming' as a way of achieving any large, urgent, non-routine task; the obsessive insistence on the expression 'task'; the distinctively military metaphors abounding in discourse about all political affairs, even civilian ones: 'people and resources are mobilised in "campaigns", and factories, farms, schools, theatres and all other institutions are engaged in a "struggle" for "victory" on their various "fronts". Exemplary performers in any field are "heroes".'[15] This point clearly overlaps with the former one, about the weakness of legal constraints. As a Polish sociologist writes: 'Political decisions are not measured against legal rules, but against their intended effects. There are legal forms which are adjusted to specific political decisions and acts, not vice versa.'[16]

The joint upshot of both points is that the political environment characteristic of Soviet-type states appears, from the evaluative standpoint inspiring my earlier assessment of the modern state in general, highly aberrant and, to put it mildly, unsalubrious. From the same viewpoint, I would make two additional points about the role played in that environment by its dominant feature, the Communist party. One point, to use unashamedly normative language, makes things appear somewhat less bad than suggested so far; and the other makes them appear much worse.

First, the good news. The commandeering, imperious, impatient, arrogantly dogmatic role I have attributed to the party is not all there is to it. For in the Soviet-type system the Communist party is typically also the locus of an intense, demanding form of political participation, of mutual involvement of individuals in talk; it is a place where public affairs of all kinds are continually scrutinised and discussed, information is disseminated, ideological themes are raised and entertained, existent states of things are monitored, the performance of official bodies is criticised.

Of course these processes are activated, controlled and manipulated, at all levels, by the party's higher officials; and of course these constitute, more and more so as one ascends toward higher organisational levels, an exclusive body of privileged, unaccountable oligarchs. Yet it should not be forgotten that the party as a whole may comprise millions of men and women (over 15 million in the case of the CPSU, that is over 7 per cent of the Soviet Union's adult population). These millions, much as they get manipulated and made to jump to their leaders' orders, and motivated as they may in turn be by petty ambition and/or by servility, yet week after week give of their time and their energy to what is, when all is said and done, political activity, focused on public concerns.

In the course of such activity, futhermore, those millions people reach out to and communicate with other millions – with whom they share a work setting, an occupation, a place of residence, leisure or cultural interests – in order to make *them* aware of the party line about those concerns. At peak times – say, in the run-up to a national congress – the party becomes a veritable beehive of incessant activity. True, 99.99 per cent of this activity does no more than provide a sounding board for the decisions of the leadership; but the resulting process of echoing and amplifying the notes issuing from above is lengthy and sustained; it diffuses information and generates awareness; it reaches all corners and crannies of the environing society. And under certain, rare circumstances it may simulate, in however inadequate a fashion, that confrontation of independently formed, openly competing views about policy which (once more) the inexistence of a properly constituted public sphere denies to the population at large.

Now for the bad news. The overt activities of the party are complemented by the diffuse, covert activities of secret police organisations (whose command posts are filled by members of the *nomenklatura*) and of a number of volunteer busybodies and informers. Normally the population are aware that this goes on, and understandably feel compelled to keep to themselves any potentially dangerous knowledge or curiosity about political matters they might have, or share it with others only under very restrictive conditions. They are thus denied opportunities to realise how widely their concerns may be shared, let alone to act upon them in concert with others. The political awareness and sophistication of people at large is thus severely thwarted; ignorance, cynicism and apathy about public affairs flourish, complemented in many people by an intense, sometimes morbid involvement in private concerns, in unrealistic aspirations to and fantasies of escape. These can be seen as responses to the fact that Soviet-type states encounter and indeed engender profound, frustrating problems in the management of their societies; but they are also produced by what is in many ways, to use again expressly evaluative language, a highly unsalubrious political environment.

VI

Nature and prospects of communist party-states

If we now seek a comprehensive characterisation of communist party-states, we can choose from a whole range of conceptual formulas proposed by students and observers.[17] Among these I find most persuasive that suggested by T. H. Rigby, who characterises the Soviet Union, in particular, as a 'mono-organisational society'.

Essentially, Rigby argues, there are three way of controlling the social process, and in particular of coordinating social activities: by means respectively of custom, of contract or of command. (The reader, parenthetically, may see an analogy between this tripartition and that applied in chapter 1 to the notion of social power: normative, economic, political power. There is a further, insufficiently noted analogy between both tripartitions and Weber's one concerning types of stratification units: estate, class, party. But let us continue with Rigby.)

> It is probable that all three modes of coordination can be found to some
> degree in all societies. Nevertheless it does seem that one mode or another
> tends of predominate in most societies; and further, that as societies become
> technologically more developed and more complex, coordination by
> contract and command tends to replace coordination by custom . . .
> Custom-dominated societies will be called *traditional societies*; contract-
> dominated societies will be called *market societies*; the command-
> dominated societies will be called *organizational societies*.[18]

Societies of the last-named kind, however, come in two main ideal-typical varieties: those where organising – that is, the building and operating of coordinated chains of top-down command/obedience relationship – is undertaken autonomously by a plurality of social units, which then relate to one another largely through contracts, on the market; and those where all organising is done by, within, and on behalf of, a single, all-encompassing entity, with the intent of making its control over the social process as comprehensive and effective as possible.

The Soviet Union constitutes an approximation to this second variety, where 'nearly all social activities are run by hierarchies of appointed officials under the direction of a single overall command'.[19] It represents an attempt to treat a huge, increasingly advanced and complex society as a single organisation, receiving all its critical impulses from above, via a single, extensive and imperious command structure, which does not have to reckon with the interests and strategies of any independent social forces – because *there aren't any* independent social forces with which to reckon.

This basic design was coupled, in the lengthy historical phase of Stalinism, with a massive exercise in absolute, ruthless personal tyranny, leading to a situation in which 'there was no sphere of social activity, from retail sales to internal security, and from farming to the arts, which was not directed by a chain of command culminating in Stalin'.[20] But it is not the case that a mono-organisational society as to be run, at the top, by a dictator, or for that matter that such a dictator has to display the ghastly human qualities which Josef Stalin brought to his rule. The basic design of the mono-organisational society can be realised also in a situation such as that of the Soviet Union today. Here, as I see the matter, the supreme leadership belongs not to a single individual, but rather to a small but not inconsiderable number of top oligarchs, committed to collective leadership, who accord one of themselves the role of *primus inter pares*, to be played under considerable constraints. (Reforms under consideration in the Soviet Union in early 1990 might however increase the personal leverage of that *primus*.)

It is important to appreciate that, although both in its premises and even more so in its concrete realisations, this design profoundly contrasts with significant features of the Western historical experience, it also echoes an aspiration toward three, overlapping Western values: the commitment to modernisation; the emphasis on economic achievement, on the mastery of society over nature; and the search for rationality. In this perspective, the construction of a mono-organisational society appears as a way of accelerating economic modernisation and eliminating what is perceived as the source of much irrationality in earlier modernising experiences – the nature of capitalism.

Capitalism entrusts the development of the whole society not to the planned pursuit of collectively agreed (and/or imposed) goals, but to the the uncoordinated interactions between a multiplicity of private enterprises, each seeking to maximise its profit by exploiting the economic power it possesses *vis-à-vis* its labour force. Under these conditions, social development is intrinsically casual (or, in Marxian/Marxist language; spontaneous) and divisive. In the mono-organisational society, instead, social development is intended to become purposive and unitary. For it is, in its entirety, directed and controlled by a political agency – the party-state – which possesses and enacts a comprehensive, infallible blueprint of such development.

There are, alas, enough things wrong with the assumptions thus made as to how to realise the values I have mentioned, to make their realisation most improbable, as the experience of the Soviet Union and of other similar systems shows, these days more clearly than ever before. In the first place, the party-state cannot suppress *all* social division, and thus guard and pursue the interests of a unified society. For its very presence divides society into that part which gathers to itself all political power, and that part over which that power is wielded. Unavoidably, the party-state rules over (the rest of) society, and in this capacity it becomes the self-sufficient holder of imperious interests of its own, which render it an implausible instrument for envisaging and realising those of the larger society. In the second place, the Communist party's claim to possess an intrinsically, uniquely valid vision of the nature and goal of social development, in the light of which it alone can determine a society's correct path toward fulfilling that goal, is a piece of arrogant nonsense. Thirdly, in trying to enforce that claim – as its exclusive possession of the sole form of social power allows it to do – the party-state systematically frustrates, disables and suppresses lively, spontaneous social forces. (Thus, paradoxically, it often creates a social vacuum which offers it futher pretexts to intensify its rule, with yet more damaging effects for the vitality of the social process. And so on – unless the spiral is broken by revolutionary development such as those of 1989.)

I have repeatedly emphasised the political aspects of the third phenomenon; for the inexistence of a public sphere is at the same time a cause and a consequence of the systematic suppression and repression of social forces – a critical aspect, for where only political power exists, forces which cannot express themselves politically are condemned to impotence. As two Polish critics of the East European post-war approach to industrialisation put it, 'the effective realisation of such a process of industrialisation required that all classes and social strata be deprived of the means of defining their interests and fighting for their implementation or in their own defense.[21]

Here, I would like to focus briefly on the economic aspects of that phenomenon. As it turns out, the attempt to rationalise the economic process by entrusting it to the conscious, comprehensive direction of politically activated and empowered planners, rather than to the unplanned interactions between a plurality of competing, self-interested market units, produces at best contradictory results.

Central planning can yield positive outcomes on some counts, if one ignores the colossal human costs with which it has been associated, in particular, in its most massive (and successful) ventures – Soviet industrialisation in the late twenties and thirties, and Soviet reconstruction in the late forties. (After all, as I have pointed out, even Western countries experiment with varieties of central planning in wartime.) But its results are systematically inferior on other counts, and particularly when it comes to securing efficient allocations of the factors of production,[22] to those yielded by a market system – and not just by an ideal market system, but also by those approximations thereto constituted by real capitalist economies. (From the little I understand about such matters, it seems that in purely theoretical terms an out-and-out 'ministry of production'[23] could produce as efficient allocations as an out-and-out market system. But, of the known approximations to the former, the best do not give as good results as the worst approximations to the latter.) In the real world, in conclusion, economic processes function more rationally – and thus yield greater wealth – on the market than under planning.

But this is a threatening conclusion for communist party-states, for they depend for their own legitimacy in the eyes of the citizenry on their ability to promote economic growth, to provide a steady and improving flow of goods and services. It could be suggested that they share that dependency with liberal-democratic states; but, in fact, theirs is even greater, exactly because they, unlike liberal-democratic states, expressly and aggressively take sole charge of the economic process.

In any case, in so far as the Soviet-type state is unable to deliver on economic promises, this threatens it deeply; for, as Harding writes,

> welfare inducements and welfare sanctions constitute its most potent and pervasive weapons of social and political control, and their efficient management is the principal guarantee of its stability. Resort to extensive coercion is not intrinsic to its structure but symptomatic of its [early stages of development] or of a failure of the graduated hierarchy of sanctions available to its mature formation.[24]

But – to phrase sharply what seems to me the greatest contradiction besetting the Soviet-type state – while such a state is committed to economic success, it is doomed to economic failure, at any rate in so far as its economic performance is measured against that of advanced capitalist economies, characterised by the increasing variety of the goods and services they provide via increasingly sophisticated material and organisational technologies.

The seriousness of the contradiction becomes apparent once one reflects that the above clause 'in so far as' does not provide a let-out. For three reasons the Soviet state cannot but compare itself to the leading capitalist economies: because of the fateful connection between industrial-technological capacity and military preparedness; because a society projecting itself (as Soviet society does) as the model for universal social development must at the very least hold its own in terms of economic performance; and because for too long now the Soviet state has sold itself to its citizenry by promising to catch up with and overtake the standard of living of advanced capitalist countries. (The ambiguity of the expression 'for too long' is intentional, for it points up a further contradiction. I mean by it both that the promise has been made for too long *to be believed* by those to whom it is made, and that it has been made for too long *to be surrendered* by those who make it.)

If the argument advanced so far has any validity, a Soviet-type system by its very nature, *qua* mono-organisational society, produces (comparative) economic failure, at any rate when it seeks to promote a more advanced industrial order. To be able effectively to pursue economic success it would have to renounce and subvert its most critical institutional principle – the centrality and supremacy of a single political agency (the party-state) which runs the whole society as a single organisation via relationships of command and subordination. The maintenance of that principle, I have suggested, systematically and inexorably frustrates and suppresses potential social forces, beginning with those which, if left to themselves, might through their market strategies reactivate the economy. On the other hand, if such forces were allowed expression they would sooner or later challenge the exclusion from the social scene of all forms of power except political power. Furthermore, they would compel the loci of political power to open themselves to the monitoring, the criticism, the attempts at influence of a public sphere encompassing a plurality of mutually independent, competing political actors.

Such prospects are, on the face of it, unacceptable to parties claiming and vaunting the inheritance of Lenin's Bolshevik party. Recent events in the Soviet Union, Eastern Europe and China suggest, at any rate to their more conservative elites, the dangerous implausibility of what could be called the Bucharin hypothesis – the idea that the party can promote a revival of decentralised, market economic power, and benefit from the resultant revitalisation of the economy, without seeing its political supremacy challenged. And, of course, the most radical approach to economic reform – the out-and-out restoration of private property in the means of production, of the capitalist employment relationship – remains for the time being unthinkable. Among other reasons, its corollary – the integration of the socialist economies in the world economy – would probably, at any rate in the short-to-medium run, lower the living standards of the working masses, as well as causing extensive unemployment, and other social problems endemic to capitalist countries.

So, 'what is to be done?' Probably the best approach consists in experimenting with less radical forms of decentralisation of economic power, for instance with cooperative property, or with the increased autonomy of managers from planning and party organs. This seems the approach envisaged by Gorbachev's *perestroika*. But, as I have already suggested, its realisations are for the time being few and not particularly considerable and consequential.

It would be foolish to try and forecast what further realisations will be forthcoming. Undoubtedly, what I would personally judge to be Gorbachev's serious commitment to thoroughgoing *perestroika* is meeting fierce resistance from strong and diverse forces. For that resistance does not arise only from the obstinate attachment to power and privilege of the *nomenklatura* personnel, but also from habits ingrained over three generations in the broad mass of the population.

For instance, a serious attempt to approximate market relations would require withdrawing the huge (and thus financially ruinous) subsidies on basic necessities – such as housing, elementary foodstuffs, fuel – and exposing millions to sudden, harsh deprivations. It would entail allowing uneconomically run enterprises to go bankrupt – but there are thousands of those, and again they employ millions.

Furthermore, a functioning market system presupposes that many individuals possess a self-reliance, an ambition to make one's way by one's own wits, a capacity for calculation and risk-taking, an ability to evoke and manage others' efforts, that very few people have had a chance to develop in the Soviet Union, and that almost all others find morally suspicious or indeed repulsive, and would rather see punished than rewarded. Finally, habits of sustained, purposive work have been largely extinguished, in the working masses, by the lack of visible correspondence between one's efforts and one's rewards, and have been widely replaced by a sullen dependency and by a lack of trust in the possibility of serious improvement in one's situation that would generate diffidence even toward the most well-meaning reformers.

Thus, the range of vested interests which can be counted upon to resist thoroughgoing change is vast. Furthermore, even those sections of the population ranged behind the would-be reformers – for instance the intellectual strata, the non-party managerial element – need to be rewarded for their support in the (relatively) short run, or they will lose their confidence in reform and their credit with uncommitted sections. But the short run looks very unpromising, both for objective reasons (you do no achieve a turnaround in the short run in a system as massive and diverse as the Soviet economy) and because the promise of change has aroused excessive, unrealistic expectations.

Meanwhile, the promise of extensive reform has unleashed centrifugal forces – chiefly, the nationalistic aspirations of ethnic groups, sometimes locked together within ethnically mixed territories – which threaten the very existence of the Soviet Union as a multi-national entity. Like its historical predecessor, the Tsarist empire, the Soviet Union may be too vast and ethnically too diverse to remain united otherwise than through the imposition of a strong, highly centralised political framework (and of its corollary, the supremacy of the Russian over all other ethnic components).

The question is, whether the political centre can be divested of some of its prerogatives (particularly those concerning the conduct of economic and of cultural life) without jeopardising also its capacity to impart political guidance to the social process at large and thus to hold the Union together. As they seek to answer that question, the would-be Soviet reformers might discover an unpleasant corollary to a positive answer: the development and the increasing autonomy of forms of social power other than political power, which restrict the scope and the discretion of that power. In the past, Western rulers often found that they could live with those restrictions, but they operated in a historical field where, as I have suggested in chapter 5, the well-established institutional traditions and entrenched social forces characteristic of a strong civil society *imposed* such restrictions upon them.

The contemporary situation in the Soviet Union has no close parallel to these circumstances, and it is for this reason that on so many counts the Gorbachev initiative so reminds the outside observer of the Russian tradition of revolution from above. This can only make one uneasy; for in a situation of stagnation and decay, or indeed one approaching breakdown (for such is the impending prospect of the Soviet economy according to the Soviet leaders themselves), it is tempting to use political power ruthlessly in order to exercise maximum leverage on the society; and whatever feats such use of power may accomplish, it cannot favour the development of something approaching the Western civil society.

Yet the significance of *glasnost* is precisely that it tries to induce at least one aspect of such a development – the emergence of a public sphere. This is important; for if a willingness to experiment with new arrangements is not a sufficient condition for effective change, it is a necessary condition of it. And *glasnost* is in turn necessary to produce that willingness, by awakening the 'institutional imagination' of a society too long locked into a flawed but arrogantly self-assured and rigidly imposed design. However, at the same time it increases expectations and allows the voicing of contrasting, impatient claims, the unavoidable disappointment of most of which is liable to induce a sense of impotence and cynicism. What balance can be established between these conflicting effects of *glasnost* remains to be seen.

10

Contemporary Challenges to the State

At the close of the twentieth century, the prospects of the state appear mixed, both in the liberal-democratic systems and in the party-states. In both, although to a different extent and in different ways, the state performs an utterly central role in the management of social affairs, absorbs and manages a huge amount of societal resources, receives and processes a vast number and variety of demands.[1] In both, however, the ways in which states do these things has for some time been the object of greater concern and criticism than has been usual during much of the state's historical career.

In liberal democracies, in particular, shifts in the electoral fortunes of opposing parties and the associated changes in the composition of governments often modify only marginally the repertories of on-going state action and make only minor kinks in the curves expressing the ever-growing size and diversity of those repertories. For this reason (among others) critical attention has shifted its focus away from the policy preferences of specific parties and coalitions, and toward what has been widely seen as an underlying, bipartisan, inertial tendency of the state to grow. In the same way that the State had been praised by some as the beneficient protagonist of the prosperity of the first 25 years or so since the the end of the Second World War, it was blamed by some for this or that aspect of the phase of (relative) stagnation and disarray that followed.

Furthermore, new problems arose on the horizon of Western societies which, according to many observers, the state was by its very nature ill-equipped to confront. This final chapter will identify some of those problems, as well as a few others, indicating that under contemporary conditions it becomes increasingly difficult to give coherent expression to the institutional mission of the state.

I

The nuclear revolution

Time and again, in the course of the argument so far, we have had to consider aspects of the nature and development of the state expressing the persistent, fateful connection between the state and the phenomenon of war. In this part of the book I connect with the advent of total war the much enlarged role that in the early part of the century the state came to play in the management of the economy and of class relations. And the Russian revolutions of 1917, which had as their long-term outcome the establishment of the first and most durable party-state, were themselves the direct outcome of the disastrous impact of the First World War upon the Tsarist empire.

At the end of the Second World War, with the 'nuclear revolution',[2] the centuries-old connection between war and the state takes an unprecedented, paradoxical turn. Thermonuclear devices are of such breath-taking, terrifying destructiveness, and the related delivery systems have such speed and range of operation, that they cannot be conceived of, let alone made use of, as just another kind of weaponry, merely more effective and lethal than others. When they are in the possession, as they have been since the early fifties, of rival, potentially hostile powers, these cannot consider them as normal instruments of policy, for they can only use them to deter one another from using them and thus visiting horrifying, unbearable destruction upon each other. And it is difficult to conceive a realistic scenario in which such powers would wage war against one another without the logic of armed conflict at some point compelling each to resort to nuclear warfare.

Yet war has ever been the ultimate way of resolving disputes between sovereign entities contending over interests they define as vital – interests of such significance that it made sense, in some kind of rational calculation, for a given state to wage war and risk military defeat rather than renounce its pursuit of those interests and concede the advantage to a rival state. For three reasons the nuclear revolution makes nonsense of such a calculation. First, it replaces risk with certainty; second, it subjects both parties to such certainty; third, it condemns them, if they do wage war, to an outcome of such utter awfulness that it cannot be conceived of as *just* a military defeat. (The formula 'mutual assured destruction', with its telling acronym MAD, neatly conveys all these changes in the nature of war in the nuclear era.) Thus, to the extent that it can no longer be resorted to in the conflicts among great powers, which have the political control over the world as their stake, the mechanism of war, 'the great balancing mechanism' of the modern states system[3] – has become unavailable.

The concrete significance of this phenomenon should not be over-estimated. True, atomic weapons have not been used on human populations since Nagasaki. Yet, it is reckoned, between 1945 and 1985 some 20 million casualties have resulted from about 150 conventional wars.[4] Also, the impossibility of resorting to out-and-out warfare with one another has not kept the two chief nuclear powers, the US and the USSR, from pursuing in other ways their conflicting power interests. Their rivalry has found expression, for instance, in wars by proxy; in attempts to promote subversion within the rival or its client states; above all, in economic competition. For all this, it remains true that since Nagasaki, it has become impossible for the states that matter to wage the war that matters. And this persistent impossibility opens up a number of questions concerning the contemporary prospects and circumstances of the state.

One question is, of course, whether that impossibility will persist. One of the forces sustaining the nuclear armament race has been the stubborn pursuit by both sides of a technological advance allowing it to maintain and increase the certainty of the other's destruction, in the event of a nuclear conflict, while eliminating the certainty of its own, or significantly reducing the amount of destruction it must expect to endure.

Very likely, no nuclear power can realistically expect to hold such a position of advantage to such an extent and long enough to have its own way with another by either threatening or effecting a nuclear attack on it. But – leaving aside that there would be little to say, from the standpoint of human values, for so reinstating what used to be the normal political uses of military superiority in the pre-nuclear era – a redoubtable question is whether top political decision-makers might not *think* their side does enjoy such an advantage, and act on that conviction, whether warranted or not. A further one is whether there may not occur circumstances in the contemporary political environment in which a top decision-maker sufficiently discounts the gravity or the certainty of nuclear destruction for his/her own country to pull whatever nuclear trigger he/she controls – a situation which nuclear proliferation makes less and and less unlikely. The same can be said of another situation, where a nuclear power accidentally fires a nuclear device at another's territory, with localised effects, but in circumstances leading other powers to retaliate in kind.

On all these counts, the fate of the human species and indeed of the earth itself are frighteningly in jeopardy in the nuclear era. This fact inspires, among others, considerations bearing on this book's theme, although they can be barely sketched here. One may suggest, for instance, that although in the nuclear era all-out war has lost whatever rationale it may have previously possessed as the last resort in deciding inter-state disputes, this does not sufficiently secure humanity against its reoccurrence. For, as a Swedish statesman advised his son centuries ago – consider to what insignificant extent the world is governed by reason! Thus, securing humanity requires that states cease to be the main units of the world's political environment, and/or that the states system radically changes, by instutionalising new, peaceable ways of settling significant conflicts between states and for policing their coexistence.[5]

A different line of reasoning concerns the ways in which states are internally affected by what one might call the nuclear interdiction of war. For – to recapitulate – states had long been defined by their ability and perhaps proneness to make war; for centuries they had promoted their own growth by invoking the relationship between military threats and opportunities on the one hand, and fiscal requirements on the other;[6] historically, the military capacity of individuals had constituted the very core of citizenship. Thus, one can presume, the nuclear interdiction of war since 1945 must have affected states deeply.

On the fact of it, a number of facts confirm that presumption. Whoever considers, for instance, the geographical position of Australia, the enormous extension and the absolutely vital demographic and productive significance of its coastline, and the demographic situation of neighbouring countries, cannot but marvel at the ridiculously puny number of armed ships the Australian Navy maintains today. Yet, while the same observation can be applied to all Western states – including Japan – other than the USA and, to a lesser extent, the United Kingdom, it is difficult to say whether this is because of those states' awareness of the nuclear interdiction, or because of their reliance on the United States (via SEATO and NATO or otherwise) for their defence.

In any case, for whatever reason, since the Second World War states in contemporary advanced societies have sought to re-define and re-justify themselves by emphasising their non-military mission, and particularly their ability to sustain and guide economic development and to moderate some of its undesirable effects. As I have indicated, even their rivalries, which the nuclear interdiction of war has kept from eventuating in open enmity, have found expression in (among other things) economic competition.

In principle, one must salute this as a positive development. In my view, at any rate, it is (mostly) A Good Thing that advanced industrial countries (those most likely, after all, to blow up the world should they wage war) have, over the last several decades, set much store by their ability to assist the growth of their respective gross national product, to reduce some of the social strains, economic iniquities and cultural distortion attendant on industrialisation, and to present a model for economic development to other countries. But, as I have repeatedly indicated, this extensive involvement in societal management has had numerous negative side effects (among which I have previously singled out the growing disjunction between policy and democratic – as against bureaucratic – politics). Also, lately it has not been as effective as previously. There are many reasons for this, and some of these will be mentioned in the next section, which considers a second major challenge to the state in the contemporary situation.

II

The crisis of territoriality

Again, we are dealing with phenomena directly affecting the very core of the state as a political entity: not, as in the previous section, its relationship to war, but its relationship to a territory, to a geographically distinct part of the globe, which constitutes the unique physical base and referent of the state's institutional mission, its very body, the ground of its being.

For quite some time this essential territorial reference of the state has been under pressure from a number of phenomena, and this pressure has grown momentously over the last few decades. What is at stake is each state's ability to monitor competently, and to intervene effectively in, a growing range of aspects of social existence, in spite of the fact that such aspects decisively affect the wellbeing of its population, the resources available to the state, and its ability to form and carry out policy.

To adopt an expression that is frequently used in current social science discourse – in an increasingly obvious and intense fashion since the end of the Second World War, the contemporary world is witnessing a process of *globalisation*. That is, a complex of economic, technological, ecological and cultural structures and processes display their effects on the scale of the planet, or at any rate have a radius of action that ignores, or denies relevance to, any given state's territory.

Globalisation has its own specifically political aspects. To remain for a moment on the topic of the last section, we may note again that since the Second World War, two major blocs have been formed. Each bloc has claimed or sought to operate worldwide, and within each, one power has enjoyed unchallengeable military superiority over all others, placing them in a position of military and diplomatic dependency which not long ago would have been deemed incompatible with their claim to constitute independent members of the comity of nations.

This situation is partly the result of what could be called the globalisation of military power. Advanced nuclear weapons systems can indeed operate worldwide, for they can deliver their payloads to any place at all on earth, and do so within a very short time. They are thus capable of making the whole earth uninhabitable, and of threatening the very survival of the human species (among others). You cannot get any more global than that.

There is another, less overt, form of globalisation of military affairs. Some years ago, an author whose name unfortunately I have forgotten spoke of the Bomb, the tank, the sub-machine-gun, as exemplifying the three main kinds of military capacities in the contemporary world. There is a kind of hierarchy of territorial significance associated with the different destructive powers of each of these deadly devices – the first in the hands of superpowers and with the whole world as its radius; the second in the hands of conventional armies, operating at the regional level; the third in the hands of guerrilla fighters, operating chiefly at the local level.

But for some time now, according to some interpretations, the phenomenon of international terrorism has subverted this hierarchy. It operates with relatively little destructive power, yet its radius of action is potentially worldwide, and characteristically it results from and seeks to affect conflicts of more than regional significance – say, the Middle Eastern question. A new kind of warfare is being waged by political-strategic centres which possess only a minimal, covert and mobile territorial base (on the basis of the hospitality tendered them by this or that state), and yet which definitely seem to operate on the global stage, extending their threat, say, to the worldwide network of communication and transport managed by *all* airlines. Time and again, states, which are essentially regional powers, have appeared to be relatively defenceless against this threat.

To return to that trio of weapons, the Bomb is the distinctive military resource of super-states; the tank that of the other states; the sub-machine-gun that of forces seeking to subvert a given state's regime or leadership. But the explosive timed to go off on a cruising aircraft, the highjacking of an airliner, the bomb by means of which an Armenian terrorist group blows up a Turkish consulate in France, Australia or Switzerland – these military actions have only an accidental relationship to the state territory within which they are planned or executed, and do not necessarily express enmities having their source or their target in any given state.

But the aspects of the globalisation process which are of interest here are not only those of a political nature; and by considering other aspects our argument may refer to the notion, raised briefly at the beginning of this book, of a plurality of forms of social power.

Unavoidably one thinks first of all of the economic sphere. This sphere has recently witnessed a remarkable acceleration, widening and intensification of the interdependencies generated already for centuries by the world market. Furthermore – and this is the significant point for our argument here – these interdependencies are now, to a much greater extent than before, expressly established and purposefully managed by centres of economic power of such magnitude that they transcend and override (or can even determine) the political activities of individual states or even coalitions of states.

The key units of the contemporary economy are international corporations which operate in fact on a global scale, and whose structure and modes of operation minimise both the interference of states with their strategies of investment and the states' control over the accumulation and deployment of their resources. They operate plants in different parts of the world, and can vary the pattern in which the outputs of those plants complement or replace one another in a given final product. They can thus take advantage of the fiscal and development policies which states pursue in order to compete with one another and also frustrate the defensive strategies of states and unions.

Often these corporations operate telecommunication systems coupling satellites and computers, which practically abolish distance in transmitting information. This technology not only constitutes the backbone of their worldwide managerial structures, it also conveys enormous flows of financial resources, which heavily condition the national economies and the states' economic policies. In spite of this no state can effectively monitor and control those flows, even through its central bank (always in any case a somewhat refractory instrument of state policy). These corporations, furthermore, settle their differences through mediation and arbitration arrangements of their own making, which again makes them jurisdictionally independent of states, or for that matter of the arrangements states have evolved for the settlement of international disputes.

In these ways and others, many significant centres of economic power in the contemporary world, including many of those at the leading edge of technological innovation and possessing the largest resources, have loosened their relationship to individual states. They have become for many critical purposes extraterritorial in their constitution, in their activities and in the logic of their operations. They can, to a significant extent, play various states off against one another in seeking advantageous locations for their activities, and thus maintain their independence of each.

These same units, furthermore, are the protagonists of other more or less frontier-transcending processes which play an increasing part, across the world, in shaping people's mental lives, their preferences and fantasies, their sense of what is possible or impossible, true or false, right or wrong, worthy or unworthy, desirable or undesirable.

Because – among other reasons – the social and material technology required for purposefully managing and directing these processes is very expensive, international corporations tend to play a key role in them. By creating and broadcasting a continuous flow of sparkling, captivating imagery, they can to an extent determine the answers to three critical, overlapping questions: what do people know, or think they know? how are people entertained? how do people choose to expend their own resources (from time to money to attention to moral commitment)? And the corporations' impact on those answers tends to be, if not often global, then generally transnational.

To such an extent, in the contemporary West, has the conscious production of what is called in French *l'imaginaire* become a business, that one is tempted to conclude that, whether within or across countries, the centres of economic power have today entirely subjugated to themselves what we have earlier called normative power, that is the form of social power resting on somebody's control over others' beliefs and values. Culture-shaping processes, from this point of view, have become a significant but subordinate part of economic ones in the West; and a similar argument could be made for their subordination, in the Soviet system and in other one-party regimes, to the logic of political power.

But such a conclusion, I would argue, is a hasty one. Critical cultural processes continue to unfold, in the contemporary world, with considerable autonomy from both economic and political power; and also these processes challenge the territoriality intrinsic to the state. I have in mind primarily two very different sets of processes: on the one hand those pertaining to the production and diffusion of scientific knowledge, which are increasingly the concern of international networks of researchers; on the other, those which guard, and occasionally modify, the legacies of world visions, of values, practices, understandings of the meaning of existence for the individual and of the identity and destiny of groups, which the great eras of religious prophecy of the past have bequeathed to the modern world.

One can legitimately raise strong doubts concerning the effective autonomy of the contemporary 'scientific estate', both in the West and in the Soviet system. Governments and business forces seem to agree that science is too important to be left to the scientists. In particular, advanced, state-of-the-art research is often enormously costly, and when successful it produces knowledge which is critical for military and industrial innovation. Thus its practitioners have no choice but to accept political and economic constraints upon the inner dynamic of their vocation. For all that, there *is* such an inner dynamic, resting ultimately on the power of the mind to challenge and transcend established images of reality, and to compel reasoned agreement around new ones. And, ever since its beginnings, modern science has periodically reasserted its transnational identity, its vocation for the disinterested pursuit of truth, and occasionally sought to limit the use and abuse of its findings for political and economic advantage. Finally, in many fields contemporary scientists semi-autonomously manage a structure of communication and (to a lesser extent) a flow of rewards of their own making, and are in that sense extraterritorial.

In any case, perhaps a stronger case for the autonomy of cultural processes, to the effect that centres of normative power may persist or indeed emerge anew in the contemporary world, can be grounded on the second set of phenomena. The best example of these is the rise of Islamic fundamentalism; but some aspects of the revival of Christian fundamentalism, and of other contemporary reappraisals of the Christian message, can be considered as more attenuated instances of the same process. In both these cases, albeit to a different extent, religious vision has inspired large numbers of people to define themselves, to identify their interests, in ways which go counter to the spirit of the age, or indeed seek to re-form that spirit, to generate new collective identities. These often cut across national and territorial boundaries, and to that extent again jeopardise the states' jealous insistence that all significant commonalities and routine frameworks of interaction be inscribed within their own frontiers.

Whether or not one attributes the phenomena discussed so far in this section to forms of social power other than the political, a final set of globalisation processes, which again affects the state's territoriality, arises from a realm of phenomena which the social sciences have not yet learned to address competently – the realm of the interaction between the human species and the rest of nature, and in particular what is commonly called the ecological question.

This question concerns the extent to which the products, intentional or unintentional, of the activities of human populations, which necessarily make use of natural resources, and thus and otherwise affect the environment, are overstraining or damaging that environment's capacity to reproduce itself, to endure as a viable biological setting for those very activities, and as a store of resources upon which they can safely continue to draw. As is well known, there are serious grounds of doubting that, even today, human populations are in a stable, sustainable equilibrium with their environment and that such equilibrium can be maintained if human populations go on expanding and raising their standard of living at the current rate.

In the framework of our theme here, the point of these concerns is that a state's territory may no longer be, if it ever was, a framework appropriate for identifying, moderating or suppressing the strains imposed on the natural environment by the ongoing production and consumption activities of its population and those of other states. For territories (including territorial waters) have become vulnerable to the damaging environmental effects of what goes on outside them, as a product or by-product of other populations' activities. Those effects are often truly global, although the connections between their ultimate source and their localised manifestations may be numerous and hard to trace.

In any case, even when those connections can be traced, it may be the case that no state has the faculties and facilities required to deactivate them and keep them from transmitting damage. Basically, because it is politically ordered on the basis of territorially bounded states, the globe lacks the political structures necessary to confront the biological threats represented by environmental depredation, and by other ecological processes which ignore state boundaries – best exemplified by the Chernobyl disaster, acid rain, the pollution of the oceans, and the rapid diffusion of AIDS, or for that matter the international drug traffic, which is primarily a business, but on some counts can be seen as a worldwide epidemic.

In turn, the most sophisticated and effective political structures the globe possesses, those embodied in states, are bypassed and deprived of relevance by those processes. At best, states operate downstream from them, and do not effectively attack at source the problems they cause. At worst, it is actually state undertakings that directly cause the damage – as, again, with the Chernobyl disaster or (less dramatically) with a state's decision to build new highways in order to accommodate private car traffic and foster its growth instead of strengthening the public transportation system. More widely, to the extent that states have become hooked on economic development, or cannot withstand economic blackmail on the part of their business elites or international corporations, governments may be unwilling to attack the ecological problems at their source, or may simply seek to divert their effects toward the territory of other states.

To sum up the argument in this section: the notion of society as normally used in sociological argument reflects historically distinctive circumstances, associated with the advent of modernity.[7] Here the great majority of the significant social, economic and cultural processes go on within territorially bounded units, each hosting a population which tends to define itself as a nation, and each politically managed by a state. Activities crossing the boundaries between states are relatively insignificant, largely constituting a spillover from those carried out within states, and are relatively easily handled politically via the interactions of states. In these circumstances one can speak of a 'world society' only in a relatively weak sense of the term. Today, however, such a society exists in a much stronger sense, being held together by a multitude of processes – economic, cultural, ecological – which are intrinsically, not occasionally and marginally, transnational.[8] This contemporary world society cannot be meaningfully understood – nor can it be effectively regulated – as if it constituted only the sum total of those activities originating within states and which states can control as between themselves. And since the states are still *the* political protagonists of the contemporary world, this means that an increasingly massive, rapid and complex flow of diverse, highly significant, potentially damaging processes crisscrossing that world cannot, to a sufficient extent, be politically managed.

III

The threats to unity and the displacement of rationality

As I have stressed, both the state's connection with war and its territoriality are intrinsic to its very nature as a political entity, and in that sense the contemporary phenomena affecting them could be said to threaten the *hard* aspects of its institutional identity. Other phenomena could then be said to affect some *soft* aspects of it, that is, the more culturally laden – and more specifically modern – ways in which the state defines and justifies itself. Here the focus must be on a state's internal activities; for it is chiefly the manner in which a state manages politically its own territorially bounded society that makes it historically distinctive.

A number of aspects of the contemporary situation have eroded two characteristics of the state which had earlier established its distinctiveness – and its superiority – as a form of institutionalised political power centre: unity and rationality.[9] There is considerable conceptual overlap between these two expressions, and many of the concrete phenomena relevant to one bear also on the other. But they differ enough to warrant considering them separately. This can be done very briefly, for most of those phenomena have already been considered in previous chapters.

Unity characterises primarily the state's structure, designed to connect systematically all social units engaged in political activities within the territory to a single centre. In that design, the centre exercises supreme political initiative, and activates and controls all those other units, treating them as components in a complex division of political labour, which it unitarily ordains and monitors.

Rationality characterises primarily the state's mode of operation. In the state, *arbitrium* and the appeal to tradition, which had long been the primary ways in which the conduct of rulers had been oriented and justified, are to be supplanted by purposeful, reflexively articulated choice between rationally assessed alternatives of action.

To begin with unity – and to limit ourselves, once more, to liberal-democratic states – one can see that several twentieth-century developments have seriously compromised this presumed feature and virtue of the state's structure. As I said much earlier in the book, it has become totally unrealistic, in particular, to conceive of the state as making up 'an organisation', as suggested in the definition by Tilly which we considered in the second chapter. Even if we consider just a state's administrative apparatus, we must today think of it as making up instead a vast, diverse, complex organisational environment.[10] The units of this are themselves discrete, largely autonomous organisations. These are strongly insulated from effective guidance and supervision on the part of higher-level units, and routinely engage in competition among themselves, or form coalitions with one another in order to evade and resist the feeble attempts of those higher-level units effectively to perform their official guiding and supervising role.

This loss of unity among the administrative components of the state's structure is due not only to their proliferation and diversification, and to the attendant, ever-growing distance between them and the purported centre of unitary initiative and control. It also flows from the fact that many administrative units, as I have already pointed out, establish close, privileged relationships with organised social interests, or that these, in turn, seek to use administrative units as their own bridgeheads within the state apparatus.

These two phenomena, which sometimes occur together, constitute routes to what is called neo-corporativism – an expression (with several variants) which implicitly points to a tendency for contemporary state structures to regress toward political arrangements similar to those preceding the emergence or the maturity of the state. For the essence of medieval and *ancien régime* corporativism had always been to parcel out political power among relatively autonomous power centres, expressing and advancing the distinctive and conflicting interests of different sections of the population. The same contention is present, even more explicitly, in the recurrent use of feudal terminology – particularly the expression fiefdom – to characterise, on the one hand, the extent to which state agencies have become isolated from and competitive toward one another, and on the other, the usurpation of public prerogatives by centres of private (particularly economic) power.

In the original constitutional design of most liberal democracies, a legislative, representative body (often composed of two chambers) would counter those feudal tendencies of the administrative apparatus by initiating, authorising and monitoring all state action. But this arrangement, whereby the legislature safeguarded the unity of the apparatus, progressively failed on both sides of the relationship.

On the one hand, as we have already seen, the ever-growing size and complexity of the apparatus, and the increasingly diverse content of its tasks, made it impossible for its operations to be effectively monitored and controlled by the legislature. On the other hand, the increasing constitutional significance of organised parties progressively deprived the legislative bodies of their autonomy.

The great issue became, what party, or what party coalition, controlled the legislature? As this expression suggests, the legislature itself has become a medium through which parties or party coalitions process their own policy initiatives by mustering their own elected members; it no longer constitutes a forum where open-ended debate over the opinions entertained by single members could produce contingent, previously un-programmed decisions.

On two counts the massive, overwhelming presence in the parliamentary arena of organised parties makes it an implausible site for a unified, comprehensive, authoritative overview of the state's resources and activities. First, particularly in two-party systems, each party uses whatever transitory or durable electoral and parliamentary superiority it possesses as a means to advance its own cause, and particularly to secure for its leaders and followers privileged access to governmental positions and to the many advantages they can confer. Second, particularly in multi-party systems, the leading bodies of all parties, or at any rate of all larger ones, share an interest in handling their coalition arrangements, the resulting policies and the distribution of the spoils, outside the parliamentary arena, and thus sheltered from the scrutiny of public opinion. Both each party's single-minded pursuit of its own advantage, and the conspiracy among several parties in jointly increasing the discretion of the respective elites, end up pre-empting the realm of decision originally assigned to the legislative bodies, and denying them autonomy and significance as centres of unitary political initiative and control.

Structured originally (but alas not permanently) as a unitary system, the state was also supposed to rationalise the social process, to adopt and follow intrinsically valid criteria in performing the political functions which had become its exclusive prerogative. Not for nothing is the great European debate about *ratio status* (*raison d'état*) largely coeval with the diffusion of the term 'state' itself and its equivalent in various European languages. But the upshot of that debate was too limited in its scope: it consisted, essentially, in the negative conclusion that a ruler might have to disregard the dictates of religion and morality in pursuing the realm's greatness and security; positively, it saw too exclusively the ruler's personal qualities of leadership (his *virtú*, in Machiavellian vocabulary) as the source of the rationality to be applied to that pursuit.

As the institutionalisation of political power advanced, and the political enterprise became more diverse and continuous, the rationality which was to orient it had to seek another source, less personal, more public, more accessible to a plurality of state agents and more capable of being systematically acted upon by them. As I see the matter, this search found four successive solutions to the problem of whence the state would derive the criteria that were to rationalise its activity – successive, because while each solution to an extent was manifested in distinctive, significant aspects and phases of the state-building process, each in the course of events became less plausible, and another had to be found.

The first solution was associated primarily with the absolutist era, and articulated in particularly sophisticated manner in the German territories: it considered law to be the chief source of the state's rationality. Knowledge of the laws and mastery of juridical method were the principal qualifications allowing state agents, at all levels, to formulate and apply correct answers to most problems arising in political practice. The formation of laws would be the prime expression of sovereignty, and could draw inspiration from rational legal principles, embodying the dictates of God and/or of Nature themselves. The totality of the laws valid in a given state, furthermore, made up a single, coherent system, and as such guaranteed in turn the unity of the state.

This view of law, and the reliance upon it for making the state's activity rational, has been thoroughly discredited since the time in which it originated. It has become difficult for us even to comprehend to what extent, for a few generations of European intellectuals and state-makers in the eighteenth century, law constituted the form of universally valid knowledge *par excellence*. States still frame and apply laws, but even jurists have given up the pretence that these laws form, in any reasonably useful sense of the term, a system. In the public mind, most laws do not appear to express any kind of intrinsically valid rationality, but rather to embody one sectional interest which has gained an advantage over contrasting ones purely through its superior capacity for influence and pressure.

For a time, when confidence in the law as an intrinsically rational system had waned, the reference to laws could still be seen as a plausible way of rationalising the day-to-day operations of the state (personally, I still consider it widely plausible for that purpose) while acknowledging that it could not address the prior problem of what laws should be framed and more generally what policies the state should pursue. What rationality, then, could preside over these decisions? The answer to this question associated with the liberal phase of state-making acknowledges that those decisions are a matter of opinion, rather than of established knowledge; but entrusts the choice between competing opinions to an open-ended process of discussion, of discursive confrontation among those holding them.[11] The key to a rationally operating state is an enlightened, informed, reasoning public, whose every member is free to address others in order to form his/her own opinion and to influence theirs. This process, particularly when it culminates in various bodies of opinion competing for the suffrage of the members of a wider public, produces in the end – via the subsequent decisions of elected representatives – rational inputs into the formation of policy, and, once policy is formed, legal rationality takes over.

Once more, this was historically a significant answer, but not lastingly so. It rested on the assumption that rational political discourse could only be carried out among a minority of a country's adult male population, qualified for sustaining it by its possessions and education – an arrogant assumption to begin with, and in any case one subsequently made irrelevant by the entry of the masses into politics, and by the attendant development of organised parties, with consequences which I have already mentioned for the nature of the parliamentary process.

Today, furthermore, the notion that an open-ended, discursive confrontation between contrasting political opinions would necessarily yield a rational choice between the related policy options has become as implausible as the notion of a unitary, rational legal system. As I have already noted, the overlapping activities of informing, entertaining and persuading mass publics have become big business, and the process of opinion formation has been taken over by organised interests and by their agencies specialising in manipulation. Too often, even in the context of electoral campaigns, the significant issues confronting the polity are not even identified, let alone discussed with sufficient clarity to allow the public to make up its own collective mind about them: instead, campaigns concentrate on the so-called personalities of leaders.

A third solution to the problem of how to make state action rational can be seen in a certain construction of the process of democratisation that we may label cybernetic.[12] The essence of that process lies in the extent to which the state opens itself at all levels to inputs of demand and support on the part of the population, so that its action can attend to the population's multiple, varying interests and preferences. In order to do so, the state multiplies its organisational articulations throughout society, each of them constituting both a listening post and a proximate source of authoritative guidance, assistance and discipline. In this view, what makes state action rational is its responsiveness to social needs, rather than its accountability to public opinion.

There is a great deal to be said for this view, which is to an extent embodied in the development of the welfare state. If what I have earlier called the nuclear interdiction of war threatens the most ancient justification for the state's very existence, this notion of what could be called a serviceable state suggests an alternative, down-to-earth, secular understanding of the state's institutional mission. However, the increasing complexity of advanced industrial societies makes it implausible to expect much rationality from a state operating according to that understanding. Social demands are too multiple, varying, impatient and contradictory; a state effectively opening itself to them can develop no coherent policy. Its resources are liable to be overstrained and dispersed; its several agencies form cosy alliances with sectional interests, or alternatively, manipulate these in order to secure their own autonomy in respect of both any given interest and the political centre.

A fourth solution to our problem has relatively ancient roots in some aspects of Enlightenment thinking about public affairs, but has periodically reappeared during subsequent times, and enjoyed a particularly intense revival after the Second World War. In this solution, which could be called technocratic, only science can reliably provide rational inputs into the policy-making process.[13]

Once the overriding goal of this process is identified with the promotion of economic development, one can leave largely to staffs of experts the questions of how best to secure it, minimise the attendant social and environmental strains, distribute its burdens and advantages, manage its promotion. Those staffs employ the new techniques of economic planning, social accounting and forecasting, analytical policy-making and so forth, and transmit the results of their inquiries to the agencies to which they are attached. The task of politicians is to generate consensus around the policies those results identify as optimal, and whose pursuit is thus intrinsically rational, whether or not the public (or, for that matter, the politicians themselves) understand how those policies are determined.

More widely, bodies of sophisticated professional knowledge are increasingly drawn upon in the selection and training of state personnel, and routinely guide their activities, imparting an intrinsically rational orientation to the operation of the agencies to which they belong.

Once more, the technocratic solution has become embodied in valuable aspects of the structure and activity of contemporary liberal-democratic states. For instance, it has – in some more than in others – moderated the previous exclusive reliance on law as opposed to other sources of knowledge and forms of reasoning about the circumstances, the objectives and the consequences of public action. It has created a livelier interchange between the world of science (including the social sciences) and that of politics, and reduced the politicians' reliance on partisan considerations or on bodies of superannuated ideological discourse.

But one may well doubt whether a thoroughgoing rationalisation of state action has resulted from these and related technocratic developments. Basically, our scientific knowledge of the social environment, and of its interaction with other environments (the natural and the psychological ones in particular) is simply not advanced enough to offer policy-makers (and their staffers) a reliable basis on which to operate. For one thing, those bodies of relatively well-established knowledge that exist are too complex, abstract and disparate to allow much meaningful communication between their practitioners and the policy-makers, let alone wider publics.

Given this, the appeal to the authority of science in justifying policy choices is, in many cases, unwarranted, and sometimes constitutes a cover for otherwise formed, intrinsically controversial preferences. After all, the enterprise of science itself, even in the natural field, is being carried out today under the auspices of powerful political and socio-economic interests; and many of its leaders, even though they may have emerged through their professional accomplishments, often can perform their leadership role in the public world only by seeking to be coopted among other social elites, and by joining one or the other of the alignments they form. This is all the more so in the social science fields, where technocratic ideas are more openly and aggressively entertained and promoted, and where mostly they are less tenable. (As a provocative question goes: '*whose* social scientist are you?')

Furthermore, even where the claims of decision-makers and their advisers to the possession of significant policy-relevant expertise are better grounded, they often implicitly serve to deny a say to mere citizens, in spite of the fact that the policies in question often presuppose moral preferences which every citizen, as such, is perfectly qualified to entertain and entitled to express. Thus – to echo an argument developed earlier – the appeal to technocratic rationalisation of state action becomes a factor in the contemporary uncoupling of *policy* from democratic *politics*.[14]

In any case, over the last two decades, the expectations (hopeful or fearful) concerning that form of rationalisation have been considerably reduced. Consider, for instance, to what extent the policy undertakings, both military and civilian, hatched by the Kennedy and Johnson state planners have failed, or the international crisis of Keynesian economic policy. Such developments have, if not shown the technocratic emperor to be naked, then considerably torn his clothes.

IV

And yet . . . and yet . . .

Thus far this chapter has summarised a number of arguments (most of them much more extensively developed in a large body of literature) to the effect that in the contemporary situation the state is undergoing a serious crisis. Let us recapitulate.

The basic phenomenon of war, which has constituted a fundamental *raison d'être* for the state throughout its historical career, is currently placed under an interdiction by the very nature of nuclear armaments, at any rate as concerns, to repeat my earlier statement, the war that matters between the states that matter.

The territory, which has always constituted the essential physical basis of the state's institutional mission, is increasingly traversed or bypassed by vital economic and cultural processes and affected by ecological phenomena which are intrinsically trans-territorial. World society is, day by day, acquiring a new, compelling reality, via a complex of systemic interactions and equilibria which the state cannot effectively survey and regulate.

Organisational developments internal to the state compromise its claim to constitute a unitary set of political arrangements. Powerful administrative units engage with one another in games of bureaucratic politics, which far from being restrained by political directives, dictate their content. Representative political institutions, supposedly central to the operation of the state as a whole, lose their autonomy *vis-à-vis* parties, which both compete with one another for their control and conspire with one another to prevent them from effectively monitoring and guiding the political process.

Finally, the institutional formulas with which the state has experimented over the last few centuries in order to impart rationality to its activities, have successively failed to deliver on their promise.

Persuasive as these arguments may be, one should not exaggerate the extent to which they imply that the state phenomenon has run its course and outlived whatever social justification it might have had in the past. After all, as a great sociologist once wrote to me, 'the visible, i.e. institutional aspect of society is *always* decaying' – and the state's massive visibility makes it particularly liable to exhibit flaws and failures which attract disproportionate attention on the part of its critics and opponents.

Furthermore, some of the points developed above may overstate the extent to which the state is in crisis. Take the last argument, to the effect that successive answers to the problem of how to rationalise state activity have successively failed. They have, but each of them represented an approach which has lasting significance, both because of its intrinsic merit and because some of the related arrangements are still to a certain extent in operation. For instance, the persistent import of the absolutist project to rationalise state operations by means of laws is that today state agents are still under an obligation to cite the legal principles and rules justifying most of their activities. The persistent product of the liberal rationalising strategy of subjecting divergent opinions and policy options to public controversy is that even now most state policies, even when not decided in public, must exhibit their contents and document their results through publicly accessible documents; and so forth. Although individually all these rationalising projects have had little success, together their institutional legacies to the contemporary state constitute a powerful restraint upon *arbitrium*, and miscreant politicians and administrators often pay them a backhanded compliment by going out of their way to avoid been *seen* to violate them.

Previous sections of this chapter may also have given the reader the impression that states are wholly inert and passive in the face of phenomena that, arguably, threaten the premises of their existence, for example, the increasing globalisation of economic processes. Most of them, indeed, may be inert and passive, but they need not be. For instance, inter-state arrangements can and do moderate the effects of the mobility of capital and of other economic resources, and/or establish wider jurisdictional frameworks within which states can jointly monitor and control the activities of multinational corporations, or for that matter the flow of employee labour between countries.

Having thus discounted some unwarranted readings of the considerations presented above, let us return to a paradox stated at the beginning of the chapter. The contemporary situation seems to pose a number of serious threats to the institutional identity of the state. Yet, at the same time, the state, even in liberal democracies, is systematically increasing the number and the scope of its activities.

One can also remark that, while the state seems to be undergoing something of a crisis in the countries both of the West and of the Soviet system, for decades now in other parts of the world powerful social forces and political movements have been struggling to establish states, to institutionalise state-like arrangements for the performance of political activities. In a sense this is a further globalisation process, successful to the extent that today only a very few, marginal portions of the earth – and a decreasing part of the oceans – find themselves outside the jurisdiction of some state.

In this book, I have chosen not to discuss this phenomenon – the spread of the state system to parts of the globe previously ruled through non-state arrangements – because I lack familiarity with the form it takes in those parts of the world, but also, to an extent, because of a feeling that *si duo faciunt idem, non est idem*, the same thing done by two different parties is never quite the same thing. I have difficulty enough comprehending and conveying the reality of the state's presence and activity in one-party regimes of the Soviet bloc's industrial societies; to comprehend and convey what 'the state' is really like in Nigeria, or Thailand or even Honduras, is beyond my ken. This, I repeat, not only on account of my lack of relevant knowledge, but, furthermore, on account of a West-centric feeling that the notions themselves of state and of the states system still bear a relationship, however remote, to cultural assumptions originally unique to Western Christianity,[15] which the newer states of Africa and Asia cannot realistically be expected to share.

For all that, it remains true that the State has been aggressively globalised, since the Second World War, becoming the dominant form of institutionalised political power. And this phenomenon, I repeat, stands in a paradoxical relationship to all those pointing to a crisis of the state in the West.

To return, then, to Western liberal democracies – what pragmatic conclusions may one draw from the many symptoms of that crisis? Do these authorise the view that the state should retreat and retrench?

This is not the place to address those questions; I am, after all, trying to write a social science book, not a political scenario nor a tract for the times. But I have stretched the conventional boundaries of social science in an earlier chapter, to the extent of raising the question of whether the development of the state should be considered to have been A Good Thing, and I shall stretch them once more to the extent of indicating again my own feelings about those questions.

I say 'again' because those feelings are probably apparent from earlier chapters, and have been echoed in this one. I find much that is wasteful and dangerous about the state's current operations and its continuing growth. But a great deal of this, in my view, results from the growing disconnection between the state and politics, or rather from the neutral-isation of democratic politics and its replacement by bureaucratic politics, neo-corporatist politics, invisible politics. If that disconnection can be repaired, that might in turn remedy some of the disturbing aspects of today's relationship between state and society.

The alternative of arresting the state's development, or indeed 'rolling back' the state, seems to me not only difficult to realise but also intrin-sically unpromising. For into the social vacuum left by retreating political power would immediately rush other forms of social power, particularly those huge agglomerations of private economic power, the great business corporations.

These have considerable past human attainments to their credit, at any rate as far as the Western countries (and Japan) where they still have their main bases of operation are concerned. But their record is not unmixed – witness, for instance, their impact on the environment.

Furthermore, they have largely subordinated to themselves, by turning it into big business, the production and circulation of cultural goods and services; and, as both sponsors and prime beneficiaries of scientific advance, they control to a disturbing extent, and thus effectively privatise, the production and distribution of an intrinsically public good, human knowledge. In fact, one may argue, they have done a very good job of guiding and putting to their own use the development and the strategies of the state itself, although in these particular operations they sometimes have had as junior partners the unions and other minor centres of economic power.

A major reason for doubting the feasibility of a major retrenchment of the state is that, as I have already pointed out, modern economies require complex, expensive and sophisticated infrastructures which can only be provided by the state.

On account of the utter centrality of economic processes to contemporary social life at large, it seems to me absurd to expect the state to refrain from monitoring, regulating and intervening in those processes. The notion that if it persists in doing those things, the state would unavoidably do grievous damage to that unique device, the market, irreparably robbing it of its wondrous virtues, is nonsense. Real markets seem to preserve those virtues to a remarkable extent, in spite of the many and diverse ways, not of the state's making, in which they differ from the ideal market – in spite, chiefly, of the formation of oligopolies, or of the extent to which major corporations no longer depend on the market for their finances or for setting the prices of their products. In the light of this, I see no compelling reason why all and only the state's attempts to monitor, regulate and intervene in real markets should necessarily threaten those virtues.

The problem is to identify *which* of the ways the state monitors, regulates, and intervenes in real markets do *what* damage if any, and should, if that damage is excessive, be abandoned. One should mistrust any doctrinal, conclusive solutions to that problem. For instance, there is a great deal of justified consensus, today, to the effect that state ownership and management of business firms is one of the most wasteful forms of state intervention. Yet only a few decades ago some large industrial holding companies in which the Italian state was the majority stockholder played a major, positive role in promoting the country's industrial modernisation.

A further consideration is that states should not decide their economic policies (let alone other policies) with an eye only to their economic effects. Even policies inflicting some degree of damage to the integrity and efficiency of market processes might conceivably be justified in the light of other values they protect and promote. In particular, through their policies which implement the principle of citizenship, states constitute today the major sources and symbols of commonalities which encompass many people and extend over several generations. Thus, to arrest the dynamic of that principle would diminish the variety of a society's institutionally sanctioned affiliations and modes of conduct. In a more and more unreservedly marketised society, individuals would be left to regard each other solely, at best, as diffident, arm's-length cooperators or puny components in – or insignificant opponents of – this or that corporate giant.[16]

Opposing the facile formulas of anti-statism does not entail endorsing the present trends in state-society relations. What is required are more discriminating processes for selecting state policies, which would complement and correct – eliminating them is impossible – the now prevailing processes: bureaucratic politics, neo-corporatist collusion, the calculation of narrow, partisan advantage, the overriding priority assigned to business interests.[17] My own preference (repeatedly foreshadowed throughout this book) is for processes involving, and resting upon, the reactivation of the public sphere, the encouragement of open debate about public issues, the fostering of citizens' awareness, involvement, articulateness.

Again, this is not the place to justify at length this preference or to specify how it could be pursued. But, lest it be considered to be *exclusively* what it *largely* is – a wishful aspiration, fondly entertained against much evidence of its impracticality – I shall indicate very briefly one aspect of it, which is relatively concrete and feasible. It concerns the most powerful contemporary mass medium, television. My argument is that perfectly legitimate and feasible state policies could turn television into, among other things, an instrument for rendering the citizenry, as I have said, aware, involved, articulate; and that only the state's unwillingness to challenge powerful vested interests makes television, instead, a powerful means for keeping it unaware, uninvolved, inarticulate.

Television broadcasting systems, at any rate as far as they operate within a given state's territory, are intrinsically subject to state regulation. The wavelengths on which they operate must be assigned to them by some kind of public authority; and since generally anybody who owns a set can freely access what is being broadcast, it is a matter of public policy whether those systems are to be financed from advertising revenues or from some kind of publicly enforced fee system. Thus, the ways in which they operate can in principle be restricted and controlled by the state or some other political body. Such restrictions and controls can in turn – again, as a matter of policy – either encourage or discourage the use of broadcasting systems also to inform the public about public affairs, to generate an audience for political controversy, to (again) render the citizenry aware, involved, articulate. It is thus as a matter of policy that in three countries I know something about these possibilities are not fulfilled, and television does not begin to make the enormous contribution it could make to (re)generating a liberal-democratic public sphere.

In the United States, the necessity for candidates to public office to buy from TV (and radio) stations almost all of the viewing (and listening) time these make available for political broadcasting, even during elections, has a number of deprecable consequences. Candidates must invest almost all their energies to seeking from individuals and organisations financial contributions with which to buy TV (and radio) time. They are thus compelled to place themselves under obligations to large and diverse sets of sectional interests – obligations to be redeemed by their future policies or at least by their earnest attempt to influence the policies sponsored by their more successful competitors. (In late 1989, for instance, one Republican and four Democratic US Senators were implicated in the so-called Savings and Loans scandal because, in seeking funds with which to finance their campaigns, they had become beholden to one of the protagonists of that scandal.) The time they buy is so costly that it is necessarily expended in producing ridiculously brief and shallow TV and radio presentations, consisting almost exclusively of visual and auditory messages intended to bestow 'a good image' upon a candidate, plus one or two slogans and/or jingles, whose content and format are decided by advertising consultants. What this does to the quality of an electoral campaign beggars description; and also the format of the so-called great debates between presidential candidates, which is relatively free of these commercial restrictions, does nothing to compel the contendents to seriously articulate the issues at stake in the campaign and to expound and defend their proposed policies.

In Italy, the most significant decision ever taken by the Constitutional Court, that which suppressed the monopoly of television and radio broadcasting previously enjoyed by RAI (a fee-supported, state-owned and nominally parliament-controlled system) was not followed up by legislation to regulate the resulting free-for-all. This legislative vacuum had a series of positive short-term consequences for the quality and quantity of Italian broadcasting, but its long-term consequences seem to be a great deal less positive. RAI itself, for the time being, maintains a monopoly in the broadcasting of news; but the political elite, after establishing three competing TV channels within RAI, each to be treated largely as a patronage resource and a public relations outfit for one of the major parties, permits their output to be rather uninformative, for reports on and discussion of public affairs are dwarfed by the assiduous presentation of party non-events. Meanwhile, unregulated competition among private channels has led to the formation of a few cartels, which broadcast almost exclusively a mixture of entertainment schlock and of advertising messages, and thereby compel RAI to follow suit in its own entertainment programmes. In sum, Italian TV also does very little to stimulate interest in and diffuse information about public affairs.

In Britain, the long-standing antipathy of the political elite of whatever party is in power at a given time toward what used to be the best broadcasting system in the world, the BBC, has found particularly sustained and damaging expression under Margaret Thatcher's rule. I shall not review her policies and practices on this matter. But their result is that at present even the BBC has to engage in a great deal of political self-censorship, and operates under formal rules and informal pressures which make it a less and less effective medium for informing the British public and generating debate about political issues.

I have raised the matter of the public regulation of broadcasting (a matter about which I cannot claim particular competence) because I consider it significant on two counts. Methodologically, because it is clear to me that state policies different from those I have mentioned could make a great deal of difference to how that matter is handled without in the least exceeding the boundaries of liberal-democratic legality, and without mortally wounding the economic interests invested in the media business. Substantively, because how – if at all – the public is informed about topics of such general interest, defines them (or not) as political issues, and takes sides on them, is vital to my main point, which I would like to restate for the last time.

The state is in a state of crisis. But in our societies it still concentrates within itself and manages political power. It is doubtful that it does so very well by some absolute standard, but by a relative one, that is in comparison with other historically relevant arrangements for institutionalising political power, it does – or it has done so, in a number of significant instances – fairly well. (Who said that all states are bad, but the worst state of all is no state at all?) To me, the events which have been shaking Eastern Europe in the course of 1989 constitute among other things a claim to put an end to the expropriation of the national state on the part of the Communist party, a demand that the state recover its ability to express and guard the nation's collective identity.

As to political power itself, it is among other things a vital social resource, which needs to be better employed, not disposed of – not that it could be, anyway. One necessary (though not sufficient) condition of its better employment lies, I submit, in a purposeful reactivation of explicitly political processes, concerned with deciding the rightful goals and the proper modalities of public existence. For whatever reasons, for too long state structures and state policies have to an excessive extent, even in the liberal-democratic West, de-activated those processes. It is necessary to bring them to bear again on those structures and those policies.

Notes

1 SOCIAL POWER AND ITS POLITICAL FORM

1 For an overview of the controversies concerning this concept, see S. Lukes, ed., *Power* (Basil Blackwell, Oxford, 1986)
2 See for example H. Haferkamp, *Soziologie der Herrschaft* (Westdeutscher, Opladen, 1983); or K. Hondrich, *Theorie der Herrschaft* (Suhrkamp, Frankfurt, 1973). M. Mann, *The sources of social power* (Cambridge University Press, Cambridge, 1986), vol 1 proposes instead a four-fold distinction by distinguishing military from political power.
3 N. Bobbio, 'Politica' in *Dizionario di politica*, eds N. Bobbio, N. Matteucci and G. Pasquino, 2nd edn (UTET, Turin, 1983)
4 P. Berger, *Invitation to sociology*, (Doubleday, Garden City, NY, 1963), 69
5 M. Weber, *Wirtschaft und Gesellschaft*, 5th edn, (Mohr (Siebeck), Tübingen, 1976), 122ff. (English translation: *Economy and society*, Bedminster, Totowa, NJ, 1968, 212ff)
6 Bobbio, 'Politica'
7 R. Lautmann, 'Politische Herrschaft und polizeilicher Zwang', in H. Feest and R. Lautmann, *Die Polizei* (Westdeutscher, Opladen, 1971), 11
8 W.D. Narr 'Physische Gewaltsamkeit und das Monopol des Staates', *Leviathan* 8, 4, (1980), 543
9 H. Popitz, *Phänomene der Macht* (Mohr (Siebeck), Tübingen, 1986), 69
10 N. Luhmann, *Ausdifferentierung des Rechts*, (Suhrkamp, Frankfurt, 1981), 139
11 Weber, *Wirtschaft und Gesellschaft* (*Economy and society*, 592)
12 See for instance M. Levi, 'The predatory theory of rule' in *Microfoundations of macrosociology* ed. M. Hechter (Temple University Press, Philadelphia, Penn., 1983), 35–52
13 G. Sartori, 'Politica', in *Elementi di teoria politica* (Mulino, Bologna, 1987)
14 J. Weintraub, *Freedom and Community: The Republican virtue*

tradition and the sociology of liberty (MS of a book to be published by the University of California Press), ch. III, 25-6

15 Popitz, *Phänomene der Macht*, 69
16 This thesis is developed for instance in N. Luhmann, *Macht* (Enke, Stuttgart, 1975)
17 Weber, *Wirtschaft und Gesellschaft*, 30. (*Economy and society*, 55)
18 W. Humboldt, *The limits of state action* Cambridge University Press, Cambridge, 1969)
19 Have been defined as 'public' or 'collective' goods those which, when privately produced for sale, cannot be purchased in efficient amounts. P. A. Samuelson, 'A pure theory of public expenditure', *Review of Economics and Statistics*, 36 (1954), 387-9
20 For the briefest possible introduction to the contemporary literature concerning these matters, see P. Rosanvallon, *La crise de l'état providence* (Seuil, Paris, 1981), 59-62
21 M. Weber, 'Politics as a vocation', in *From Max Weber: Essays in sociology*, eds H. Gerth and C. W. Mills (Oxford University Press, New York, 1947)
22 Bobbio, 'Politica'
23 Popitz *Phänomene der Macht*, 38-9

2 THE NATURE OF THE MODERN STATE

1 C. Tilly, 'Reflections on the history of European state-making', in *The formation of national states in Western Europe* ed. C., Tilly (Princeton University Press, Princeton, NJ, 1975), 70
2 G. Simmel, *Sociologia* (Communità, Milan, 1988,) 443-4
3 M. Weber, *Wirtschaft und Gesellschaft*, 5th edn (Mohr (Siebeck), Tübingen, 1976), 30 (English translation: *Economy and society*, Bedminster, Totowa, NJ, 1968, 56)
4 On these polities, see S. Breuer, *Imperien der Alten Welt* (Kohlhammer, Stuttgart, 1982)
5 S. Finer, 'State and nation-building in Europe: The role of the military', in *The Formation of national states in Western Europe*, ed. C. Tilly (Princeton University Press, Princeton, NJ, 1975), 88-90
6 A. Giddens, *The nation-state and violence* (Polity Press, Cambridge, 1985), 272
7 N. Luhmann, 'Selbst-thematisierungen des Gesellschaftssystems', in his *Soziologische Aufklärung 2* (Westdeutscher, Cologne, 1986), 18
8 G. Tarello, 'Organizzazione giuridica e società moderna', in his *Cultura giuridica e politica del diritto* (Mulino, Bologna, 1988), 143-72
9 H. Popitz, *Phänomene der Macht* (Mohr (Siebeck), Tübingen, 1986), 37
10 Weber, *Wirtschaft und Gesellschaft*, 30 (*Economy and society*, 56)

3 THE DEVELOPMENT OF THE MODERN STATE (1)

1 This chapter and the following conduct an argument similar to that occupying the central chapters in a previous book of mine, *The development of the modern state: A sociological introduction* (Stanford University Press, Stanford, Calif. 1978). Because that book is easily

accessible to the interested reader, however, the treatment offered here – besides being much shorter – relies mainly on a different set of sources. Among these I would like to mention a set of historical entries from an excellent Italian reference work: N. Bobbio, N. Matteucci, G. Pasquino, eds, *Dizionario di Politica*, 2nd edn (UTET, Turin, 1983), which is unfortunately not available in English, and is thus much less accessible.

2   See in particular E. L. Jones, *The European miracle*, 2nd edn (Cambridge University Press, Cambridge, 1987)

3   See for example J. O Ward, 'Feudalism: Interpretive category or framework of life in the medieval West?', in *Feudalism: Comparative studies*, eds J. Ward and S. Mukherjee (Sydney Association for Studies in Society and Culture, Sydney, 1985), 40ff

4   See H. K. Schulze, *Grundstrukturen der Verfassung in Mittelalter* (Kohlhammer, Stuttgart, 1986), vol. 1

5   See O. Brunner, *Land und Herrschaft*, 3rd edn (Rohrer, Brunn, 1943)

6   G. Duby, *La société aux XI et XII siècles dans la region mâconnaise* (Colin, Paris 1953)

7   See for example G. Tabacco and G. Merlo, *Medioevo: V/XV secolo* (Mulino, Bologna, 1981), Part 1

8   See M. Mann, *The sources of social power* (Cambridge Universtiy Press, Cambridge, 1986), vol. 1

9   H. Heller, *Staatslehre*, 2nd edn (Sijthoff, Leiden, 1964), 126

10 P. Schiera, 'Società per ceti', in *Dizionario di politica*, eds N. Bobbio, N. Matteucci and G. Pasquino, 2nd edn (UTET, Turin, 1983)

11 Heller, *Staatslehre*, 128

12 M. Weber, *Wirtschaft und Gesellschaft*, 5th edn (Mohr (Siebeck), Tübingen), 1976, 637

13 N. Matteucci, 'Sovranità', in *Dizionario di politica*, eds N. Bobbio, N. Matteucci and G. Pasquino, 2nd edn (UTET, Turin, 1983)

14 For example, A. Merkel, *Juristische Enzyklopedie*, 3rd edn (Guttentag, Berlin, 1900), 163

15 F. M. Watkins, 'State' in *International encyclopedia of the social sciences* (Macmillan, New York, 1968), vol. 15

16 Matteucci, 'Sovranità'

17 Quoted in S. Schama, *Citizens* (Knopf, New York, 1989), 104

18 N. Elias, *Court society* (Pantheon, New York, 1983)

19 G. Poggi, *Development of the modern state: A sociological introduction* (Stanford University Press, Stanford, Calif., 1978), 68–9

20 See for all F. Hartung, 'Aufgeklärter Absolutismus', in *Die Entstehung des modernen souveränen Staates* ed. H. Hofmann (Kiepenheuer, Cologne, 1971), 149ff

21 P. Schiera, 'Stato di polizia', in *Dizionario di politica*, eds N. Bobbio, N. Matteucci and G. Pasquino, 2nd edn (UTET, Turin, 1983)

22 M. Raeff, *The well-ordered police state* (Yale University Press, New Haven, Conn., 1983)

4 THE DEVELOPMENT OF THE MODERN STATE (2)

1   P. Schiera, 'Stato di polizia', in *Dizionario di politica*, eds N. Bobbio, N. Matteucci and G. Pasquino, 2nd edn (UTET, Turin, 1983)

2   N. Matteucci, 'Costituzionalismo', in Bobbio, Matteucci and Pasquino, *Dizionario di politica*; see also N. Matteucci *Organizzazione del potere e libertà: Storia del costituzionalismo moderno* (UTET, Turin, 1988)

3   H. von Krokow, 'Staat, Gesellschaft, Freiheitswahrung', in *Staat und Gesellschaft*, ed. E.-W. Böckenförde (Wissenschaftliche Buchgesellschaft, Darmstadt, 1976), 465

4   J.H. Hexter, 'The birth of modern freedom', *Times Literary Supplement*, 21 Jan 1983, 51

5   E.-W. Böckenförde, 'La pace di Westphalia e il diritto d'alleanza dei ceti dell'Impero', in *Lo stato moderno* eds. E. Rotelli and P. Schiera, (Mullino, Bologna, 1974), vol 3, 33Off.

6   K. Kluxen, 'Die geistesgeschichtlichen Grundlagen des englischen Parlamentarismus', in *Parlamentarismus*, ed. K. Kluxen (Kiepenheuer, Cologne, 1967), 103

7   See for example E. Halévy, *History of the English people in the nineteenth century* (Barnes & Noble, New York, 1934), vol 1

8   H. Taine, *Le régime moderne* (Hachette, Paris, 1909), vol. 1, 319

9   M. Weber, *Wirtschaft und Gesellschaft*, 5th edn (Mohr (Siebeck), Tübingen, 1976) 173. (English translation: *Economy and Society*, Bedminster, Totowa, NJ, 1968, 295)

10 See M.S. Giannini, *Pubblico potere: Stato e amministrazioni pubbliche* (Mulino, Bologna, 1986), 134

11 H. Heller, *Staatslehre* 3rd edn (Sijthoff, Leiden, 1964), 114-15

12 C. White, *Russia and America: The roots of divergence* (Croom Helm, London, 1987), 130

13 F. Rossolillo, in 'Nazione', *Dizionario di politica*, eds N. Bobbio, N. Matteucci and G. Pasquino, 2nd edn (UTET, Turin, 1983), 701-5

14 Max Weber, 'Politics as a vocation', in *From Max Weber: Essays in sociology*, eds H. Gerth and C.W. Mills (Oxford University Press, New York, 1947)

15 See chapter 6.

16 See W.H. McNeill , *The pursuit of power: Technology, armed forces, and society since AD 1000* (Basil Blackwell, Oxford, 1984)

5 CONTROVERSIES ABOUT THE STATE: ATTEMPTING AN APPRAISAL

1   See M. Hastings, *Victory over Europe: D-Day to VE Day* (Little, Boston, Mass., 1985)

2   M. Weber, *Wirtschaft und Gesellschaft*, 5th edn (Mohr (Siebeck), Tübingen, 1976), 29 (English translation: *Economy and society*, Bedminster, Totowa, NJ, 1968, 54)

3   N. Luhmann, *Macht* (Enke, Stuttgart, 1975), 17

4   E. Rotelli and P. Schiera, eds, *Lo stato moderno, 1: Dal medioevo all'età moderna* (Mulino, Bologna, 1973), 11

5   M. Weber, *Wirtschaft und Gesellschaft*, 572 (*Economy and soicety*, 983-4)

6   H. Popitz, *Phänomene der Macht* (Mohr (Siebeck), Tübingen, 1986), 91-2

7   R.A. Nisbet, *Community and power* (Oxford University Press, New York, 1962)

8   R. I. MacIver, *The web of government* (Macmillan, New York, 1949)
9   Quoted by E. Barker, *Church, State and Study* (Methuen, London, 1930), 168
10 J. A. Vann, *The making of a state* (Cornell University Press, Ithaca, NY, 1984), 161
11 Pistone, 'Ragione di stato', in *Dizionario di politica*, eds N. Bobbio, N. Matteucci and G. Pasquino, 2nd edn (UTET, Turin, 1983)
12 A. Passerin d'Entrèves, *The notion of the state* (Oxford University Press, Oxford, 1967)

6 CONTROVERSIES ABOUT THE STATE: ATTEMPTING AN EXPLANATION

1   See R. Unger, *Politics: A work in constructive social theory* (Cambridge University Press, Cambridge, 1986), vol. 3
2   For a brief, thoughtfully critical account of this line of interpretation, see B. Badie, and P. Birnbaum, *Sociology of the state* (Chicago University Press, Chicago, Ill., 1983), ch. 2
3   See A. Gouldner, *The coming crisis of Western sociology* (Basic Books, New York, 1970), ch. 9
4   S. P Huntington, *Political order in changing societies* (Yale University Press, New Haven, Conn., 1968), 1
5   See A. Gouldner, 'Reciprocity and autonomy in functional theory', in *Symposium on sociological theory* ed. L. Gross (Row, Peterson, Evanston, Ill., 1959), 241–70
6   M. Levi, 'The predatory theory of rule' in *Microfoundations of macrosociology*, ed. M. Hechter (Temple University Press, Philadelphia, Penn., 1983), 35–52
7   See R. Unger, *Politics*, vol 3
8   A. R Zolberg, 'Strategic interactions and the formation of modern states: France and England', in *The state in global perspective*, ed. A. Kazancigil (Gower, London, 1986), 72–106
9   For an exhaustive (and exhausting) review of these versions see B. Jessop, *The capitalist state* (Robertson, London, 1982)
10 See G. Poggi, 'The modern state and the idea of progress', in *Progress and its discontents*, eds G. Almond *et al* (University of California Press, Berkeley, Calif., 1982), 323ff.
11 Zolberg, 'Strategic interactions and the formation of modern states'
12 G. Poggi, *Development of the modern state: A sociological introduction* (Stanford University Press, Standford, Calif., 1978), p. 162, note 29
13 See B. Moore Jr, *Social origins of dictatorship and democracy* (Beacon, Boston, Mass., 1966)
14 See for instance B. de Jouvenel, *On power: Its nature and the history of its growth* (Greenwood, New York, 1981); or A. De Jasay, *The state* (Basil Blackwell, Oxford, 1985)
15 See D. Gerhardt, 'Regionalismus und Ständeswesen als ein Grundthema europäischer Geschichte', in *Alte und neue Welt in vergleichender Geschichtsbetrachtung*, ed. D. Gerhardt (Vandenhoeck & Ruprecht, Göttingen, 1962)
16 See for instance E. Weede, 'Der Sonderweg des Westens', *Zeitschrift für Soziologie*, 18, 3 (June 1988), 172ff

17   See the arguments – reviewed and assessed by Albert O. Hirschman in his *The passions and the interests: Political arguments for capitalism before its triumph* (Princeton Unversity Press, Princeton, N.J., 1977) – by means of which some contemporary observers predicted that the commercialisation of the economy would force the holders of political power to exercise their power in more moderate and restrained fashion.

18   See G. Poggi, *Calvinism and the capitalist spirit* (Macmillan, London, 1983), ch. 6

19   J. Habermas, *Strukturwandel der Öffentlichkeit* 5th edn (Luchterhand, Neuwied, 1971)

20   B. Anderson, *Imaginary communities* (Verso, London, 1988)

7 LIBERAL DEMOCRACY IN THE TWENTIETH CENTURY (1)

1   So called because it was enunciated for the first time (in 1883) by the German economist Adolf Wagner.

2   John Burton, *Why not cuts?* (Institute of Economic Affairs, London, 1985), 26

3   R. Mayntz, *Sociologia dell'amministrazione pubblica* (Mulino, Bologna, 1982), 62–3

4   R. Rose, 'Priorities of government. A developmental analysis of public policies', *European Journal of Political Research*, 4 (1976), 247–89

5   Mayntz, *Sociologia dell'amministrazione pubblica*, 64–9

6   See for all D. Ashford, *The emergence of welfare states* (Basil Blackwell, Oxford, 1987)

7   Data calculated by Louis Fontvieille, as reported in: Pierre Rosanvallon, *Crise de l' état providence* (Seuil, Paris, 1981), 161

8   See S. E. Finer, 'State and nation-building in Europe: The role of the military', in *The formation of national states in Western Europe*, ed. C. Tilly (Princeton University Press, Princeton, NJ, 1975), 84ff

9   See for instance K. Middlemas, *Politics in industrial society: The experience of the British system since 1911* (Rowman, New York, 1979)

10   See G. Wright, *The ordeal of total war, 1939–1945* (Harper, New York, 1985)

11   A. Peacock and J. Wiseman, *The Growth of Public Expenditure in the United Kingdom* (Oxford University Press, London, 1961)

12   The supply – demand imagery has been employed to discuss related matters, for instance, in P. Dunleavy and B. O'Leary, *Theories of the state: The politics of liberal democracy* (Macmillan, London, 1987), ch. 3

13   See for instance F. G. Castles, ed., *The impact of parties: Politics and policies in democratic capitalist states* (Sage, London, 1982)

14   See S. Berger, *Organizing interests in Western Europe* (Cambridge University Press, Cambridge, 1981)

15   G. Lenski, *Power and privilege* (McGraw-Hill, New York, 1966), ch. 7

16   E. Gellner, *Plough, sword and book: The structure of human history* (Basil Blackwell, Oxford, 1988), 235

17   C. Lindblom, *Politics and markets* (Basic Books, New York, 1977)

18   G. Germani, *The sociology of modernization* (Transaction Books, New Brunswick, NJ, 1981), 118ff

19   This is often revealed, especially when the social circumstances of people are brutally disrupted by natural or social emergencies. For a fictional treatment of such a case see the famous novel by Franz Werfel, *The forty days of the Musa Dagh*; for an autobiographical account, see L. Gilkey, *Shantung compound* (Harper, New York, 1975)

20   Hence the connection between increasing state power and the new quantitative and qualitative aspects of the phenomenon of deviance. See A. Giddens, *The nation-state and violence* (Polity, Cambridge, 1985), 120

21   See Giddens, *The nation-state and violence*, concerning the growing significance of surveillance

22   R. Scott, *Organizations: Rational, natural, and open systems*, 2nd edn (Prentice-Hall, Englewood Cliffs, NJ, 1987), 9

23   N. Luhmann, *Politische Theorie im Wohlfahrtsstaat* (Olzog, Munich, 1981), ch. 2

24   N. Luhmann, 'Moderne Systemtheorien als Form gesamtgesellschaftlicher Analyse', in *Theorie der Gesellschaft oder Sozialtechnologie: Was leistet die Systemforschung?*, eds J. Habermas and N. Luhmann (Suhrkamp, Frankurt, 1970), 22–23

25   N. Luhmann, 'Reflexive Mechanismen', in *Soziologische Auklärung*, ed. N. Luhmann (Westdeutscher, Stuttgart, 1970)

26   See R. Rose and M. Peters, *Can government go bankrupt?* (Basic Books, New York, 1978)

27   Francis G. Castles, ed., *The impact of parties: Politics and policies in democratic capitalist states* (Sage, London, 1982)

28   See Giddens, *The nation-state and violence*, chapter 5, for an excellent account of the conceptual and empirical relations between these two orders of phenomena

29   D. Parisi, *Non solo tecnologia: Scienza e problemi di 'policy'* (Mulino, Bologna, 1988)

30   See for example the critique of the 'new professions' whose social standing is closely associated with the welfare state, in B. Berger and P. Berger, *The war over the family: capturing the middle ground* (Doubleday, Garden City, NY, 1983)

31   See D. A. Stockman, *Triumph of politics: Why the Reagan revolution failed* (Harper, New York, 1986)

32   See S. Bowles and H. Gintis, *Democracy and capitalism: Property, community, and the contradictions of modern social thought* (Basic Books, New York, 1987)

33   M. Weber, *Wirtschaft und Gesellschaft*, 5th edn (Mohr (Siebeck), Tübingen, 1976), 383. (English translation: *Economy and society*, Bedminster, Totowa NJ, 1968, 636)

34   See D. Bell, *The cultural contradictions of capitalism* (Basic Books, New York, 1978)

35   Robert McNamara was the president of the Ford Corporation and famous for his technocratic prowess when, early in 1961, J. F. Kennedy appointed him Minister of Defense in his cabinet.

36   See J. Barbalet, *Citizenship* (University of Minnesota Press, Minneapolis, Minn., 1989)

8 LIBERAL DEMOCRACY IN THE TWENTIETH CENTURY (2)

1   See for instance J. Marchal, 'Wage theory and social groups', in *The theory of wage determination*, ed. J.T. Dunlop (Penguin, Harmondsworth, 1957), 148–70

2   N. Luhmann, *A sociological theory of law* (Routledge and Kegan Paul, London, 1986)

3   Paul Starr and Ellen Immergut, 'Health care and boundaries of politics', in *Changing boundaries of the political: Essays on the evolving balance between the state and society, public and private in Europe*, ed. Ch. Maier (Cambridge University Press, Cambridge, 1987), 221–54, here, 222

4   The concept of bureaucratic politics has been used particularly in the analysis of foreign policy making; see for instance G.T. Allison, *Essence of decision: Explaining the Cuban missile crisis* (Little, Brown, Boston, Mass., 1971)

5   See for instance H. Heclo and A. Wildavsky, *The private government of public money: Community and policy in British political administration* (University of California Press, Berkeley, Calif., 1974)

6   G. Roth, *Politische Herrschaft und persönliche Freiheit* (Suhrkamp, Frankfurt, 1987), part 1

7   See F.G. Castles, ed., *The impact of parties: Politics and policies in democratic capitalist states* (Sage, London, 1982)

8   See R. Inglehart, *The silent revolution: Changing values and political styles among Western publics* (Princeton University Press, Princeton, NJ, 1977)

9   J.A. Schumpeter, *Capitalism, socialism and democracy* (Allen & Unwin, London, 1943) For a comprehensive, thoughtful reassessment of the role and significance of parties, see A. Ware, *Citizens, parties and the state* (Polity, Cambridge, 1987)

10   See for instance W. Streeck and P. Schmitter, eds, *Private interests government: Beyond market and state* (Sage, London, 1986)

11   See M. Levi, *Of rule and revenue* (University of California Press, Berkeley, Calif., 1988)

12   See R. Rose and T. Karran, *Taxation by political inertia: Financing the growth of government in Britain* (Unwin, London, 1987)

13   See R. Rose and M. Peters, *Can government go bankrupt?* (Basic Books, New York, 1978)

14   N. Luhmann, 'Subjektive Rechte', in his *Gesellschaftsstruktur und Semantik: Studien zur Wissenssoziologie der modernen Gesellschaft*, vol. 2 (Suhrkamp, Frankfurt, 1981)

15   C.B. Macpherson, *The life and death of liberal democracy* (Oxford University Press, New York, 1977)

9 A NEW TYPE OF STATE

1   I owe nearly all I know about the Soviet Union to repeated conversations with Victor Zaslavsky; and if I had been willing to follow up more of his criticisms and suggestions in producing the later drafts of this chapter, it would present a much more plausible account of the present conditions

and prospects of the Soviet Union than I am able to offer in what follows.

2   A. Ware, *Citizens, parties and the state* (Polity, Cambridge, 1988), 35–6
3   See L. Schapiro, *The origins of the communist autocracy: Political opposition in the Soviet state. First phase, 1917–1922*, 2nd edn (Harvard University Press, Cambridge, Mass., 1987)
4   A. J. Polan, *Lenin and the end of politics* (University of California Press, Berkeley, Calif., 1984)
5   A. Gouldner, *The coming crisis of Western sociology* (Basic Books, New York 1970), 304ff; see also F. Parkin, *Marxism and class theory: A bourgeois critique* (Columbia University Press, New York, 1979), ch. 3
6   See A. Nove, *The economics of feasible socialism* (Unwin, London, 1983)
7   J. Hough, *The Soviet prefects: The local party organs and industrial decision-making* (Harvard University Press, Cambridge, Mass., 1969)
8   See C. Lindblom, *Politics and markets* (Basic Books, New York, 1977)
9   V. Zaslavsky, *The neo-stalinist state: Class, ethnicity, and consensus in Soviet society* (Sharpe, Boston, Mass., 1982)
10   Ibid.
11   C. Konrad and I. Szelenyi, *The intellectuals on the road to class power* (Routledge and Kegan Paul, London, 1979)
12   N. Harding, 'Conclusion', in *The state in socialist society*, ed. N. Harding (SUNY Press, Albany, NY, 1984), 309
13   E. Guicciardi, *La giustizia amministrativa*, 5th edn (CEDAM, Padua, 1953)
14   T. H. Rigby, 'A conceptual approach to authority, power and policy in the Soviet Union', in *Authority, power and policy in the USSR*, eds T. H. Rigby, A. Brown and P. Reddaway Macmillan, London, 1980, 9–31
15   Ibid., 20
16   G. Ekiert, 'Conditions of political obedience and stability in state-socialist societies: The inapplicability of Weber's concept of legitimacy', *Center for research on politics and social organization*, Working paper series (Harvard University), 12–13
17   For a rapid (and not comprehensive) review, see L. Pellicani, *Gulag o utopia? Interpretazioni del comunismo* (Sugar, Milan, 1978)
18   T. H. Rigby, 'Traditional, market, and organizational societies and the USSR', *World Politics*, 16, 4 (July 1964), 539–58; here, 540
19   T. H. Rigby, 'Stalinism and the mono-organizational society', in *Stalinism: Essays in historical interpretation*, ed. R. Tucker (Norton, New York, 1978), 53–76
20   Ibid.
21   Cited in N. Harding, 'Socialism, society, and the organic labour state', in *The state in socialist society*, ed. N. Harding (SUNY Press, Albany, NY, 1984), 1–50. (Quote at p. 50. The authors are the Polish dissidents Kuron and Modzelewski.)
22   See for instance F. Feher, A. Heller and G. Markus, *Dictatorship over needs* (Basil Blackwell, Oxford, 1984), part 1
23   See A. Barone, 'The ministry of production in a collectivist state', in *Collectivist economic planning*, ed. F. A. von Hayek (Routledge, London, 1935)
24   Harding, 'Conclusion', 309

10 CONTEMPORARY CHALLENGES TO THE STATE

1 See S. Chodak, *The new state: Etatization of Western societies* (Lynne Rienner, New York, 1989)
2 M. Mandelbaum, *The nuclear revolution: International politics before and after Hiroshima* (Cambridge University Press, Cambridge, 1981)
3 O. Hintze 'Dallo stato nazionalborghese allo stato impresa', in *Crisi dello stato e storiografia contemporanea*, ed. R. Ruffilli (Mulino, Bologna, 1979), 48
4 L. Freedman, *Atlas of global strategy* (Facts on File, New York, 1985), 51
5 See Palme Commission on Disarmament and Security Issues, *A world at peace: Common security in the twenty-first century* (Stockholm, 1989)
6 See G. Ardant, 'Financial policy and economic infrastructure of modern states and nations', in *The formation of national states in Western Europe*, ed. C. Tilly (Princeton University Press, Princeton, NJ, 1975), 164ff
7 M. Mann, *The sources of social power* (Cambridge Univeristy Press, Cambridge, 1986) vol. 1, ch. 1
8 N. Luhmann, 'Weltgesellschaft' in *Soziologische Auklärung 2: Aufsätze zur Theorie der Gesellschaft*, ed. N. Luhmann, 3rd edn (Westdeutscher, Opladen, 1986), 51ff
9 See R. Ruffilli, 'Introduzione', in *Crisi dello stato e storiografia contemporanea*, ed. R. Ruffilli (Mulino, Bologna, 1979), 7ff
10 R. Mayntz, *Sociologia dell'amministrazione pubblica* (Mulino, Bologna, 1982), 103ff
11 See J. Habermas, *Strukturwandel der Öffentlichkeit* (Luchterhand, Neuwied, 1962)
12 This approach was sketched – without of course using the expression 'cybernetic' – by Durkheim in his *Leçons de sociologie*; see E. Durkheim, *Professional ethics and civic morals*, (Routledge, London, 1958)
13 On the question of technocracy, see W. Schluchter, *Aspekte bürokratischer Herrschaft* Suhrkamp, Frankfurt, 1984)
14 S. Wolin, *Politics and vision* (Little, Brown, Boston, Mass., 1960), ch. 10
15 Hintze, 'Dallo stato nazionalborghese allo stato impresa', 42f
16 J.C. Coleman, *The asymmetric society* (Syracuse University Press, Syracuse, 1982)
17 C. Lindblom, *Politics and markets* (Basic Books, New York, 1977)

Index

Index compiled by Meg Davis